Child Welfare in Football

Sport and those who run it have an important duty to ensure the safety and well-being of young participants. This text presents the findings of a unique research project into the experiences of a wide range of stakeholders in contemporary youth soccer, exploring issues of child protection, social policy, and the culture and governance of sport. It covers:

- The social context – twenty-first century family life, the sports policy background, and the organization, governance and culture of the English game
- Research findings – the experiences of children and young people, parents and carers, coaches, teachers, referees, Child Protection Officers, Football Development Officers, and those involved in women's, disability and professional soccer
- Issues in social policy research – methodological, ethical and management challenges
- Conclusions and implications – the benefits and limitations of different approaches to the protection of children and young people in sport.

For researchers, professionals and decision-makers, this text provides important new insight into the impact of child protection policies, and into the potential for evidence-based practice in youth sport.

Celia Brackenridge is Chair in Sport Sciences (Youth Sport) in the School of Sport and Education at Brunel University, London. She serves on the Research Committee of the National Organisation for the Treatment of Abusers and also chairs the Research Task Force of the NSPCC/Sport England Child Protection in Sport Unit. **Andy Pitchford** is Principal Lecturer in the Faculty of Sport, Health and Social Care at the University of Gloucestershire. **Kate Russell** is Lecturer in Human Movement and Health Education at the University of Sydney. **Gareth Nutt** is Principal Lecturer in Secondary Education at the University of Gloucestershire, a football scout and a former PE teacher.

Child Welfare in Football

An exploration of children's
welfare in the modern game

Celia Brackenridge, Andy Pitchford,
Kate Russell and Gareth Nutt

Routledge
Taylor & Francis Group

LONDON AND NEW YORK

First published 2007
by Routledge
2 Park Square, Milton Park, Abingdon, Oxon, OX14 4RN

Simultaneously published in the USA and Canada
by Routledge
270 Madison Ave, New York, NY 10016

Routledge is an imprint of the Taylor & Francis Group, an informa business

© 2007 Celia Brackenridge, Andy Pitchford, Kate Russell and Gareth Nutt

Typeset in Goudy by
GreenGate Publishing Services, Tonbridge, Kent
Printed and bound in Great Britain by
TJ International Ltd, Padstow, Cornwall

Every effort has been made to contact and acknowledge copyright owners,
but the editor and publishers would be pleased to have any errors or
omissions brought to their attention so that corrections may be published
at a later printing.

British Library Cataloguing in Publication Data
A catalogue record for this book is available from the British Library

Library of Congress Cataloging in Publication Data
A catalog record for this book has been requested

ISBN10: 0–415–37232–1 (hbk)
ISBN10: 0–415–37233–X (pbk)
ISBN10: 0–203–09906–0 (ebk)

ISBN13: 978–0–415–37232–9 (hbk)
ISBN13: 978–0–415–37233–6 (pbk)
ISBN13: 978–0–203–09906–3 (ebk)

This book is dedicated
to all children who play the beautiful game
in the hope that their dreams come true
and
to all the dream-makers who care for them

Contents

Illustrations

Figures

Tables

Contributors

Celia Brackenridge

Professor of Sport Sciences (Youth Sport), Brunel University, UK

After teacher training and degree study at Cambridge and Leeds universities, I began my professional career as a teacher of physical education in a Hampshire secondary school in 1973. I soon moved into higher education, first in Yorkshire and then in Gloucestershire, where I stayed for twenty-eight years before taking my chance in the private sector and running my own research-based consultancy company from Scotland. In the 1970s and early 1980s I played, coached and administrated club, national and international sport: a combination of practical experience and teaching sociology raised my feminist consciousness. I became a co-founder and first chair of the UK Women's Sports Foundation in 1984: this led me to investigate the injustices of sexual exploitation, harassment and abuse in sport. Child protection in sport was a logical next step for my attentions and became a quest throughout the 1990s. I have always seen the world through interdisciplinary lenses, drawing mainly from sociology, psychology and pedagogy. Recently, I have attempted to moderate my positivist leanings and to adopt the tools of social constructionism to interpret research findings. Most of all, I am committed to social change through the mechanism of evidence-based policy. Working on the project that underpins this book offered me a significant opportunity to achieve this aim. Whether or not I have succeeded will be for the readers and later generations to judge.

Andy Pitchford

Principal Lecturer, University of Gloucestershire, UK

As a Lecturer in Sport at the University of Gloucestershire, I am one of those very fortunate people who are able to spend their working days talking and thinking about their hobby, which in this case happens to be football. I am from the Nick Hornby generation of mildly obsessed middle-class males who could not necessarily play very well but who put their energies instead into writing and generally navel-gazing about the beautiful game. I spent the early 1990s helping to produce fanzines and also, in a more serious vein, working as a sports development officer in London. In this role I helped to manage community football programmes and this sparked an interest in the youth game that has culminated in the publication of this book.

After securing a PhD in 2000, I spent a period as a contract researcher in the University's Leisure and Sport Research Unit, and it was there that I became involved with the FA's Child Protection Research Project. Although I still have research interests in community football, and in the politics of higher education, I have now returned to a teaching role. I have a family of young children, each of whom demonstrates considerably more footballing talent than their father and, as a consequence, I am now helping in a voluntary capacity in grass roots junior football.

Kate Russell

Lecturer in Human Movement and Health Education, University of Sydney, Australia; BASES Accredited Sport and Exercise Scientist (Psychology), Chartered Psychologist, Division of Sport and Exercise Psychology

Following my psychology degree at Lancaster and some PE teaching in Lancashire, I undertook a PhD at Coventry University, where I later joined the staff. My doctorate involved investigating the role of body satisfaction and identity development among female rugby, cricket and netball players. The key findings – the transiency of body satisfaction and the role the body takes on the sporting field in developing a positive body image – are still key factors that drive my research interests today. As a sports psychologist, coach and competitive sportswoman, I see evidence of the impact sport can make on young and adult participants alike and value the role that it can play. After joining the University of Gloucestershire in 2001, my interests developed to include the issue of child protection in sport and the role and responsibilities sporting organizations have in managing this. As a psychologist on the research team, with a leaning towards the social construction of identity and experience, I have utilized my skills as both a quantitative and qualitative researcher to focus on the effect of sport and exercise on a variety of psychological aspects. I hope to highlight how factors such as identity and self-esteem are constructed through the footballing experience.

Gareth Nutt

Principal Lecturer, University of Gloucestershire, UK

I am currently in the Department of Education where I am the PGCE secondary course leader for the Gloucestershire Initial Teacher Education Partnership. After graduating from Loughborough College of Education in 1974, I taught physical education in secondary schools for fourteen years before returning to Loughborough to complete a master's degree in physical education and sports science. While employed as a teacher, I worked as an official and team manager for the local schools' football association and as a coach at the Centre of Excellence of the local professional football club. My involvement with professional football has since extended to scouting for a Football League club where my responsibilities involve team and player assessment for the first team squad. During my time in Gloucestershire, I have undertaken a variety of course leadership responsibilities in Initial Teacher Training but I have never forgotten my PE roots. I still retain a research interest in the changing nature of teachers' work and its impact on the role of physical education teachers.

Foreword

The research project which underpins this book was unique.

The Football Association (FA), working with Professor Brackenridge and her team, embarked on a pioneering study into child protection in football in order to provide an objective, evidential basis for the continued review and development of the FA Child Protection Policies, Procedures and Strategy.

What this book and its conclusions confirm is the need for a constant focus on a child-centred approach, across all levels of football, to create a safer football environment for young people.

The Child Protection programme has and continues to have an impact on the game's cultural environment. The research project identified evidence of this in 2002. The FA Learning Child Protection and Best Practice programme has reached 150,000 participants and the FA Criminal Records Bureau Unit has processed 68,000 disclosures: this has contributed to creating a safer environment for children in football. Raising awareness of the importance of safeguarding children has meant that many more adults in football are better informed and willing to act to address inappropriate and abusive behaviour. The current roll-out of Welfare Officer training will provide additional support and guidance to underpin consistent management of poor practice concerns in the grass roots clubs.

Professor Brackenridge has been at the forefront of child protection in sport for many years. Her dedication and commitment have made an immense contribution which is widely recognized.

The work of Professor Celia Brackenridge and her team was exemplary. Circumstances were sometimes challenging for both the FA and the research team, and I would like to record my deep gratitude for the professionalism and willingness that enabled us to collaborate in the production of an important research project.

Football in particular and sport in general are better informed as a result.

Tony Pickerin
Former Head of Education and Child Protection
The Football Association
June 2006

Acknowledgements

This project was undertaken by a team of researchers which, in addition to the main authors, included the following persons who each made a distinctive contribution to the work: Joy D. Bringer, Zofia Pawlaczek, Claudi Cockburn, Liz Kinder, Annie Kerr, Adrian Ibbetson, Jacquelyn Allen Collinson and Heather Sheridan.

The project that provided most of the empirical data reported here was funded by the Football Association: the authors are very grateful for its permission to reproduce the data and the image on the front cover. We would like to express thanks to all those engaged in the game who took the time to respond to questions during the research project and who gave generous help during our quest for information. In particular, we wish to record our thanks to Tony Pickerin for writing the foreword, his staff based at Lilleshall for their friendliness and hospitality, Jenny Myers of the NSPCC and Keith Daniell of The Media Group TV for their support and assistance, Brenda Read for her research on cultural change and Yvonne Williams for her helpful support.

Abbreviations

ACPC	Area Child Protection Committees (now Safeguarding Board)
AOTT	Adult Other than Teacher
ASBO	Anti-Social Behaviour Order
BSS	Brazilian Soccer School
CASC	Community Amateur Sports Club
CCPR	Central Council for Physical Recreation
CCRPT	Central Council for Recreative Physical Training (now CCPR)
CEHR	Commission for Equality and Human Rights
CFA	County Football Association
CLC	Children's Legal Centre
CPO	Child Protection Officer
CPSU	Sport England/NSPCC Child Protection in Sport Unit
CRB	Criminal Records Bureau
CYPU	Children and Young People's Unit
DCMS	Department for Culture, Media and Sport
DfES	Department for Education and Skills
EFDS	English Federation of Disability Sports
ESFA	English Schools' Football Association
FA	Football Association
FACA	Football Association Coaches' Association
FDO	Football Development Officer
FFEVTS	Footballers' Further Education and Vocational Training Society
FIFA	Federation of International Football Associations
FITC	Football in the Community
FL	Football League
HEI	Higher Education Institutions
ICC	International Co-ordinating Committee of World Sports Organizations for the Disabled
ICFDS	International Confederation of Futebol de Salão
IFC	Independent Football Commission
IOC	International Olympic Committee

IPC	International Paralympic Committee
IPDC	(Women's) International Player Development Centre
JTM	Junior Team Manager
LMA	League Managers Association
MAPPP	Multi Agency Public Protection Panel
NASL	North American Soccer League
NCB	National Children's Bureau
NCF	National Coaching Foundation (now Sports Coach UK)
NCH	National Children's Home
NPFA	National Playing Fields Association
NGB	National Governing Body of Sport
NSPCC	National Society for the Prevention of Cruelty to Children
ONS	Office for National Statistics
PFA	Professional Football Association
PHU	Partially Hearing Unit
PL	Premier League
RESC	Research Ethics Sub-Committee
scUK	Sports Coach UK (formerly National Coaching Foundation)
SEN	Special Educational Needs
UEFA	European Football Association
UGlos	University of Gloucestershire
UN	United Nations
UNCRC	United Nations Convention on the Rights of the Child
UNCHR	United Nations Convention on Human Rights
WFA	Women's Football Association
YMCA	Young Men's Christian Association

Introduction

Celia Brackenridge

Sometimes in the life of a researcher there is a moment that takes their breath away. This is very rare, for research is mostly a long-drawn-out, slow procedure filled with administration and tedium, hours of planning, budgeting, analysing figures and words, and writing, editing, and rewriting. For me, the moment came when I least expected it. In September 2000 my office at work was being refurbished and I had nowhere to go so I was at home one day, working on some administrative document of the type that dogs all academic managers in that particular month. The telephone rang: it was the college office ... 'Can you call the FA? They want to talk to you.'

Within two weeks, I had met with Tony Pickerin, then the head of the English Football Association's (FA) Education and Child Protection Department, to discuss their research requirements. Tony wanted me to conduct an impact study on their Child Protection programme across the entire country and at every level of the game from the Premier League at the top to local village clubs at the bottom. It took a further three months to agree a research design and more than another year to translate the design into an operational plan and agree a budget and a contract. The project itself did not start until January 2002.

The long gestation period was an education in itself, an object lesson in organizational politics. It provided me with glimpses of the road ahead and with enough early warnings to realize that this would be not only the most exciting but also the most challenging research enterprise of my career. The opportunity to conduct fully funded longitudinal qualitative and quantitative research, in this case over five years, represents manna from heaven to the social researcher. Better still, this project was commissioned before the FA's Child Protection programme was rolled out, rather than part-way through or at the end, as so often happens with monitoring and evaluation studies. But, for all the excitement surrounding the breaking news of a £1.3 million research award in the college, there was also a lingering feeling that this might be a life-changing experience for me, as project leader, and not necessarily a positive one.

The FA is the largest and most powerful sport governing body in the UK and guardian of the country's national game. In the late 1990s the FA had an estimated 40,000 affiliated clubs for children and young people within their remit. I knew this because, in 1996, Tony Pickerin had attended the first national conference on child protection in sport that I had organized at the then-Cheltenham and Gloucester College of Higher Education (which later became University of Gloucestershire). As he left at the end of the day he said quietly to me, 'I need to talk to you'. It was clear that the sport was beginning to come to terms with its duty of care for this vast army of young players, but it was some four years before we spoke again, following that momentous telephone call.

When the authors of this book came together as a research team it was from different academic and professional starting points but from a shared concern to improve children's and young people's experience of sport. I initially came from a professional physical education background and was, at the time, head of the college's Leisure and Sport Research Unit, with over a decade of research on child protection in sport behind me. Andy Pitchford had studied at the University of Southampton and then worked as a sports development officer in Bromley before taking up his lecturing post at Cheltenham. He was a lifetime football supporter and, as the parent of a young family, especially committed to safeguarding the younger generation of soccer players. Kate Russell, trained as a sport psychologist, brought to the team strong skills in quantitative methods and a keen interest in gender and sexuality issues in football linked to her own doctoral research on body image in women's sport. Gareth Nutt was also a physical education specialist, in charge of initial teacher education in PE at the college, but using most of his spare time serving as a scout for a Football League club. He therefore had particularly useful insights into the pathways that aspiring young players follow into the professional game. It is fair to say that many other colleagues queued up to participate in the project because of its prestige and the football cachet. In the end, however, the core team settled well and other members were gradually added to cover the geographic spread that the research demanded.

It is important for us to acknowledge the contribution of the other researchers since we worked together closely throughout the project, in virtual proximity despite being separated widely in actual space. Annie Kerr, from the north west, had strong practical and academic experience of child protection and equity issues in disability sport. Claudi Cockburn, taking on the London area, related very well to young people and brought high energy and impact to the project. Zof Pawlacek, from Sunderland University, a social scientist who has since emigrated to Australia, was an unpredictable, fun and challenging colleague. Liz Kinder, Child Protection and Welfare Officer for both the Youth Sport Trust and the FA's National Development Centre for Women's Football at Loughborough, brought experience of young people in bucketloads to the team: Liz had been both a secondary school PE teacher and in charge of pastoral care. Her very practical and down to earth approach enlivened and enriched the research team hugely. Joy Bringer, a doctoral student at Gloucestershire, brought her considerable methods expertise to bear on the programme and helped with data analysis. Adrian Ibbetson, who joined the group for the second year when Annie was taken seriously ill, fitted in perfectly. His role at Central Lancashire University gave him access to an academic and a practical footballing heritage and he used this, together with his own social science perspectives, to bring great wisdom to our work. Two research assistants also helped with collating the data: Heather Sheridan's quiet, unassuming efficiency was invaluable as the mass of material grew to mountainous proportions, and Jacqueline Allen Collinson's background in research administration, combined with her auto-ethnographic research skills and relentless positivity made her a perfect addition to the group in the second year.

We have chosen to foreground our own experience of the research project from time to time in this book rather than to conceal it, since, like Sparkes (2002), we believe that the research process is an inherently political one, shot through with value positions and vested interests yet all too often presented as a neutral activity. It is therefore consistent with our commitment to reflexive sociology that we should represent both the research *process* and the research *product* here. All of us kept research diaries during the project: some chose to share these with their co-researchers and others kept them purely as records of personal thoughts. The diaries were partly cathartic and partly a means to log the journey and keep the sequence of events clear so that when each annual report was drafted we could refer back to them if necessary.

In order to fulfil our commitment to positioning ourselves in the unfolding story of this project, we have included occasional reflexive commentaries. Through this confessional device we hope to illustrate how the professional and the personal often blend together in the research world, and to uncover some of our own presuppositions and prejudices. Another purpose of adopting a reflexive style is to encourage the reader to stand back from the bald facts and findings of the research and to question their own role in the construction of knowledge about child protection in football in particular, and about football and its place in our society more generally. For example, how far do researchers act as change agents in the organizations that they study? To what extent does football's response to child protection reflect general attitudes to human rights and welfare in the game? What do the findings of this work tell us about the expression of children's rights in sport (David 2005) more widely? Can contract researchers ever maintain academic and ethical objectivity when reliant on funding from the subject of their investigations? It seems to us that these, and many more questions, are legitimate enquiries about a project such as this.

It is important for us to acknowledge certain limitations in the way we have chosen to present and interpret the material in this book. In particular, none of us is legally qualified which explains, in part, why we give little attention to the fine details of the legislation related to abuse and protection of children. Others are far better qualified than we are to tackle this task. Also, the law is a moving target that affects both policy and practice: the introduction of mandatory police checks through the agency of the Criminal Records Bureau (CRB), for example, has caused enormous upheaval and controversy in sport. We could have written a separate book on this theme alone, but instead chose to take a wider approach and simply to embed some of the data about it within the text. We refer the reader to the FA's own publications and to the reports from the Independent Football Commission (IFC 2005, 2006) for further detail on this. Another result of focusing on stakeholder groups rather than on social themes is that issues of race and class might appear to have been minimized or overlooked. We did not make a deliberate choice about this but, because of the way the research was commissioned and designed, we had relatively little focused data on these subjects. For this, and any consequent criticisms, we must accept responsibility.

This book is divided into three parts. In Part I we set out the context of the project by, first, situating children and young people within contemporary debates about the sociology of the family and, second, mapping the landscape of child protection and safeguarding in the modern welfare state. It is somewhat ironic that, at a time when so much legal and policy attention is focused on the needs of children and young people, they appear to be silent partners in sport. We therefore pay particular attention to their place, or absence, within the sport policy process and to the need for their voices to be heard. The social and institutional evolution of the game of football is then examined in order to shed light on how it has come to be adult-dominated. The multiple forms of the sport, from 'soccer tots' and mini-soccer to commercially driven competitive leagues, reflect the market diversification and commodification that have characterized football, and many other sports, in recent years. This commercial picture forms an important backdrop to the seemingly innocent forms of children's soccer and, as will become apparent, is inextricably bound to them. Part I closes by focusing more narrowly on the nature of the FA and its child protection agendas. We outline both the purposes of the research project whose findings inform this book and also the processes – managerial and intellectual – through which the project was initiated, shaped, negotiated and, finally, begun.

Part II presents the data from the research, focusing on each of the major stakeholder groups in turn. Deciding how to break up and present the findings here was a source of many possibilities and great debate. For example, we could have chosen a thematic structure since many of the emergent themes recur in each stakeholder group. We could also have chosen a geographic substructure, or one based on the performance level of the clubs or on the stakeholder group being studied. In the end, we felt that a generalized stakeholder approach would be best, since the FA's own policy objectives were largely focused in this way. The work of Child Protection Officers and Football Development Officers impinges on much of the material reported in these chapters and, for this reason, they are not considered separately.

We begin Part III by addressing head on, in Chapter 13, the ethical and management issues that confronted us before and during our contractual relationship with the FA. In order to lay bare the potential successes and weakness of the research, we all – researchers and the FA Child Protection staff – undertook to conduct what we termed 'bracketing interviews' at the start of each year of the research. Looking back afterwards at the extent to which predictions were or were not accurate caused wry smiles and quite a lot of anguish, but the device proved its worth over and over again.

The book closes with further conclusions about the difficulties of implementing child protection on behalf of children and young people in sport and weighs the benefits and limitations of different approaches to this task. In particular, it asks how, in sport, we can move from treating children as objects to treating them as subjects, and from viewing them as stakeholders to viewing them as rights holders. The Child Protection in Football project was initially conceived as more than simply a study of Child Protection, rather as a study of cultural change in a very large organization of great national import. The extent to which the FA and its smaller partners in sport grasp this opportunity will say much about their real commitment to meeting social justice objectives both in and through sport. The way that sport treats its young people reflects its true value base. To this extent, child protection merely holds up a mirror to sport.

Part I

Context

Chapter 1

Families and football in the twenty-first century

Andy Pitchford

Football really is the family game. Our national sport offers every member of the family an opportunity to get involved through playing, spectating, coaching or just helping out the thousands of clubs that operate from grass roots to the professional levels. Pre-school versions of the game now help to encourage the under-fours to get kicking;[1] boys and girls as young as five can enjoy mini-soccer, while parents and grandparents can access courses to help them learn the fundamentals of football coaching.[2] Even those parents or carers with a more casual, 'taxi-service', kit-washing connection with the sport can benefit from the Football Association's own education resource, *Soccer Parent*.[3]

If a parent wants a child to enjoy the atmosphere and excitement of professional football, there is no longer any need to pass the infant over the heads of the crowd to the front of the terraces once inside the stadium. Instead, specially designated, comfortable all-seater family stands are ready and waiting to welcome them at the vast majority of professional grounds. The match day programme is likely to incorporate a family or kids' page, and parents and children alike can take further comfort from the presence of any number of 'father figures' on the touchline or in the directors' boxes. Most FA Premiership matches will involve some kind of family interest or intrigue, with the Redknapps, the Fergusons, the Wright-Phillips, the Lampards or the Glazers likely to be centre stage for some years to come.

Football's connections with families are, however, nothing new. A fairly cursory glance through any of the life stories of professional players published in the past thirty years will reveal touching accounts of the importance of supportive families. In these texts, parents are depicted as role models or inspirational figures, encouraging their offspring through even the darkest days. For example, Jack Matthews, the 'Fighting Barber of Hanley' (Miller 1989), Philip Robson, the Langley Park miner (Robson and Harris 1991) and Fred Hughes, the Barrow-in-Furness shipbuilder (Hughes 1980) are admired for their love of the game, their commitment or their ability to instil discipline and respect. Mothers, too, receive praise for their love and warmth, even on occasions for their unexpected contributions to football management. The example of Cissie Charlton's involvement with the school football team during and after the rise of her sons is indicative of the coaching and leadership roles that many mothers appear to have undertaken in the 1940s and 1950s (Harris 1971, McKinstry 2002).

These close connections between football and the family also help to reinforce the idea that the world's most popular sport is overwhelmingly a force for good in society. For over a century and a half, football has been perceived as character building, a source of discipline and commitment, and as healthy and wholesome. As we will see, agencies aiming to enhance education, social inclusion, rehabilitation, community development and citizenship, all use football as a social intervention, harnessing its apparently positive characteristics in order to bring about social change.

Despite our familiarity with this rather rose-tinted view of the sport, it is probably clear to all of our readers that both families and football are rather more complicated fields than are suggested by this nostalgia and rhetoric. This book is an attempt to question this kind of interpretation, and to unpack and examine some assumptions about both of these spheres in the hope that we might better understand the experiences of those children and young people who currently engage with the sport.

Unlike the authors of many sports textbooks, we are not particularly concerned about the quality of future Premiership players or the potential of any future England international teams. The focus in the pages that follow will be on children, their lives, motives and experiences. We want to emphasize the notion that children's experiences are worthy of consideration in their own right, rather than of secondary importance to the 'real', serious business of adult life (James and Prout 1990). Put another way, we feel that the experiences of an eight-year-old girl playing mini-soccer are as valid, as interesting and as important as those of any international player or adult spectator.

In order to begin to help us think in this way, and to encourage our readers to think more critically and sociologically about children and sport, we have devoted this first chapter to a consideration of families and children. Within this discussion, we also consider the impact of families on the ways in which children play, and the ways in which they engage with organized sport in general and football in particular.

New formations for families

To understand more about children and their play, we need first to establish the position that they currently occupy in the family and in society more generally. Unfortunately, just as the number of potential team formations in football has multiplied in the past twenty-five years, so too have the formations of families. Understanding where children fit in these new formations can be challenging, as the dominant 'nuclear family', which was presented by many sources as the only acceptable norm in the twentieth century, appears to be fragmenting and diversifying into a variety of new arrangements.

Parallel with this fragmentation, however, has been a growth in the number of experts observing from the sidelines. The past twenty-five years have seen the diversification of sociology into new specialist areas, including the analysis of the family and childhood. As with many of the branches of sociology, the early pace setters in scholarly investigations of the family and parenting were from the structural–functionalist tradition. Such writers as Murdoch (1965), Parsons (1971) and Fletcher (1973) were concerned with the connections between family formations and the broader requirements of our social system. During the 1970s and 1980s, the more conservative assumptions of these scholars were challenged by Marxist and feminist critiques of the power relations that underpin macro- and micro-social structures. Oakley (1974, 1976), McIntosh (1978) and Jeffreys (1990) were therefore concerned with the subordinate position of women in a range of economic and cultural settings, and the role of the state in supporting a form of patriarchal capitalism that restricted the ability of women to resist and challenge this situation. The influence of these writers has been considerable, bringing into clearer focus the connections between: the economics of domestic work; authority within the family; gender role socialization and conceptions of childhood; and the role of gender, class, ethnicity and physical ability in the construction and maintenance of power in society as a whole, and in the particular family units under analysis.

In more recent years, writers have become increasingly interested in the difficulties faced by the traditional nuclear family form, with some searching for new family formations and new sources of identity, and others reaching out for ways to rescue and refresh what remains of the older tradition (consider Mount 1982, Cheal 1991, Bernandes 1997). Contemporary analysis of the family continues to focus predominantly on this 'breakdown thesis', the idea that the traditional nuclear family is fracturing in various ways. While for critical and feminist theorists this fracturing is due to shifts in key power relations and a subsequent renegotiation of economic and decision-making roles, concern in the public sphere is dominated by moral panics over rising divorce rates, increasing illegitimacy and the heightened visibility of child abuse cases. These concerns are echoed by many 'New Right' theorists and socio-biologists, who argue that the nuclear family and associated traditional gender roles are morally and biologically desirable.[4] According to Collier (1999), much recent family legislation has been underpinned by the desire of politicians to protect the remnants of the nuclear family and to construct new conceptions of parenting which comply with the values of the traditional model.

While these arguments reflect popular sentiment in some quarters, the dominant sociological response to them is to try to understand the move to new and varied family forms by looking at broader economic and social shifts. Cheal (1991), for example, describes our society as 'late capitalism' or 'postmodernity' (also discussed in Chapter 2). On this reading, changing approaches to parenting and family life are the outcome of the interplay of subtle historical and cultural processes. These range from advances in medicine and contraception, to the emancipation of women and to the increasing sophistication of processes that enable businesses to make a profit. Within this setting, families are undergoing a gradual process of transformation, from a 'unit of production', to a 'unit of consumption'. Many of the activities and functions traditionally associated with families – such as education, advice, day care, emotional support and counselling, food production and domestic cleaning and maintenance – are increasingly the concern of the service or voluntary sectors (Ritzer 1998). Where families have, in the past, produced or provided these functions, it appears that many now buy them from a commercial supplier. This 'commodification' of family life has implications for the ways in which family roles are negotiated, for the relationships between parents and provider institutions, and for the means by which family members share experiences and build identities. Increasingly, for example, it seems likely that bonds between family members will be shaped by shared leisure pursuits rather than shared productive enterprise. Furthermore, these leisure pursuits are more likely to be provided by institutions or commercial agencies than to be the product of enterprise within the family or local community (see Cross 1993).

The idea of the family focusing increasingly on leisure is reflected in accounts inspired by Bourdieu (1986, 1990) in which individuals and families are locked into a quest for social advancement that requires them to accumulate goods and status symbols in order to demonstrate their position in the social hierarchy. Using children as the carriers of these markers, or as the source of investments which might secure such markers in the future, is regarded as an important strategy in contemporary society (see, for example Wynne 1998).

If these shifts in the family can, to an extent, be attributed to the increasing confidence of women in various contexts, many authors claim that they also reflect the increasing insecurity of men. As Collier (1999: 41) argues:

> Increasingly, and in diverse contexts, questions are being asked about the nature of 'responsible' fathering. Do 'families need fathers'? 'What is a father's role?' What, ultimately are fathers 'for' at a time of profound economic, cultural and technological change which is demanding new adaptations, new forms of attachment and, of course, the mobilisation of new subjective commitments to modes of belonging and integration such as legal 'marriage' and the heterosexual 'family'?

This insecurity is associated with the gradual undermining of such apparent 'certainties' as monogamy, family size, the sharing of income, co-residence, the raising of legitimate children, and 'the superiority of the conjugal bond' (Cheal 1991: 74). What it means to be a father, and what it means to be a mother, appear to be increasingly complicated questions. Presumably, then, life is also increasingly complicated for the children concerned.

Society's interest in children has never been greater. Franklin (1995) notes how children's rights 'came of age' in the UK following the publication of the *United Nations Children's Charter* in 1989. Legislation in Britain, such as The Children Acts (1989 and 2004) and beyond, began to advance children's rights and force organizations and institutions to accept responsibility for their welfare and promotion. This shift in the legal landscape has been reflected in the growth in writing by sociologists seeking both to empower children and to challenge those everyday notions that lead to children experiencing exploitative or abusive relationships. Children are, clearly, subject to the power of other generations in various ways: but they are also subject to the power of the state, and of educational and cultural institutions and the individuals who work within them. As Jenks (1996) argues, the adult world which our society prioritizes may not always be as good, rational, kind or worthy as the grown-ups might like to suggest.

The new sociology of childhood, or sociology *for* childhood as portrayed by Mayall (2000), aims to prioritize and emphasize the voice of the child. Building on the work of James and Prout (1990), Rose (1991) and Qvortrup (1991), scholars are increasingly analysing a range of issues affecting children currently in the public domain, from the role of the state in the development of legislation and social control, to child abuse and child protection, and to the 'scholarization of childhood' – the idea that children are subjected to heightened levels of formal education at an increasingly early age (see Kirk 1999, for example). Underpinning this kind of analysis is the notion that children are active agents, not simply passive beneficiaries, whose experiences should be valued in their own right. Childhood, in this view, is not merely a preparatory phase for the 'real business of life' but a realm that adults should consider more seriously and respectfully, even if the messages received might reflect attitudes quite different from our own. The sociology of childhood is therefore a field that seeks to look up, from the position of the child, rather than down from the position of the academic or adult stakeholder.

Clearly, football is an arena in which children's experiences and voices could be more fully considered; indeed, we have already argued this point elsewhere (Brackenridge *et al.* 2004, Pitchford *et al.* 2004). However, to understand more effectively how a child arrives on the pitch in the first place, and to consider how adults can shape both the experience of football and the decision-making processes which surround it, we now turn to an analysis of the interactions between families, play and sport.

Squeezing play: families and children's leisure

The new family formations that we have already noted above appear to be impacting heavily on play and on children's ability to engage with their chosen leisure or sporting pursuits. Managing children's play in single-parent families, in dual-income families, in 'reconstituted families', with step-parents, distant parents, and with stressed and anxious parents (see Pahl 1995), brings new and complex challenges.[5] As Kay (2004) argues, these complexities are likely to be experienced quite differently depending on the position in the social hierarchy of the family concerned. Surviving and prospering in families requires time, tolerance, patience, knowledge, understanding, cash and security resources that are not distributed equally among the population. In our increasingly commercial, 'commodified' society, cash can be deployed in attempts to resolve a wide range of child-minding and child-rearing issues but, at the same time, cultural expectations may make these kinds of choices hard to make and to justify.

Alongside this rising complexity, it appears that adults are increasingly anxious about children. Jenks (1996) argues that the uncertainties of modern living have consequences for adults and their sense of identity. Where in the past men, particularly, would find cultural meaning through the value, integrity and longevity of their work, the 'death of the job' and the flexibility of modern economies mean that such identity formation is more problematic. Although women are more able to access and progress within labour markets than in the past, they still face considerable difficulties in negotiating a sense of identity that reconciles the often-competing expectations of families, friends and partners. Faced with the unsatisfactory nature of these realms, Jenks suggests that many adults make considerable investments in children in order to secure their own sense of belonging:

> The trust that was previously anticipated from love, partnership, class solidarity and so on, is now invested more generally in the child ... As we need children we watch them and we develop institutions and programmes to watch them and oversee the maintenance of that which they, and only they, protect.
>
> (Jenks 1996: 51)

Investing in children, and attempting to maximize their potential in various ways, leads to a situation where adults survey, supervise and constrain children more than ever before. Prout (2005) argues that this reflects broad shifts in the ways that children experience the world, specifically 'domestication', where children are increasingly relocated from public spaces to special, protected places; and 'insularization', which describes the restriction of children's mobility, and the creation of special 'islands of childhood' to which they are transported – usually by car – by their parents and carers. Ensuring that children remain within safe environments reflects what Furedi (2001) describes as 'parental paranoia', as carers react with concern to media-heightened tales of 'stranger danger' and the uncertainties of traffic, weather, animals and technology in the outdoor world. Although Furedi argues that the majority of these fears are actually unfounded, the general culture of anxiety forces parents to do their utmost to protect their children, and to continue to ferry them across society's shark-infested waters.

Other writers go further, claiming that these 'islands' are frequently commercial spaces, where parents pay for their children to be educated and entertained. Mayall, for example, suggests that these commercial islands allow parents to assuage the guilt that they harbour as they restrict the freedom of their offspring:

> Childhood as apprenticeship, as preparation, as separate from the economic mainstream of adult activity is an important component of modern UK ideas about childhood. In the eyes of some adults, modern childhood is less a time of freedom and exploration and more and more restricted; parents think that they must compensate for this by providing organised leisure time for their children
>
> (Mayall 2000: 20)

This 'organized leisure' contrasts sharply with a culture where children have traditionally taken responsibility for their own play. Hendrick (1997) demonstrates how the twentieth century witnessed societal shifts leading to increased urbanization and compulsory schooling. In turn, these developments led to children experiencing more profound distinctions between work and play, with their free time increasingly subjected to new forms of information technology and the mass production of consumer goods – specifically toys. Outdoor play, self-directed play, and the risk-taking and self-development associated with these realms, appear to have been in gradual decline in recent decades as a result.

Resolving whether this organization and commodification of play is good or bad for children is a complex question (Cooke 2001). What does seem clear, however, is that many organized play environments are actually designed with the interests of adults, rather than children, to the fore. McKendrick et al. (2000), for example, in their study of commercial playgrounds and soft play areas, demonstrate how children played only a marginal role in the decisions which led to visits to such areas, and how the marketing and design of the spaces prioritized adult needs to 'buy' time for themselves and suitably safe and supervised play for their children.

Clearly, sport in its various guises and manifestations, is of considerable relevance here. Holiday camps, classes, after school clubs, academies, schools of excellence, training, fixtures, events and tournaments are all examples of organized play. On the surface at least, it would appear that most of these environments are organized by adults, but whether they prioritize the needs of adults or children is rather more open to question. Although much is made of the empowering potential of sport, few people seem prepared to examine the extent to which children may experience freedoms and responsibility in these realms. In Chapter 3, we explore the various ways in which football contributes to this picture, locating the growth of mini-soccer particularly, in a context where children's free play has been transformed into an organized, rationalized business.

Analysing the sporting family

It would be wrong, though, to imagine that sport has only recently been used in this way. Since the 1880s, sports have been used in educational settings and beyond as a way of connecting with children, as well as organizing, disciplining and more generally 'civilizing' them (Hargreaves 1986). Histories of youth movements (for example Smith 2001, Collins 2003) and Muscular Christianity (Watson et al. 2005) demonstrate how sports have been used at various times to occupy children, with broader economic and social shifts accounting for the fluctuating profile and energy of the agencies involved. This theme is developed further by Burstyn (1999), whose analysis of the historical development of male sporting institutions offers a rare illumination of the relationships between sport and shifting family forms. The growth in institutionalized sports in the nineteenth century can be attributed, for Burstyn, to the need for fathers to be engaged in colonial or capitalist enterprises, and therefore to be absent from the home for long periods of time. Thus the

> ... absence or remoteness of the familial father in turn created an emotional and pedagogical need for extra-familial social fatherhood to prepare boys for the competitive, public world of men ... Sport provided a mass form of surrogate fatherhood and male socialisation, as the place of the family father underwent massive change.
>
> (Burstyn 1999: 52)

The extent to which these kinds of relationships can be found in sport today is of great interest to us. For example, does the increase in single-parent families place a burden on sports clubs to provide more contemporary forms of this surrogate parenting? Do families from different levels of the social hierarchy use sport in different ways? Unfortunately, current literature on the inter-relationships between children, the family and sport offers us few pointers. Burstyn's interpretation is unusual, and it clearly demonstrates the notion that understanding children in sporting situations requires a wider ranging and more critical appreciation of the position of children more generally in society. This approach is not the norm in the sociology or the psychology of sport. These fields are dominated either by the analysis of professional sport, and thereby overlook the role and importance of the majority of sports settings which house children and young people, or they are concerned with the ways in which families and family members can support elite sports development. In other words, they ask what families can do for sport, rather than what sports can do for, or to, families and children.

Interpreting sports in this way leads to parents and families being presented as just one aspect of the socialization process (Kay 2004). The needs of the sport, or at least the needs of athletes as determined by their ability to achieve their sporting potential, are the priority. Rather than ask about the extent to which adults impact on children's sense of enjoyment in these settings, the important questions are about the extent to which adults help or hinder young athletes as they develop. Implicit here is the notion that the real business of sport, and the real business of life, is the competitive adult realm. Everything else is preparation for the main event, whether it is the World Cup, the Premiership, the Olympics or World Championships: ultimately all other aspects of life are subordinated to these aims.

Parents are typically assessed in relation to their ability to impact positively on these developmental processes (see, for example, Gibson 2002, Jambor 1999, and Stroot 2002). The work of Hellestedt (1987, 1990) has been of great influence here, and has helped scholars to consider the ways in which the self-interest of parents can, in various ways, have a deleterious impact on the development of young athletes. While these concepts or 'over-involvement' and 'under-involvement' offer a useful basis for categorizing potentially abusive relationships (Brackenridge 2001a), the position of parents in youth sport remains largely unexamined and untheorized. Instead, a 'common sense', functionalist account of barriers, constraints and sporting pathways continues to dominate, with parents and children depicted as bit-part actors in the main event, the acculturation of young people into long-term sporting careers.

In a sense, this lack of attention to family matters in sport is surprising. As Brackenridge (2000) notes, the use of 'the family' as a metaphor is common across many sporting organizations. It may well be possible to depict football as the 'family sport' but many other sports agencies attempt to offer individuals feelings of belonging and security by employing frequent references to the family and its central characteristics. Underlying these attempts to legitimize sports and to present them as wholesome, supportive environments, is a 'family ideology' in which patriarchal authority, exploitative gender relations and an emphasis on competitive 'sibling rivalry' may be central (see Chapter 4). The work of Simson and Jennings (1992) and Jennings (1996) exposes the 'Olympic Family' in this respect, while Messner (1992) draws our attention to the ways in which the hierarchical structures of many sports institutions reflect the structures of the traditional nuclear family. These structures are manifested in their most extreme form in 'fraternities' or 'families' in US and UK higher education institutions respectively but it is clear that in many professional and amateur sports clubs 'father figures' are able to wield considerable influence, demanding loyalty and exerting emotional, financial and, on occasion, physical sanctions on family members who deviate from the priorities of the leader or group. Although these connections could provide a rich terrain for sociological enquiry, the discipline has yet to make substantial forays in this direction.

Commentary on families and parenthood is equally limited within the subsections of the sociology of sport that relate directly to football. Some useful insights for our enquiry are, however, offered by contributors to debates on sports spectatorship and spectator violence. Although the growth of this field centred largely on the figurational analysis of Dunning et al. (1988), more recent anthropological and ethnographic contributors have focused on the role of football in identity construction for individuals and communities. Whilst many texts (for example, Bale 1993, Williams *et al.* 2001) point to the historic position of football clubs at the centre of geographic, religious or ethnic communities, both Armstrong (1998) and Robson (2000) argue that shifts in dominant conceptions of masculinity result in a particular emphasis being placed on football for the construction and maintenance of masculine identities. We have already observed how the complexities of modern life are creating difficulties for men and women as they develop their family lives, with fathers in particular confused about their roles and requirements. This apparent 'crisis of masculinity' is, furthermore, linked to insecurities inherent within the contemporary class structure and the fracturing of established class foundations. In the absence of the clear messages that were once transmitted by these social structures, it appears that males may increasingly attempt to attach themselves to leisure pursuits – particularly football – as a source of identity and meaning.[6]

Summary

The purpose of this first chapter has been to encourage readers to think about children and football in a slightly different way, and to consider how we might understand the experiences of children in the sport more effectively. For those writers who have helped to establish the sociology of childhood as a respected field, this understanding is most likely to be underpinned by the employment of research methods that empower the children concerned, and that prioritize the voices of the participants. We consider some of the strengths and weaknesses of the methodological alternatives in this respect in Chapter 4 but, at this point, it is worth noting that some sports sociologists have started to employ the kind of ethnographic and qualitative research strategies likely to yield worthwhile results in this area.

Interestingly, a number of these strategies have concerned children in the state education system (Renold 1997, Skelton 2000), and young people in high performance settings in football, specifically those who have been participants in the Youth Trainee Schemes (see Parker 2000, 2001), and Football Association Centres of Excellence or Academies (Cushion 2001, Oram 2001). Although most of the subjects in these studies were in the older 16–18 age range, such projects have at least begun to raise questions about the relationships between children and the institutions which represent the professional branch of the sport. These issues have been pursued further by Daniel (2004) and Thorpe (2004) who consider the relationships with respect to children in younger age groups. Whilst these studies and their research strategies are to be welcomed, they still represent analysis of the tip of a very large iceberg.

Of far greater significance than the Professional Game, at least in terms of numbers of participants and associated adult volunteers, is the participant game, described by the Football Association as 'The National Game'. Although we will consider the professional game in some depth in Chapter 8, most of our attention in the chapters that follow will be focused on youth leagues, junior sections, 'lads and dads' organizations, outreach programmes, community organizations and voluntary sports clubs.[7] It is in these settings, in particular, that we want to consider in more detail the current state of play between adults and children.

Given the shifting formations of families, it seems pertinent to ask how contemporary families engage with football, and to examine whether families prioritize the needs of adults or children when they become involved with the sport. To what extent, for example, might mothers and fathers use youth football as a source of identity in an increasingly complex world? To what extent does youth football represent a commodified leisure experience which families buy into in order to satisfy a range of economic and social needs? To what extent do families support children so that they can play football in the manner and circumstances that they are most likely to enjoy?

Consideration of the data we present in Part II will also enable readers to reflect on the extent to which children's voices are currently prioritized within the institutions that operate and regulate youth football. What, for example, are the experiences and motives of children currently engaged in football at varying levels of the sport? What do they want from the sport and what do they enjoy about participation and performance?

As we will discover in Chapter 3, the organization of football in England is so fragmented and disparate that children are likely to experience the sport quite differently depending on the agency that hosts their play. Local authorities, commercial providers, professional football clubs, voluntary clubs, state youth clubs, uniformed youth organizations and churches, for example, are all engaged in the provision of football for children. Identifying the organizers, and interrogating their motives, is therefore a worthwhile exercise if we are to understand the extent to which children are likely to feel empowered in these settings, and the extent to which these environments are dominated by adult requirements or assumptions.

Despite the lack of any critical reflection on these themes from a UK perspective, the beginnings of the kind of reflexive framework we would like to encourage have been published in the US. Aicinena's (2002) study of youth football, despite its apparent lack of academic rigour, poses many relevant questions, while Dyck's (2000) ethnographic study of 'soccer dads' could be replicated, with much potential, on this side of the Atlantic. Although professional 'soccer' has still to develop effectively in the US, the amateur, participant sport has been expanding rapidly for the past thirty years. Indeed, the commercial markets for youth soccer are considerably more mature than in the UK, with many significant agencies competing for customers in the particularly lucrative coaching and holiday camp sectors.

We will consider in more depth in Chapter 3 the ways in which the UK markets for organized youth football have developed in recent years. Before then, however, we will examine some of the legal and policy frameworks which currently impact on children in sport and the various agencies that claim to prioritize their welfare.

Notes

1   Consider *Soccertots*, the softplay/football product for under-fives in nursery and pre-school care, offered as a franchise by the International Confederation of Futebol de Salão.
2   Premier Skills, a West Midlands coaching company, offers specific courses for parents and grandparents to support 'back garden football'.
3   Details of the Football Association's *Soccer Parent* product are available at www.TheFA.com
4   'New Right' theory describes those scholars who have influenced Conservative (UK) and Republican (US) politicians in the past thirty years or so, emphasizing a mixture of free market, 'business first' policies and the promotion of traditional values in relation to parenting and child rearing. Mount's (1982) work is indicative of this approach.
5   'Reconstituted families' describes those families which have 'split' and reformed in new and varying units.
6   For an effective articulation of these themes, consider the film *Fight Club* and its reflections on the use of games and sports as antidotes to the frustrations of contemporary lifestyles.
7   Community amateur sports clubs (CASCs) to give them their formal, legal title.

Chapter 2

Child protection and the sports policy agenda

Celia Brackenridge

Since the late 1990s and the rise to power of New Labour, sport in the UK has experienced a plethora of social inclusion and equity initiatives for race, disability and gender (Sport England 2004a). Through the mechanism of 'standards' (prescriptions for service delivery and performance outcomes), the public and voluntary sectors have co-operated in efforts to institutionalize social inclusion and to make organizations accountable for their funding from the public purse. This form of soft social engineering has attracted criticism from some quarters as interference by the 'nanny state' and obsession with 'political correctness'. For others, it is simply a means of reducing inequality and enhancing diversity and fairness in society.

Child protection (CP), which in England refers to the protection from abuse, neglect and maltreatment of young people under the age of eighteen, has been broadly defined as part of the inclusion agenda for sport but does not sit entirely comfortably alongside the other strands of the Commission for Equality and Human Rights (CEHR 2006). These strands are: race, age, gender and gender reassignment, disability, religion or belief, and sexual orientation. Nonetheless, within the FA from 2002, CP took a prominent place under the broad umbrella of ethics and equity in a department that was later, in 2005, renamed Equality and Child Protection. The change in title symbolizes and reinforces the importance of this work for the organization. As a founder member, in 1985, and first chair of the UK Women's Sports Foundation, I was well placed to compare the policy struggles of these two areas of inclusion and to ponder on their relative success or failure in changing the nature and culture of modern sport.

Drawing on the work of Parton (1985, 1996 and 2005), I start this chapter by tracing the discursive drift from 'child protection' to 'safeguarding' that has occurred in English social welfare provision in recent years and consider the implications of the new safeguarding agenda for sport. I then go on to explore possible frameworks for analysing how sport organizations have responded to the exposure of 'child abuse' in their midst and, in particular, how sport has begun to grapple with the new rights agenda for children. Using David's work on human rights in sport (2001 and 2005), constructions of childhood and children's rights are examined and a range of potential rights violations that sport poses to children and young people is identified. Since I regard abuse as rooted mainly in power relations and differentials (see Brackenridge 2001a, Chapter 5), I am especially interested in the way that conceptions of 'participation' vary inside and outside sport, and what this means for the autonomy of the individual child athlete. I therefore focus on the contradictions of giving voice to children in an era of burgeoning scientific knowledge about and political pressure for 'talent development'.

It is important to set child protection in this wider sporting context before turning to the details of the FA project since we should never forget that sport is simply one part of the political, economic and social fabric of our society. I close the chapter by arguing that the child protection work of the FA, and within sport more generally, is part of a process through which concerns about children and youth are becoming institutionalized as a response to the pressures and uncertainties of late modernity.

From child protection to safeguarding

Nigel Parton (2005), arguably the UK's foremost commentator on child welfare and social policy, suggests that the government's Green Paper, *Every Child Matters* (Chief Secretary to the Treasury 2003) and the passing of the Children Act 2004, marked a turning point in official responses to children's services in England and Wales.[1] Subsequent reforms have been far reaching. These reforms were rooted in the work of social services and the police to reduce threats to children from inside and outside the home but, in the public mind, *extra*-familial threats have always assumed greater importance and shock value (Critcher 2003). Because of this, the 'parental paranoia' (Furedi 2001) mentioned in Chapter 1 has also impacted on sport, with parents and carers now more active than ever in the delivery and management of their children's sporting activities (see also Chapter 6).

Notwithstanding the long-term consistency of annual statistics on child abduction and murder (Home Office 2004, Duffy 2001), a string of child maltreatment tragedies, including the death of Victoria Climbié (Laming 2003) and the murders of Sarah Payne in July 2000 and of Holly Wells and Jessica Chapman in August 2002, have prompted a crisis of confidence in society's capacity to care for and protect children in both home and out-of-home settings. Such cases fuel fears of 'stranger danger' among less discerning members of the public. Parton (2005: 1) argues that England is not alone among its Western counterparts in facing the tragedies of child abduction and murder, yet:

> It is England that has embarked on the most radical and ambitious process of change. The pace and nature of change seems of a different order to elsewhere and is more self-consciously related to attempts to 'modernise' services and practices.
>
> (Parton 2005: 1)

Table 2.1 The drift from child protection to safeguarding

Era	Changing focus	The state	The family	Social assumptions
Late 19th century	• Social and moral welfare equated	• Non-interventionist support of the family in bringing up children • Social work low profile except in extreme cases	• Ensuring health and development of the child	• Family and state interests coalesce • Interest of children and parents coterminous • Local geographic and kinship communities = moral entities
Mid 20th century	• 'Battered baby' syndrome • 'Non-accidental injury to children'	• Attempts to rebalance child welfare policy and practice in the light of new evidence	• The family as 'haven' challenged through medical evidence • Coping with childcare under the strains of fracturing of family ties and structures	• Family no longer able to cope as a private sphere therefore need for greater state role
Late 20th century	• 'Child abuse and child protection' • 'Significant harm and the likelihood of significant harm'	• Risk, need and impairment assessments drive decisions about intervention • Information and communication technologies facilitate monitoring and information sharing	• Increasing individualization of social and family relations	• Greater opportunities for children are counterbalanced by increased risks to their own and others' security • Regulation is justified as a means to increasing the child's autonomy
Early 21st century	• 'Safeguarding and promoting the welfare of the child'	• Children and youth recruited and controlled through the social inclusion agenda • Emergence of the 'preventative state' (Parton 2005:6)	• Rights of the child supersede rights of the family	• Early intervention pays social and economic dividends

After Parton 2005

The policy responses to this crisis of confidence have also reflected a change in emphasis from worrying about prevention and recurrence of abuse within family settings (i.e. the immediate protection of the individual from harm) to worrying about lack of personal development and consequent failure to optimize the civic and economic contributions of all individuals (i.e. the future safeguarding of society from an unproductive or criminal workforce) (see Table 2.1). This change of emphasis from the private to the private *and* public domains is also reflected in some of the political and legal attention being paid to the issue of child welfare.[2] Issues of adult justice and youth justice have begun to colonize children's services (Piper 2005a). This has led to a much more interventionist approach to these services, sometimes directly through the law, taxation or mechanisms like anti-social behaviour orders (ASBOs) but often through 'softer' incentive schemes and/or financial sanctions. Examples in sport include the many award-based and kite marking programmes for sport organizations, such as Clubmark, Preliminary, Intermediate and Advanced Equity Standards (Commission for Racial Equality 2000a, 2000b) and the withholding of funds from those unable or unwilling to comply with such standards.

At the same time as the public was being shocked by high-profile cases of child abuse and murder, the moral panics (Thompson 1998) associated with crime and disorder (notably *male*, *youth* crime and disorder) fuelled both political and policy changes. The child welfare and crime/disorder discourses became merged into one – the safeguarding discourse – in which the protection and control of children could be addressed together. The twin objectives of current social care and future economic productivity could thus be achieved under the one, safeguarding, banner. The question is, however, safeguarding what or whom?

The five key outcomes of the government's agenda, *Every Child Matters: Change for Children* (DfES 2004a), are:

- to be healthy
- to stay safe
- to enjoy and achieve
- to make a positive contribution
- to achieve economic well-being.

So, although the government's social inclusion agenda is now explicitly focused on children's rights and welfare, it is also aimed at reducing worklessness and offending, and increasing evidence of citizenship (Piper 2005a). So, this renders the concept of 'at risk' very unclear. Who is at risk, and from whom?

Cynics might suggest that greater intervention and control in the lives of the young will protect not them but adults who fear for their own security. Equally, safeguarding might apply to protecting youth from themselves by reducing their freedoms, increasing surveillance over every aspect of their lives through various forms of a policy panoptican (Foucault 1979), and structuring their time to deflect them from destructive deviance. 'Youth' has long presented a perceived generalized threat to adults and to society, partly through its difference but also through its energy and innovativeness (Cohen 1972). The current guiding principle of children's rights is 'in the best interests of the child' (Piper 2005b), similar to the benign rule in medicine and health promotion of 'do no harm': but we should perhaps ask whether state interventions are not more accurately described as being in the best interests of the state? Traditional conceptions of freedom through constraint, or positive freedom, offer a rationale for this interventionist approach to social policy but jar for those who regard it as simply an extension of 'nanny-ism' (Furedi 2005) (see also Chapter 1).

Sport offers an almost perfect vehicle for addressing both children's rights and social control but I suggest that the latter is the dominant discourse in youth sport today. Children are certainly engaged in sport, and especially football, in large numbers but whether their best interests are served, and whether they have autonomy as athletes is highly debatable.

The terminology associated with child protection in sport has always been contested, with some sport organizations preferring to adopt the term 'welfare' for their nominated officers, some agreeable to 'child protection' as a label and yet others hedging their bets by appointing Child Protection/Welfare Officers. None yet, to my knowledge, has followed the discursive shift identified above by calling them 'Safeguarding Officers' but perhaps it is only a matter of time before this happens, since the second Action Plan of the NSPCC/Sport England Child Protection in Sport Unit, dated from the spring of 2006, is already named *Strategy for Safeguarding Children and Young People in Sport* (CPSU 2006). It is likely that, in choosing such names and titles, sport is merely following the wider trends in children's services.

These different terms constitute part of the repertoire of interpretive discourses that may be uncovered in the child protection and safeguarding world (for example 'welfare', 'protection', 'safeguarding'). Each discourse may reflect a different set of beneficiaries and each may indicate a different approach to policy design, delivery and evaluation. Whether those who run sport organizations are consciously critical of the meanings attached to these labels, or how they influence thought and action, is a moot point. I suspect not. But words have powerful significance for actions and for the ways in which we define, explain and attempt to resolve problems. It would be a great shame if sports personnel did not engage in critical debate on these matters, especially at a time when sport is centrally positioned as a servant of political policy (Sport England 2006).

Notwithstanding the new safeguarding agenda for sport (CPSU 2006), the term 'child protection' (CP) is adopted throughout this book, since this was the term in currency at the time of the football research project that underpins this book, and was the name used by the FA in its own policy documentation at that time. I suggest that uncritical acceptance of the safeguarding label plays directly into the government's youth control agenda in ways that might actually reduce rather than enhance the possibility of sport organizations achieving *any* aspirations for individual development and autonomy among their athletes. For this reason, at the end of this book I return to this theme and examine whether the narrow pursuit of talent development, for example through Long Term Athlete Development (Balyi and Hamilton 2003), dehumanizes youth sport.

Frameworks for the analysis of child protection in sport

Just as 'modernization' has driven reforms in social services and child care under New Labour, so it has also been the major policy imperative for sport (Deloitte & Touche 2003a, 2003b). The erosion of boundaries between the private (family) and the public (state), and between the public sector and voluntary sector, have highlighted, yet again, issues of social control and personal freedom in leisure (Coalter 1989).

The establishment of the Sport England/NSPCC Child Protection in Sport Unit (CPSU) in 2001 signalled a new way of thinking about children, child abuse and child protection in sport (Boocock 2002). For me, this marked the end of a long struggle to get the social 'problem' of child abuse recognized in the corridors of sporting power (documented in Brackenridge 2001a). It also signalled a shift to a more interventionist era in child protection in sport than had been experienced previously, with the eventual introduction, in 2003, of a set of national standards for safeguarding children in sport. I have previously described this as a shift from the permissive to the prescriptive (Brackenridge 2004b): it also reflects the shift from child protection to safeguarding described earlier. For example, from 2003 the award to governing bodies of grant-in-aid exchequer funding from Sport England became contingent on them satisfactorily meeting the nine national CPSU standards within five years.

It was tempting for me to become caught up in these developments as I had been part of a group pressing the sport authorities for change. My role as 'moral entrepreneur' (Becker 1963) was fairly transparent and had attracted criticism from some quarters for taking me outside the dispassionate stance of the social researcher (Furedi 1999). But elsewhere, (see Brackenridge 2001a: Chapter 8) I have characterized these apparent conflicts as part of a broadly feminist approach to praxis.

What was the political meaning of this turn of events? And against which ideological frameworks might we start to explain it? Parton (1985) describes Carter's (1974) attempt to detail a range of alternative ideologies of child abuse, including penal, medical and social welfare. In Table 2.2 these are adapted for our purposes, with the four right-hand columns specifically applied to sport. Of course, such an analysis shows only a set of ideal types that, in practice, often overlap. The third column, for example, suggests that a traditional 'utilitarian' approach to competitive sporting success often normalizes behaviour that might

Table 2.2 Alternative child (mal)treatment ideologies in sport

	Penal	Medical	Utilitarian	Social welfare		
				Humanistic		
				a) Child-centred	b) Reforming	c) Radical
Framework	Criminal	Scientific	Competitive			
Definition	Child maltreatment	Child maltreatment	Normal coaching/ training	Child maltreatment	Child maltreatment	Child maltreatment
Attitude	Punitive	Compassionate	Accepting	Protectionist	Judgemental	Challenging
Rationale	Justice	Treatment/cure	Medal success	Child welfare/ protection/safety	Athlete rights/ empowerment	Liberation/ reform
Tools	Courts/hearings/ tribunals	Referral for medical help	Collusion and denial	Education and awareness raising	Confrontation and adaptation	Disruption and change
Discourse	'Justice must be done'	'Help must be given'	'No pain, no gain'	'Education through sport'	'We need to be kind to optimize performance'	'There must be a better way'
Practitioner examples	Police, judiciary	Doctors, clinical psychologists, psychiatrists	Some former Eastern Bloc coaches	Specialist physical education teachers	Coaches who have been through CP workshops	New Games proponents
Solution	CHANGE THE (ABUSIVE) INDIVIDUAL ⟶		CHANGE NOTHING	CHANGE THE (ABUSIVE) SYSTEM ⟶		

Adapted from Carter (1974) in Parton (1985: 17)

otherwise, outside sport, be regarded as maltreatment. One example is weight control, required by the regulations of certain sports but often seriously problematic for those who participate.

The boundary between maltreatment and assertive coaching methods is also highly contested. This was sharply illustrated by both the enquiry into the coaching methods and alleged bullying by Bill Sweetenham, head coach for British Swimming (Campbell 2006), and the aftermath of Sir Matthew Pinsent's reports for the BBC on elite level training of five-year-olds in gymnastics schools in China. Following his observation to the BBC that the training regime constituted child abuse, IOC President Jaques Rogge responded by pointing to British hypocrisy and practices in public schools (Hart 2005, Knight 2005, Orr 2005). Ironically, Pinsent's visit to China coincided with the publication of the IOC Medical Commission's own *Consensus Statement on Training the Elite Child Athlete*, that closes: 'The entire process for the elite child athlete should be pleasurable and fulfilling' (IOC Medical Commission 2005).

I need to make clear that the utilitarian elements in Table 2.2 apply more overtly to physical and emotional abuse and neglect within sport than they do to sexual exploitation. Even though there is some evidence that attitudes to high level performance in sport are punitive – and even harshly so – rather than supportive (David 2005: Part III), sexual violations are of a rather different order. The punitive and controlling nature of the utilitarian approach to sport acts as a mask for such violations, whose perpetrators thrive on secrecy and complicity with their victim athletes. It is perhaps because of the sexually contradictory and conservative status of sport that those operating under the utilitarian regime, whether coaches or athletes, find it difficult to blow the whistle on such violations. Sexual contradictions are evident in the processes of desire and sublimation that attend the training, formation and reproduction of the body as a tool of performance (Guttman 1996, Pronger 1990). Conservative values shaped many of those individuals who currently regulate and manage sport and whose loyalties often lie *within* the confines of the sport rather than being directed to moral, ethical or legal codes beyond it (Brackenridge 2001a). It is not surprising, therefore, to find them reluctant to address difficult issues, such as child abuse within their ranks.

Modern sport has always faced criticisms from those seeking to undermine physical competition: indeed, radical critics of sport abounded in the early 1970s when critical social movements were having something of a heyday including, for example, women's liberation, anti-Vietnam, student and civil rights protestors (see Brackenridge and Fasting 2002). So, the radical humanist critique shown in column six of Table 2.2 is not new. But it has been brought clearly into relief by the exposure of child maltreatment cases in sport from the early 1990s onwards. To this extent, then, this critique still offers an alternative for those who feel that sport, as currently constituted, is an undeniably abusive social practice. In practical terms, an interesting tension seems to exist between the traditional utilitarian and the humanistic reform perspectives. Is it really possible, for example, to push young athletes to their performance limits in the name of sporting success and yet still succeed in empowering them to choose their own sporting paths? Is it possible to succeed at the highest level in modern sport *without* violating safety norms? These questions will be revisited in the concluding chapter.

Childhood and children's rights

As was explained in Chapter 1, childhood is socially constructed and usually set against constructions of adulthood and the family. We are constantly confronted by strong images of childhood of the 'devils v. angels' sort that reinforce these constructions. The 'devil' construction, which emerged from escalating moral panics about youth crime and disorder, especially after the death of the Liverpool toddler James Bulger, led to calls for tougher policies on youth offending. The 'angel' construction, developed from 'welfarism' and 'adultism' (Scraton 1997), led to strongly interventionist models of child welfare and protection and to the emergence of safeguarding, as detailed above. We have, then, what Phil Scraton (1997: ix) calls a 'paradoxical fusion of care, control and contempt' rooted in Victorian philanthropy (Table 2.3). Both constructions have led to state intervention and regulation of childhood, and both bolster paternalistic attitudes to children as subjects.

We have reached a point where perceived risk of child abuse and molestation leads to perceived safety from such abuses being equated with 'adults know best', described variously as the 'protectionist perspective' (Prescott and Hartill 2004), 'ethical socialism' and the 'preventative state' (Parton 2005). Just as happened with women as leisure consumers in the 1970s and 1980s, these dominant social constructions of childhood render children an homogeneous or undifferentiated group, which fails to take account of the many social, demographic and lifestyle differentiations that are now so readily acknowledged as influencing our, adult, lives.

The modern or 'new' sociology of childhood allows us to challenge this idea and, instead, to view children as heterogeneous, active agents with individual

Table 2.3 Perspectives on childhood

Care perspective	Control perspective
Disturbed	Disturbing
Welfare and support	Justice and control
Victimized	Victimizer
Protection of the child	Protection of the public
Troubled	Troublesome
What is best for the child	What is best for society

lived experiences. Seeing children as people rather than small, and lesser, adults allows us to break away from the protectionist approach towards more of a rights-based approach or what Scraton and Haydon (2002) call 'positive rights' or welfare-based rights, located under the ideology of social welfare in Table 2.2. This perspective, among other things, regards children as active agents of social change, co-constructors of knowledge, and in power relations with adults rather than being subject to the power of adults. In short, it shifts us from a sociology *of* childhood to one *for* childhood (Prescott and Hartill 2004):

> The real potential of a positive rights-based welfare approach is its challenge to the construction of children as innocent, vulnerable and weak through promoting their right to information, expression of views and their partici-pation in decision-making.
>
> (Scraton and Haydon 2002: 325)

Despite being outnumbered by the over-sixties for the first time in the 2001 Census (ONS 2001), children and young people have assumed a central role in the UK political agenda and are now protected by several international statutes and directives. The adoption of the United Nations Convention on the Rights of the Child (UNCRC) in 1989 (ratified by the UK in 1991) gave people under eighteen years of age a full set of human rights for the first time. This point marked a crucial shift in child welfare from the traditional protectionist approach to the more dynamic, rights-based approach of David (2001). The Convention (almost) universalizes the obligation for states to implement chil-dren's rights through legislative, financial, educational and other measures.[3] These rights are wide ranging and include: non-discrimination (Article 2); free-dom of expression and thought (Articles 13 and 14); association (Article 15); privacy (Article 16); access to appropriate information (Article 17); and right to life, survival and development (Article 6).

It is not uncommon for children's rights to appear in public service charters, one example being the Scottish Executive's Charter *Protecting Children and Young People* (Scottish Executive 2004a, 2004b). The work of the state in delivering the rights agenda for children has been complemented by work in a range of vol-untary sector agencies, notably through children's charities such as Barnados, the National Society for the Prevention of Cruelty to Children (NSPCC), the National Children's Home (NCH), and many more.[4] Whether children's rights have been addressed adequately in youth sport is a point of debate. David (2001, 2005), for example, argues that the promotion and protection of children's rights in sport has been a blind spot for sport organizations, despite a large literature on children's sport more generally. He suggests this is because human rights and sport have traditionally existed as separate spheres.

Possible reasons for the apolitical status of sport and its marginalization in rights discourses have been elucidated elsewhere (Brackenridge and Fasting

2002) and go back as far as Huizinga's definition of sport as free and separate from everyday life (1938). The failure of sport to engage in rights debates has left it vulnerable, at best, to accusations of naivety and frivolousness and, at worst, to charges of negligence and discrimination.

David (2001) sets out five possible sport situations that, in addition to the usual raft of discriminations based on sex, race, class and ability, can threaten the physical and mental integrity of children:

1   Involvement in intensive early training (violation of Article 19 – protection from child abuse and all forms of violence, and Article 32 – protection from economic exploitation)
2   Sexual exploitation (violation of Article 19 – protection from sexual abuse and violence)
3   Doping (violation of Articles 24 and 33 – right to health and protection from drugs)
4   Buying, selling and transfers (violation of Article 32 – economic exploitation – and Article 35 – protection from sale and trafficking)
5   Restrictions on education because of involvement in sport (violation of Article 28 – right to education).

Ironically, at the same time as David and others are turning their attention to the possible violations of rights that occur within sport, sport is being prescribed for its health, social and community development benefits through state programmes, such as those to tackle obesity and urban crime (Physical Activity Task Force 2003, Allison 1999, Nichols 2004). While private investment in 'nurturing' youth soccer players as commodities, for example, is certainly not consistent with children's own desires to be left alone to have fun, the exhortation for physical activity and healthy living is perhaps the major example of a public sector rational recreation message today.[5&6] Managing this tension is perhaps one of the greatest challenges facing contemporary youth.

Young people's patterns of leisure consumption, which are strongly influenced by commercial cultural forms, sometimes confirm but often contradict these rational recreation messages promulgated by government. But, here again, 'adultism' dominates, for these are the lifestyles and activity patterns deemed by *others* to be appropriate and 'in the child's best interests' yet actually serving the wider needs of the state.

Silent voices

The principle that young people should participate in decision-making and be consulted about political processes is enshrined in Article 12 of the UNCRC (United Nations 1989). It states that every child who is capable of forming his/her own views has:

the right to express those views freely in all matters affecting [them], the views of the child being given due weight in accordance with the age and maturity of the child.

In the UK, there are many examples of consultation initiatives across the public and voluntary sectors. For example: government departments are required to write and implement action plans for the involvement of children and young people in their work; together with Investing in Children (a County Durham partnership), the National Children's Bureau (NCB) has promoted a number of events focused on young people's participation in decision-making (NCB 2001); and Save the Children (www.savethechildren.org.uk) has produced a guide entitled *Children are Service Users Too: A Guide to Consulting Children and Young People* (2002).[7] Quality Protects, a Department of Health programme for managers of children and families (Sinclair and Franklin 2000), children's funds, schools councils and youth councils all offer avenues for children and young people to express their views on various services outside sport.

Although the shift to private funding has de-emphasized welfare considerations in leisure service delivery (Coalter 1998), the requirements of best value have also promoted greater transparency in service allocation methods and greater community group advocacy through a range of consultation techniques (Howell and McNamee 2003: 20). The consultation directive is delivered through, for example, citizens' panels and community surveys that yield quantitative and qualitative information from service users. Leisure and sport researchers have been responsive to this political imperative for stakeholder consultation, also using focus groups, surveys and other tools of the social researcher's trade in their research across the public, private and not-for-profit sectors. But where do children and young people feature within this consultation fest?

Alderson (2004: 15) asserts that 'We try to seal [children] into a risk-free world ... To be "well looked after" is to be constantly under adult care'. In her view, adults underestimate children's capabilities, which results in consultation being a charade or just a 'talking shop'. She also suggests that the most common method of assessing service effectiveness is whether 'children appear quieter or more law-abiding' and that the intrusions facilitated by the Children Act, which posits that all children are 'at risk', would not be tolerated by adults. Her account of children's absence in decision-making reminds me of the medical notion of 'patient compliance' which is used to describe adherence to prescribed medications (Whitaker 2002). Perhaps we have something similar going on here with children in sport – 'athlete compliance' – where young people are being manipulated to consume without any consumer rights? There is an implicit list of requirements that sport demands of its participants (initiation ceremonies, weight and diet controls, obedience to authority figures, for example) that ensure compliance.

But Alderson's views are challenged by Jessica Gold (2004: 25) who asserts that, in education at least, we are experiencing a 'velvet revolution'. In 1998, for example, only about fifteen per cent of primary schools had schools councils, but by 2004 the figure had reached seventy per cent. According to Gold, thousands of secondary pupils attend training courses annually, over 20,000 copies of a handbook for schools councillors had been bought by schools by 2004 and pupils are involved in a wide range of decisions in secondary schools including building, curriculum and staffing issues.[8]

Where is sport in this velvet revolution? The Sport England *Young People and Sport National Survey 2002* found that young people's motivation to take part was higher than it had been since 1994, with seven out of ten regarding themselves as a 'sporty type person' (Sport England 2003a). There are also countless school and club-related initiatives focused on sport programmes for youth, promoted through the Youth Sport Trust, governing bodies of sport, local authorities, schools and many others. Efforts to promote social inclusion have also generated better chances for girls' sport, children with disabilities and children from ethnic minorities than were in evidence ten or twenty years ago. Sport opportunities for young people are everywhere, then, but how many of them are genuinely consultative?

A report on children's rights commissioned by the British Council (Hawtin and Wyse 1997a: 3) criticized the development of the National Curriculum for using a 'tokenistic' consultation and was especially critical of the failures to afford children rights to leisure and play:

> The child's right to play and recreation is not recognised in legislation ... Children's own priorities often point to the importance they place on the arts, leisure time and play. This importance ... is supported by the UN Convention on the Rights of the Child yet ... play and recreation is [sic] often marginalised.
>
> (Hawtin and Wyse 1997a: 4)

> The voice of the child in decision-making is often ignored ... This perpetuates the view of the child as the 'property' of adults, even if the adults view the child as valuable and precious property.
>
> (Hawtin and Wyse 1997b: 1–2)

The importance of leisure and recreation to young people emerged again in September 2003 when, following Lord Laming's inquiry into the brutal death of Victoria Climbié, the government issued its Children's Green Paper, *Every Child Matters* (DfES 2003), which set out a consultation framework for improving welfare and protection outcomes for all children and families. The main message that emerged from the consultative meetings with young people (around 750 in number, mostly between four and eighteen years old), was 'the need to involve young people in decisions that affect their lives' (DfES 2003). Leisure freedoms, facilities and leisure activities (often linked to learning) featured frequently in the children's comments. The same findings emerged when the National Children's Bureau (2004) conducted a study to find out young people's views about a joined-up framework for services affecting them (*The Guardian* 2003), although this study excluded the voluntary sector where most sport, including football, takes place. Despite the absence of leisure and sport from the Children Act, the Institute for Leisure and Amenity Management argued that it offers leisure services an opportunity to 'reinforce their contribution to health, social inclusion and educational achievement' (Ives 2004: 1). Leisure services are also largely absent partners in the Multi Agency Public Protection Panels (MAPPS) that were established by government as joined-up public safety mechanisms to protect against sex offenders. Is this another example of 'leisure blindness' – like gender blindness – always there but never noticed?

In the world of sport the term 'participation' refers to taking part in competitive sport or physical activity. In the world of social policy and welfare, however, it refers to engagement in the political process and is an expression of the general rights referred to above. To this extent, then – and at the risk of perpetuating the myth of mind–body dualism (Ryle 1949) – sport organizations engage in 'disembrained' (rather than disembodied) participation. In short, they focus more on increasing the number of participants (for which read players) but not their engagement style (for which read politicization). Sport England's *Excellence Framework* (Sport England 2004b) identifies the most important outcome for sport as 'an increase in participation in sport and active recreation'. 'Driving up participation', then, which is the mantra of Sport England on behalf of the government (Rowe 2004), refers to getting people jumping about, *not* engaging them in critical discussion, reflection or review about the quality or type of service they receive.[9] The resultant depoliticization of sport effectively maintains the status quo, excludes the voices of children and silences critics.

Even if we do actively engage children and young people in decision-making in sport, we need to distinguish between simply giving them an opportunity to participate (listening) and giving them meaningful experiences of participation (hearing) (Ollé 2002: 7). Consultation initiatives with young people include the UK Youth Parliament (UK Youth Parliament 2004), and the Children and Young People's Unit. The Unit was set up by the Prime Minister in 2000 to co-ordinate services to young people. It commissioned an evaluation of participatory practice with children and young people (Kirby et al. 2003), the key findings of which were that: organizations needed to change in order to undertake meaningful and sustainable participation; participation was a multilayered and complex phenomenon; it should apply to all areas of children's lives and not just selective areas; listening was a crucial prerequisite for bringing about change; there were many social as well as personal benefits of participation; and, that organizations needed to adopt a clear rationale for developing participatory practice from a range of possible reasons.[10]

The researchers identified three different 'cultures of participation':

- *consultation-focused organizations*: these consult children and young people to inform services, policy and product development;
- *participation-focused organizations*: these involve young people in making decisions (as well as consultations) within participation activities that are time-bound or context-specific. Often a sample rather than all relevant children are involved;
- *child/youth-focused organizations*: children and young people's participation is central to these organizations' practices and they establish a culture in which it is assumed that all children and young people will be listened to about all decisions that affect their lives.

Kirby *et al.* (2003) also put forward ten principles for children and young people's policies and services:

- centred on the needs of the young person
- high quality
- family-orientated
- equitable and non-discriminatory
- inclusive
- empowering
- result-orientated and evidence-based
- coherent in design and delivery
- supportive and respectful
- community-enhancing.

Despite the sizeable shift in general society towards participatory politics, I would argue that the opinions of children and young people have generally not been taken seriously into account in sport. (Whether this is also the case in youth football is considered in Chapter 5.) This could be because either research and/or policy innovation is lacking. For example, other than some attitudinal and activity-related items, I could not find any evidence of a young people's consultation in the third national survey of young people and sport (Sport England 2003a).

Shier (2001) proposed a five-stage model of participation (see Table 2.4) which might help us in sport. It progresses from stage 1 – where children are involved but without having an opportunity to express a view or be heard, to stage 5 – where children share power and responsibility for decision-making. Organizations and individuals graduate through a process of 'opening' (showing an interest in young people participating), then 'opportunity' (giving skills and resources to young people), and finally 'obligation' in which participation by young people becomes embedded in policy and practice. I would suggest that, if

Table 2.4 Shier's five levels of participation by young people

1	*Children are listened to*
	This requires adults to listen to children when they express a view. No effort is made to ascertain children's views on a topic. Adults have to be ready to listen to children.
2	*Children are supported in expressing their views*
	This involves adults taking positive action to consult with children. Opportunities are provided for children to have a say. Adults use a range of age-appropriate activities to enable young people to express their opinions.
3	*Children's views are taken into account*
	Children express their views and these will influence the decision. The child's views should be given due weight, even if the final decision is not what the child asked for. This level of participation is mandatory for any organization that has adopted the UN Convention on the Rights of the Child – Article 12.1 states that every child who is capable of forming his or her own views has 'the right to express those views freely in all matters affecting the child, the views of the child being given due weight in accordance with the age and maturity of the child'.
4	*Children are involved in the decision-making process*
	At this level, children become directly involved in making the decision. Organizations establish procedures to enable children to participate fully. This may involve making the organization more child-friendly, possibly by changing the times and procedures of meetings.
5	*Children share power and responsibility for decision-making*
	To fully achieve this level, adults have to give up some of their power and share it with young people. This risks a decision being made that has negative consequences and adults and children have to learn to share the responsibility for this. Organizations find appropriate areas in which children can take on this responsibility and then support them in doing so.

Source: Shier, H. (2001) 'Pathways to participation: openings, opportunities and obligations. A new model for enhancing children's participation in decision-making, in line with Article 12.1 of the United Nations Convention on the Rights of the Child', *Children and Society*, 15(2): 107–117.

we apply this idea to sport organizations, it is clear that most are probably at stage 1 at best. From the start of the FA's CP strategy, for example, aspirations to include children in decision-making were listed but, by the end of two years of data collection, we were unable to discern much evidence of this having happened (see Chapter 5).

Institutionalization of adult concerns

Policy development for child protection in sport began only in the past decade but was given a major boost by the establishment of the Child Protection in Sport Unit (CPSU) in January 2001. The Unit is co-funded by the National Society for the Prevention of Cruelty to Children (NSPCC) and Sport England.

It acts as a one-stop shop for advice and referrals in sport and was overwhelmed with work in its first few years of operation. Prior to the establishment of the CPSU, various piecemeal CP initiatives had been promoted by individual sport organizations (most notably the Amateur Swimming Association), coaching groups such as the National Coaching Foundation (now Sports Coach UK) and child welfare agencies such as the NSPCC.

There are four dimensions of protection that professionals should observe and that child protection policies and procedures in sport should account for (Brackenridge 2001b):

- Protecting the player from others: that is, recognizing and referring anyone who has been subjected to misconduct by someone else, whether *inside* sport (by another staff member or player) or *outside* sport (by someone in the family or peer group);
- Protecting the athlete from oneself: that is, observing and encouraging good practice when working with athletes in order to avoid perpetrating abuse;
- Protecting oneself from the young person or others: that is, taking precautions to avoid false allegations against oneself by team mates or their peers or families;
- Protecting one's profession: that is, upholding the good name and integrity of sport.

There are examples of interventions in sport relating to all four of these dimensions. Different stakeholders focus on different aspects of this model. Coaches, in particular, are obsessed with the possibility of false allegations – despite very little evidence of these. Child protection policies, of course, are concerned with reducing the risk of all types of abuse, bullying and neglect. Not surprisingly, however, the moral panic in sport has focused on sexual misdemeanours because of a small number of very high profile cases (Brackenridge 2001a) and since April 2001, as outlined above, all Exchequer-funded governing bodies of sport in England have been required to have in place a child protection action plan in order to qualify for grant aid. This single change, alone, has had a major positive impact on the uptake of protective interventions in sport. By 2006, all state-funded national governing bodies of sport (NGBs), many county Sports Partnerships and even the British Association of Sport and Exercise Sciences (BASES) had either met the CPSU's preliminary *National Standards for Safeguarding Children in Sport* (CPSU 2003) or developed related policies and training materials.

It is interesting to speculate exactly why organizations that are not subject to the funding criterion adopted the child protection/safeguarding message. In the case of BASES, for example, fears about false allegations of abuse or professional misconduct against sport and exercise scientists were certainly one driver. The terms 'child' and 'young people' were deliberately excluded from the title of the training workshop to reinforce the idea that welfare of the professional, that is the adult scientist, was at least as important as the welfare of the young person.

Through extensive education and training, good practice measures that challenge abusive practices in sport are gradually becoming accepted by coaches and other sport stakeholders. On balance, though, it is probably fair to say that most people involved in sport organizations have encountered a very steep learning curve in relation to abuse prevention, and that they are still trying to come to terms with proscriptions on their freedoms in the name of improved child protection. Just how different members of the football family have responded will become evident in Part II.

Contrary to our adult fears, and as will be demonstrated in Chapter 5, even very young children are capable of expressing astute judgement. Consultation is not the norm in sport, however, and I would argue that sport is well behind other social provisions on this issue, not necessarily because of its failure to consult with children – although I think most schemes do not – but because of its failure to treat seriously the results of any such consultations. Why? Perhaps it is because the vested interests of those delivering youth sport would be undermined by listening to children's voices – sport (the fun pursuit of recreational games) would not be sport (the bureaucratized, commodified and hierarchically run athletic spectacle). This, then, is a form of paternalism verging on social control, based on false assumptions about the political competence and potential disruptiveness of young people and privileging control over welfare in the new safeguarding agenda. Social control is adeptly applied in youth sport where adults choose, organize, deliver and evaluate activities and programmes without inviting comments or contributions from those who consume them – children.

What would children's sports look like if adults both listened to and heard their voices?

- Sport organizations would comply in letter, spirit and in practice with the international and national statutes on children's rights.
- They would each adopt a child's rights policy with a charter of principles in children's own words.
- Laws governing children's involvement would be enforced.
- There would be full and proper investigative procedures for examining complaints into violations of children's rights and prosecution of offenders.
- There would be independent, commissioned research to investigate, monitor and evaluate children's experiences in relation to their rights in competitive sport.
- There would be permanent, formal mechanisms for children to voice their opinions, make comments and complaints and to be represented in investigations about these.

- All staff and volunteers in sport organizations would receive training in child welfare, rights and protection in sport. (On this point, as discussed in Chapter 8, the FA has done a commendable job: over 140,000 people had attended their tailored workshop by the end of December 2005 (Law 2005).)
- All children and young people in the organization would be empowered to express their views freely in matters affecting them.
- An open ethos would be established whereby children could trust adults, and each other, and feel confident in sharing opinions or problems.
- Children would have access to any information held by the organization about themselves and their development.

If we set these outcomes against the current functioning of almost any governing body then sport is found wanting. In Chapter 15 we revisit the question of whether this also applies to youth football.

Rights discourses have been 'criticized for being no more than symbolic gesturing rather than vehicles of effective structural change' (Scraton and Haydon 2002: 323). They have also been criticized for socially and politically decontextualizing child welfare, ignoring underlying economic and historical causes and constructing welfare conflicts in ways that have to be resolved by individuals, therefore avoiding collective responsibility. Scraton and Haydon (p. 324) argue that children require both protective and proactive rights – in short, a rights-based welfare approach. In order for this to happen in sport, not only does our conventional notion of participation require reinterpretation but we also require more effort by sport researchers and policy-makers to engage children and young people in both knowledge construction and power relations.

> The danger is that everyone gets to have a say, and then the adults with power make whatever decisions they would have made in the first place ... If we believe that adults don't always know best, and that children and young people have a valuable contribution to make ... we would expect things to change after we have made our contribution, not for them to remain the same. Otherwise what's the point?
>
> (National Children's Bureau 2001: 24)

Listening to children in sport does not mean allowing anarchy on the playing field. The same limits on freedom should pertain as they do for adults but there should at least be some debate about this. The manner of play, if not the very structure of the game and the way it is managed, may well be changed through consultation. If, in seeking to develop children's rights in sport, we simply tinker with minor changes in coaching practices in order to promote child protection then we are 'moving the deckchairs on the *Titanic*' and overlooking the macro social processes by which sport as an abusive practice has developed.

Summary

In this chapter I have attempted to map out the wider social and policy context of child protection before turning to its application in sport. Children are increasingly enjoying the benefits and responsibilities associated with greater political participation in their schools and communities but I have argued that this is not yet evident in sport, where interpretations of 'participation' are narrowly defined and associated with physical rather than civic engagement. I have suggested, following the work of other social commentators, that the replacement of child protection by safeguarding is a double-edged sword for children and young people, offering them both liberating and restrictive potential. While the data for the project reported in this book were collected prior to the emergence of this new discourse, I suggest that the prescriptions associated with it will be evidenced in the ensuing chapters.

Notes

1   For anyone wishing to understand more deeply the historical conditions which have given rise to modern children's services, see Parton 1985, 1996 and 2005.

2   For a very useful review of the definitional, legal and policy issues to do with 'safeguarding', see Myers and Edwards (2003).

3   Only the United States and Somalia, among the 193 possible states, failed to ratify to the Convention during the 1990s although these countries have now signalled their intention to do so (UNICEF www.unicef.org/crc/crc.htm).

4   A good international example is Right to Play (formerly Olympic Aid) (www.right-toplay.com/overview.asp), a non-governmental organization that grew out of the legacy of the Lillehammer Winter Olympics. It is committed to sport for development with disadvantaged children and runs programmes with the United Nations, UNICEF, the World Health Organization and the International Labour Organization, among others.

5   Safe sex is another.

6   The Children and Young Persons' Act 1933, for example, controls the age at which children may start paid work, the number of hours they may work and the sorts of jobs they may do (Morgan, undated). A child of school age cannot work, for example, before 7 am or after 7 pm. Children also cannot work for more than two hours on a school weekday or more than one hour before school starts, for more than two hours on any Sunday or for more than eight hours on Saturdays. Given the intensity of training and competition hours for some children in some sports, these seem like close parallels with the labour exploitation in children's sport uncovered in Canada by Donnelly (1997).

7   In 2001 the Children and Young People's Unit (CYPU) of the Department for Education and Skills (DfES) published *Learning to Listen: Core Principles for the Involvement of Children and Young People*. Based on the UN Convention on the Rights of the Child, this document offers advice and examples of good practice for the involvement of children and young people in the planning, delivery and evaluation of government policies and services. The University of Essex hosts The Children's Legal Centre (CLC, www.childrenslegalcentre.com), a charity promoting information about children and legal issues, produces a range of materials on consulting children, confidentiality, ages of consent and other topics of relevance to sport

and leisure. The National Children's Bureau (NCB) has also published a number of documents exploring children's rights and children's views. These include: *Young Opinions, Great Ideas* (1998), written by a group of young researchers 'So that big people can see things from little people's eyes', *The Emperor's New Clothes* (2001), *Young Europe* (Ollé 2002), and *Involving Young People in the Recruitment of Staff, Volunteers and Mentors* (Michel and Hart 2002).

8   In Scotland and Wales, consultation with pupils is a statutory requirement. In England, all schools have received a booklet from the Department for Education and Skills (DfES) entitled *Working Together* which asks for information about whether pupils have been consulted on curriculum, teaching and learning, target-setting, behaviour policy and staffing.

9   One of the stated objectives of the *Excellence Framework* is to provide a platform for an inspection service in sport, should it be developed in the future. If so, sport might attract an equivalent to Ofsted (Offside?). If this transpires, then the fast-vanishing boundary between state and voluntary sector will disappear altogether. Indeed, although the *Excellence Framework* is explicitly aimed at local government agencies it states:

> ... the principles of good management are the same in any organization whatever its size or structure. The Excellence Framework is equally applicable to other organization such as National Governing Bodies ...
>
> (Sport England 2004b)

So, the National Framework for Excellence is intended also to cover other partners such as NGBs (for example through Whole Sport Plans), and thus to cross the public/voluntary divide. Importantly, user engagement and school or young people's forums feature in this document as a directive for sport and services.

10   This research report was accompanied by a handbook to stimulate organizations' thinking and to help them to develop a more participatory culture. Throughout the research project, the research team was supported by and worked with a Young Advisors Group and a Young Researchers Group. Case study groups for this research, which worked mainly with 12–16-year-olds, were selected from an initial database of organizations that met three criteria:

- they had already involved children and young people
- they had listened to them and taken action as a result
- they had a degree of organizational commitment to participation and had attempted to evaluate their activity.

How many sport groups, including the FA, would pass this initial screening?

Chapter 3

Youth football

Andy Pitchford

Do you remember so long ago
When all we had to play was Subbuteo
We didn't have cable or MTV
There was only one place that we wanted to be
Playing football all day long
Dreaming of football all night long

Everyday, staying out 'til late
With Jumpers for Goalposts
Playing with our mates

Where we used to play is a car park now
But there's an Astroturf pitch on the other side of town
And Mum's so scared if you're out after dark
'Cos there's syringes in the grass of the local park
And there's too many cars clogging up the streets
I don't understand what they've done to our meat

Everyday, staying out 'til late
With Jumpers for Goalposts
Playing with our mates
If we had powder up our noses
It was only lemon sherbert
Guess it only goes to show
Life's much better when you're young
And I don't understand why things have to change
Why can't everything stay the same?

Everyday, staying out 'til late
With Jumpers for Goalposts
Playing with our mates

Jumpers for Goalposts, yeah![1]

It is easy to dismiss the ramblings of Ron Manager, the *Fast Show*'s misty-eyed football pundit, as he laments the corruption and complexity of the modern game. 'It's a far cry from small boys in the park, jumpers for goalposts, isn't it? Mmmm. Marvellous,' he would say, repeatedly. The middle-aged always bemoan the loss of their own youth, the contrasting behaviour of contemporary children and the corruption of innocent play. On this occasion, though, I think that both Ron, and Jumpers for Goalposts, the band inspired by his quaint observations, are on to something rather important.

This chapter focuses on the changes from the ways children played football in the past, and how the organization of the sport today represents a departure from the more traditional approaches to play that are, perhaps, rather more familiar to middle-aged adults. We consider, also, the ways in which the sport's lead body, the Football Association, has sought to regulate and rationalize the ways in which children interact with football, and how the current emphasis on competitive clubs and leagues represents only one alternative for the organization of the sport in the future.

Playing football: a brief history

Kicking objects at targets has probably always been a part of children's play. It is also a form of activity that has entertained adults, in various ways, for many centuries. Histories of football identify Chinese, Greek and Roman examples of early forms of the game (Murray 1994), although these interpretations tend to focus on adult participants. Examples of children engaging in these kinds of games are less frequent, partly because the history of children's play has received very limited attention from academics and partly, perhaps, because the experience of children kicking stones and cans and balls is so common that adults deem it to be unworthy of any detailed commentary.

Evidence of the historical development of football in England is reasonably extensive, tracking the emergence of variants of the game in both the upper and working classes. From the late 1700s onwards, organized games, including forms of football, were used increasingly by public schools as means by which they could pacify and civilize their charges (Brailsford 1992) with the schools of Eton and Rugby particularly prominent in the transformation of popular, 'folk' football into a practice which was significantly different from the activities of the lower orders. In these settings, football and other team sports now offered the ruling classes and bourgeoisie a method by which they could instil discipline, commitment, militarism and patriotism in the young men who would go on to secure and lead the Empire (Hargreaves 1986). The cult of 'muscular Christianity' grew from these roots, leading to an emphasis on athleticism, leadership, good 'character' and fair play in the public schools and, gradually, those branches of the Christian faith with an interest in missionary work (Watson et al. 2005).

At the same time, and despite frequent attempts by the Puritan establishment to suppress such activities, forms of folk football remained popular among the working classes. Village or 'mob' football had formed part of working-class traditions or culture for many centuries, and often appeared at festival time as ritual celebrations such as Shrovetide football in the Midlands (Dunning and Sheard 1979). In addition to football as a traditional event, more informal, recreational versions of football were common in villages and towns, and were often seen as less violent alternatives to the pastimes of cock fighting, dog fighting or prize fighting (see Thompson 1991: 448). Some authors (e.g. Hendrick 1997) do note how children would also commonly engage in variations on the football theme, with pig's bladders or tin cans. The extent to which children 'emulated' the games they saw adults playing is clearly difficult to interpret, but it is worthwhile noting at this stage that some versions of the game may have been adopted by children on this basis, while others may have been the product of children's own decisions and imaginations.

The drive to organize, formalize and rationalize football games in the nineteenth century was led by the public schools and their 'old boy' networks, with the formation of the Football Association in 1863 an outcome of the sport's increasing popularity in these fraternities (Walvin 1993). The popularity of both traditional, informal versions, and the new codified interpretation of football, grew rapidly in the decades that followed. Variations of football in working-class cultures were affected by industrialization and the gradual movement of large swathes of the population into urban areas in the same period. Hendrick (1997) notes how these processes of urbanization can also be associated with the greater regulation of time, the enclosure of space, greater surveillance, the growth of literacy, the development of information technologies and, above all, the increase in schooling. Football games in these enclosed urban environments would take on a very different character from those experienced in more open rural landscapes.

The increasing profile of the newly codified association football towards the end of the nineteenth century, coupled with its apparent simplicity, appears to have led to its increasing prominence as a street game for children. Clearly, however, football at street level could and did take a number of forms throughout those decades of the twentieth century before vehicular access further constrained the outdoor world of children. While games could replicate the team-based competitions of association football, with variations in territories, laws and numbers of players, they could also emulate specific aspects of the sport. Regional and local variations of: 'beat the goalie', 'three and in', 'all against all'; 'World Cup'; 'defenders and attackers' and 'headers and volleys' have been played in streets, playgrounds, parks and other informal play spaces for much of the past century, alongside other interpretations of the basic target game based on individual rather than team interaction. 'Rebound', 'squash' or 'corners', for example, is a one-touch football game played against a corner formed by adjoining walls. Other skill acquisition games or practices, such as 'keepy-uppy', 'tap-ups' or variations of 'wall ball', were equally common.[2]

The point of these examples is to demonstrate that football can, and does, take many forms. The fact that there is a globally recognized, rationalized, codified sport does not mean that other versions are necessarily impractical or undesirable. Association football is such a feature of contemporary life that we rarely stop to think about how it came to be in its current form, and whether other interpretations might actually be more enjoyable or sustainable. Many of the decisions that helped to create the sport in its original and codified form were fairly arbitrary, and represented the tastes of particular schools or compromises between different factions. Adaptations to the laws of the sport since the 1860s have often proceeded on a similar basis and, as a result, debates about the suitability of the sizes of goals, areas, pitches, balls and teams continue today. We can take this observation one step further and note that some variations of football are likely to be more 'ludic' or playful, simply because of the communities of interest that impact on the activity. Where adults organize and supervise football 'on behalf of', or 'in the interests of' children, it is likely that the ability of children to direct the activity, for the activity to be an end in itself and lacking in obligation, will be diminished.[3]

If we are to take the arguments of the sociology of childhood seriously (see Chapter 1), we would do well to revise our view of football, and revise our view of the versions of football that 'count'. The common sense view would be that 'games' of football (to follow Haywood et al.'s (1995) distinctions), organized and overseen by the participants themselves, are of less importance, and less virtue, than the 'sport' of football, where participants are subordinated in a variety of ways to other communities of interest. As Gruneau wrote so concisely in 1983, play becomes sport when 'a way of playing becomes the way of playing' (p. 21). Children's football, on this view, is only of any note where it feeds into and supports the regulated, affiliated, institutionalized, adult-led practice. Children who just 'play' football, outside the parameters of the sport, are either of no consequence or need to be incorporated. Unfortunately, we know very little about the experiences of children in relation to any of the interpretations of these activities. Considering how children experience 'games' of football, how they experience the 'sport', and understanding where it is that they find the greatest challenge, satisfaction and enjoyment would mark a considerable forward step in this arena.

What we do know about children's football is that, for over a century, adults have had a great interest in using the activity as a way of organizing and structuring children's play. Allowing children to determine their own play, to make their own choices and decisions and to control games and other interactions, has rarely been in vogue in English culture. Rather, thanks to the twin legacies of the Industrial Revolution and Protestantism, the emphasis in England has been on finding ways of organizing children so that their free time becomes productive, so that they use their leisure time to become more virtuous, more disciplined, more committed, more likely to contribute to the workforce and less likely to be swayed by the temptations of the Devil (see also Chapter 2). In many strains of Protestant thought, particularly Methodism, the child was seen as inherently sinful. Education and socialization were, on this view, to be designed to 'break the will' of the child, so that he or she could be shaped into an adult of appropriate attitude and virtue (Jenks 1996). Free, imaginative play, the arena of the child's will, was not to be facilitated or encouraged. Likewise games, where they aroused the child's passions or spirits, and allowed the child to control or dictate, were held in great suspicion (Thompson 1991).

Gradually, however, branches of the Protestant faith came to understand that rationalized, organized, disciplined, submissive, adult-centred versions of games – sports, as we understand them – could harness the energies of youth and, at the same time, promote some of the values they sought to instil (Bailey 1978). In the section that follows, we consider how many of the agencies that first attempted to organize football for children were influenced by this kind of ideological position.

Organizing football

If the upper classes and bourgeoisie codified and organized football essentially for their own interests, they soon came to realize that the popularity of the sport among young people in the lower orders gave them a great opportunity to counter some of the rebellious, revolutionary, uncouth, unhealthy and pernicious tendencies that they identified within the working classes. While it would be easy to interpret the use of sport in this sense simply as an attempt to instil social control, we should remember that the motives of middle class paternalism in the late Victorian era were varied. Collins (2003: 61) observes that the often contradictory desires of 'altruism and anxiety, social reform and social control were ... characteristic of Middle Class philanthropy in the late nineteenth and early twentieth century'. Meanwhile, Hargreaves (1986) reminds us that, regardless of the religious or managerial intentions of the sponsors of the 'rational recreation' movement, the recipients of this paternalism frequently transformed sport into practices that reflected their own value systems.

Nevertheless, this period saw large-scale growth in missionary work, schooling, social care and forms of youth work, and sports – particularly cricket and football – were often used as a 'hook' in these settings (Smith 2001). The range of agencies that attempted to colonize major urban centres, and then use sports as a way of connecting with the working class masses, was extraordinary. Churches, chapels, Sunday schools, the YMCA, elementary schools, uniformed youth organizations, the Scouts, the Boys Brigade, the Boys Club movement, clubs, institutes and associations appeared across all the major conurbations in England in the late nineteenth century, sponsoring physical activity programmes and sports teams. The roots of many of the original Football League clubs in church organizations is testimony to the impact of these agencies (see Mason 1980).

The focus of the majority of these early sports development initiatives was on young males and adolescents. The Boys Club movement, for example, targeted fourteen to eighteen-year-olds, with the age of entry only lowered to eleven in the 1970s, while the Scouts were originally conceived for eleven to eighteen-year-olds, with Wolf Cubs (for the over-eights) only introduced in 1916 (Collins 2003). As we will see, society's 'gaze' over children in the under-eleven age group only really extended in the early to mid-twentieth century, meaning that any sense of organized football for this grouping was yet to develop.

Although the legacy of these philanthropic agencies was enduring, other agencies soon became involved in the organization of sports in general and football in particular. In the early years of the twentieth century, working-class associations increasingly formed their own teams and social education programmes, particularly Miners' Welfare associations and Working Men's Clubs. From the 1920s onwards, these associations grew to form the basis of the 'democratic leisure' movement, where self-regulating, independent bodies attempted to promote leisure pursuits away from the paternalist interest of the middle classes (Cross 1993). These movements tended to sit rather uneasily alongside attempts by employers to cater for the recreational needs of their employees, although signs of both movements are evident in the contemporary structures of association football for young people and children. Even royalty took an interest in facilitating football for the youth of England in this period: the 475 sites funded and maintained by the National Playing Fields Association (NPFA) were established in 1925 to act as a living memory of King George V.

Beyond educational institutions, the organization of football was therefore a complicated and contested terrain. Institutions with a range of different motivations engaged with the sport in the hope of connecting with young people, using the passion, drama and excitement that was generated to win over otherwise recalcitrant individuals and communities. This situation continued throughout the first half of the twentieth century, with state-funded youth clubs entering the scene particularly after World War II.

Although the relationship between these clubs and sport was occasionally strained, with the formal and gendered aspects of sport sometimes shunned by the co-educationalists and 'mutualists' within the movement (see Collins 2003), the profile of sport in youth agencies was heightened with the publication of the Albermarle and Wolfenden Committee reports in 1960.[1] Here, widespread concerns about the anti-social and geographically mobile tendencies of working-class youth were met by a restatement of some of the core principles of Muscular Christianity and rational recreation, with constructive, disciplined sporting activity presented as a possible antidote to these apparently 'new' social problems. The 1960s saw a reinvigoration of youth sport, manifested in the establishment of the Sports Development Council (later the Sports Council) but also in the growth of youth sections and voluntary youth clubs and organizations. The Staffordshire 'Lads and Dads' football association, for example, was initiated in the mid-1960s in response to those same concerns over working-class leisure.

Up until the 1970s, therefore, children's football could be considered in relation to three main areas of activity. The first was playground, free play and children's street games, where children would either emulate the codified, institutionalized sport or would invent their own interpretations of football. Children of all ages would engage in this activity but would be constrained by time, space, increasing urbanization and motor transport. Second, the various youth organizations would offer organized football, teams and tournaments for their target markets, predominantly the teenage, 'youths'. While much of this would take place within the confines of the clubs themselves, there were also competitive infrastructures for eleven-a-side football that incorporated leagues and tournaments. There is some evidence of youth leagues developing in the early part of the twentieth century but most of the organized competitive structures were introduced in the years after World War II, particularly after the arrival of the FA County Youth Championships in 1945 and the FA Youth Cup in 1952, both of which catered for the post-sixteen, post-school age group. Third, children's football took place in and around school.

As we have already seen, the codification of football can be traced to the public schools in the early to mid-nineteenth century but the role of organized sports in state schools has a more recent history. The 1870 Education Act led to the introduction of state-funded compulsory schooling for the under-tens, with free schooling only available after 1891. Games and sports had only a limited place in the curricula of these early elementary schools, with physical training and 'drills' afforded a higher profile. However, as Kerrigan (2000) and Bridle and Burgoyne (2004) demonstrate, teachers soon began to see the value of football, in particular, in these settings, and by the 1890s a network of schools was training boys for football and playing matches. The rapid growth in competition for boys was recognized by the National Union of Teachers, who helped to launch the English Schools' Football Association (ESFA) in 1905. This organization grew steadily during the twentieth century, creating layers of competitions and international representative sides, with the focus predominantly on boys in the under-fourteen age range, although most school teams were effectively 'all age'. Organized competitive football for schoolboys under the age of eleven does not appear to have enjoyed a high profile until the mid-1930s.

Although physical educationalists will have much to say about the merits of association football in pedagogical contexts (consider for example Evans 1993, Hargreaves 1986), the crucial point for our enquiry is to consider who organizes this activity, and why? This is for two reasons. The first is because the authority of both the adults involved and the school as an institution have implications for how young people experience the activity. Football in school contexts, whether as a curricular or extra-curricular activity, is unlikely to be playful, in the senses identified earlier in this chapter. This view is encapsulated by Hargreaves in his assessment of school sport in the 1970s:

> less academically successful, male working class pupils prefer unorganised or more commercialised physical activities and pursuits, like street football and watching professional football, snooker, fighting and pop music, in their spare time. These kinds of activities give them the opportunity to play, as they see it, more adult roles, to combat boredom better and to gain control over their own lives. They reject competition, supervision and organisation being imposed upon them and they are hostile to school sport, not because they lack ability, but because it is associated with school values and the school status hierarchy ... A lot of these boys are competent performers who like sport, but they reject the school style and ethos: for them, for example, organised school football is just not normal, enjoyable football.
>
> (Hargreaves 1986: 174)

Second, we need to recognize the role of teaching professionals in developing schools' football both within and beyond the curriculum. Supporting inter-school competitive sport was a key aspect of many teachers' expectations and experiences up until the mid-1970s, and the long and varied history of the ESFA is testimony to the energies committed by teachers in this context for over a century (Kerrigan 2004). However, from this point on, a succession of contractual shifts and industrial disputes led to the gradual withdrawal of many teachers from substantial areas of extra-curricular work (Gardner 1998, Mason 2000). While the impact of this withdrawal may well have been variable and softened, in places, by the input of 'adults other than teachers' (AOTTs), it seems clear this was a period of some significance in the development of football for children. Just as some teachers began to back away from supporting teams and clubs in after-school settings, other institutions were beginning to flex their rather lax muscles in order to enter what was soon to become a competitive, commercial marketplace.

The Football Association and football development

For most of the past century and a half, the might of the FA has had little impact on the experiences of children who play football except symbolically through the role models at the top of the game. Those young people who emulated their heroes in the playground, or who threw down jumpers for goalposts in the garden, street or park, would have had little or no interaction with the sport's lead agency. School sport, as we have seen, was predominantly overseen by the ESFA, with the FA a distant and shadowy grandparent, lurking somewhere along the branches of the family tree.

Today, however, the situation is markedly different. A weighty infrastructure of officers and administrators engages in licensing and regulating commercial, educational and training initiatives aimed at organizing the sport for adults and children in line with the FA's objectives. These objectives, laid out for the first time in the FA's *Football Development Strategy 2001–2006*, are to 'increase the participation, quality and enjoyment of football' through:

- Football for life – providing everyone with a clear lifelong journey in the participation of football
- Opportunities for all – everybody having the opportunity to participate in football
- Football in education – providing children with a quality introduction to football
- Club development – having the best football club structures in the world, providing high quality coaching and development opportunities for all.

(FA 2001: 05)

Despite this rather grand rhetoric, and the considerable budgets with which it can be associated, the position of the FA in relation to children playing football is rather more complicated and contested than might be imagined. As a National Governing Body of sport (NGB), the FA has a vested interest in the rationalization of the sport at grass roots level. NGBs survive and develop in the first instance through the membership or subscriptions which clubs or organizations pay in exchange for those essential services that underpin competitive structures. Where groups of people play games or sports but do not affiliate or subscribe to the umbrella organization, NGBs miss out on income and are unable to exert any control over the activity. As a consequence, NGBs in general, and the FA in particular, are locked into a constant struggle to incorporate and affiliate rogue players, teams or clubs. By virtue of these fundamental requirements, NGBs are inevitably bureaucratic institutions with an aversion to what we might otherwise interpret as 'play'. It is in the interests of the FA to organize and package the game in such a way that it maximizes revenue and ensures institutional – and therefore adult – control over people who play football.

Despite this internal logic, the FA has only recently begun to assert itself in the context of children's football. Up until the mid-1970s, the success of the ESFA in sustaining competitive structures, the ongoing tension between the amateurism of the NGB and the closed world of the professional sport, and the inertia of the FA's own infrastructure, meant that it retained a considerable distance from the junior sport. Engagement with the youth game was confined to the licensing of over-sixteens' competitions and the affiliation of the first youth leagues that developed on a local and county basis from the 1950s onwards. To a certain extent, the gradual shift in the Association's position can be traced to the careers of a number of key individuals, and the relationships which they fostered, or otherwise, with their key partners.

Walter Winterbottom is well known as the first 'coach' of the England team, but on his appointment to the role in 1946 he was additionally given the title of Director of Coaching at the Football Association. This role recognized the importance of England's readmittance to FIFA and its entry to the 1950 World Cup, and Winterbottom set about developing layers of representative sides at 'B', under-twenty-three and youth (under-eighteen) levels (Shaoul and Williamson 2000). Crucially, Winterbottom had been both a teacher and a professional footballer with Manchester United, a CV that allowed him to make effective connections between the professional and amateur realms. His links with coaches at professional clubs smoothed the way for the introduction of two coaching awards, the Preliminary Coaching Award and the Coaching Licence or 'Full Badge'. Winterbottom was replaced in 1962 by another former teacher, the Loughborough-educated Allen Wade, who helped to establish a regional infrastructure for coaching in England. Wade and his new colleagues, most of whom shared his college background, maintained open relations with the Professional Game but this openness gradually withered and a more frosty relationship ensued with the appointment of Wade's assistant, Charles Hughes, to the post in 1982 (Conn 1997). While Hughes, another Loughborough-educated teacher, became famous for his application of scientific management to coaching (Larson 2001), he also recognized the income earning potential of coaching courses and materials and kick-started the slow growth of the FA's developmental departments. At the same time, the notion of appointing specific individuals to lead sports participation initiatives was increasing in prominence in local authorities (Collins 1995), and 'sports development', as an institutional function and potential career path, was gradually gaining momentum.

The early 1980s saw the FA come under increasing criticism for the unsatisfactory performance of its international sides, despite the growing influence of the FA's coaching courses, and the prominence of Hughes in promoting 'direct' systems of play. The FA's National School of Excellence was launched as a result in 1984, and ran at Lilleshall National Sports Centre until 1999. An analysis of the shifts in elite youth development systems is offered in Chapter 9 but, at this stage, we need to note that the merits of the School were much debated during its lifetime, raising the profile of the relationships between the FA and the Professional Game. These debates increased in intensity as the influences of the Professional Game within the FA grew, with the eventual compromise between the reluctant regulator and its major stakeholders brokered in the form of the FA Premier League (Conn 1997). In the wake of this development, the FA Council sanctioned institutional restructuring, aimed at increasing turnover and securing a range of commercial partners for future development. Hughes was replaced in 1996 by Howard Wilkinson, another former teacher but also a manager with an impressive track record in the Professional Game.

Wilkinson published his *Charter for Quality* a year later (FA 1997), and this led to the eventual demise of the National School, the introduction of FA Academies and Centres of Excellence, and a range of quality assurance procedures aimed at improving the experiences of young people in football club settings. Chief among these were the proposed restriction of younger children to small-sided football, and the 'kite marking' of clubs, schools and holiday schemes. Since the late 1990s, the work of the FA has been characterized by investment in county and quasi-state agency football development officers, the development of new coaching awards, the development of facilities and club infrastructures, and an apparent emphasis on 'child-centred' coaching techniques and strategies, aimed at enhancing both enjoyment and skill levels through the increased organization and observation of the sport. The FA's then-Education and Child Protection Department, originally based at Lilleshall, then incorporated within the Association's Sports Equity and Ethics Division, grew incrementally alongside these initiatives.[5]

Fuelled by income from television deals and associated sponsorships, the FA expanded all of its functions dramatically. Although the fluctuation in these income streams has led in recent years to a high profile turnover of chief executives and considerable insecurity among the workforce, the increasing gaze of the football authorities over young people has continued unabated. The introduction of 'mini-soccer' as the recognized game for the under-elevens in the late 1990s has contributed to a boom in junior clubs for the younger age groups. The six- and seven-a-side versions of the sport were originally intended for delivery through FA licensed 'mini-soccer centres', where some of the more challenging aspects of competition – including parental behaviour – could be more monitored and controlled. Instead, the brand was quickly adopted by the voluntary sector, with thousands of mini-soccer teams registering competitively for the first time, and junior/mini-soccer leagues expanding rapidly.[6]

This growth reflects the idea that football for children is changing, and that increasingly young people are experiencing the game as a packaged, adult-supervised, organized experience. While this notion fits with the apparent commodification of family life and leisure depicted in Chapter 1, it gains further ground when set against the growth of the commercial, charitable and quasi-state sectors in football delivery.

The first commercial football coaching products to hit the market took their inspiration from the United States. Here, in an attempt to promote the new, professional North American Soccer League (NASL), agencies in the States began to introduce 'soccer' into established summer camp structures with great success. Many British trainee teachers, armed with an FA Preliminary Award and an aspiration to travel, provided the workforce for these soccer camps, and by the late 1970s the basic formats had been shipped to Britain. The Bobby Charlton Soccer Schools, arguably the most successful British operation, started life in 1978, and the commercial market for football coaching has exploded since. A cursory glance at any local football scene in holiday periods will reveal a range of agencies, including established companies, 'one-man bands', entrepreneurial voluntary clubs and professional clubs in the guise of the national Football in the Community programme.

Football in the Community was a brand initiated by the Sports Council in the mid-1980s in response to both inner-city unrest and the apparent growth of spectator violence. Pilot projects in the London region, notably at Millwall, revived the idea that football could impact positively on the lives of young people. Outreach work, community projects, stadium access and coaching courses, all contributed to the schemes which developed further at clubs across the capital and beyond. A number of partners, including the Professional Footballers' Association (PFA), supported the projects and in 1992 an expansion programme was funded and overseen by the players' union. By the end of the 1990s, all ninety-two FA Premier League and Football League clubs, and a number of progressive non-league clubs, housed Football in the Community schemes, the majority of which were funded and managed through the educational arm of the PFA, the Footballers' Further Education and Vocational Training Society (FFEVTS). Given that some of these schemes employed up to fifteen members of staff, the impact on football markets for children was considerable.

While Football in the Community has contributed significantly to the growth of organized football coaching courses, the programme's successes in facilitating social inclusion and community development led to a range of other charitable and welfare agencies using football as a focus for social interventions. As a result, local authorities, social enterprises, charitable trusts, health promotion agencies and educational establishments all use football as a means of connecting with young people (SkillsActive 2004). Some of these agencies simply use football as a 'hook', while others attempt to deliver football in a variety of formats in order to meet their objectives. These attempts include programmes that aim to facilitate more child-centred activity, enabling children to make decisions about competitive structures, teams, rules and outcomes. *Strikes!*, the programme operated across a number of leisure and sports centres by Birmingham City Council, is one example of this approach from the local authority sector, while *Soccervation*, a coaching company from Dorset, offers football delivery and coach education with these same aims.

Further complicating the terrain is the proliferation, since 2000, of commercial coaching companies which have attempted to diversify their football coaching product by branding themselves in relation to the footballing culture of other countries. The most prominent example of this approach is Brazillian Soccer Schools (BSS), a franchise founded by coaching entrepreneur Simon Clifford. BSS focuses on technical coaching inspired by futebol de salão, the Brazilian small court game played with a weighted ball. Clifford also founded the International Confederation of Futebol de Salão (ICFDS), which has helped the game to gain ground in a number of countries across the world. Alongside the Brazilian influence, Dutch and Italian style coaching companies have also entered the market.

Thus, the massive increase in the coaching and supervision of children in football is only partly attributable to the FA. While the FA has contributed markedly to this growth, the reality is that it has no control over considerable swathes of the football landscape. Many of the agencies engaged in coaching children are explicit in their dismissal of FA strategies and techniques, and have often started life as alternatives to the NGB's mainstream. In some areas, the perennial mutual suspicion between the Professional Game and the FA precludes effective 'joined-up thinking', with the sport at the mercy of unstable and fragmented stakeholders. For the FA's Football Development Officers, employed at the level of the FA's county offices, this environment is particularly challenging, and the task of developing effective 'local football partnerships' and other co-operative arrangements can often be daunting.

Summary

It seems clear that at the beginning of the twenty-first century, children are experiencing football in a wide range of settings, and that an activity which was once dominated by free play and school competitions is now subject to increasing adult control and supervision through the growth of the voluntary sector and commercial coaching markets. Jumpers for goalposts have indeed given way to packaged football experiences and to what, for adults at least, might be deemed to be a serious business. Implicit in our discussion so far has been some suspicion about the benefits of these new settings for children, but this is based upon assumptions about children's needs and desires, and the idea that play – where children feel a sense of ownership and make decisions – is at least as valuable as formalized, institutionalized sport. These assumptions have not been subjected to any sustained interrogation, but we hope that this chapter can at least encourage people to enter the debate. We hope also that in later chapters the views of our respondents can shed some light on these complexities.

It is also worth noting at this point that the way in which football for children is organized in England is peculiar to this country. While the commercial markets for football appear to be less well developed in Europe, our emphasis on intense competition between teams representing small communities or geographic areas is also distinctive. The diversity of youth football, with teams and clubs drawn from the full range of voluntary and welfare organizations, can offer considerable opportunities for the sharing of good practice, but it can equally encourage insularity and competitiveness. Many junior football 'clubs' are in fact single teams, focused on the input of a particular adult coach, manager or parent (see FA 2003). This can mean that any number of clubs can co-exist and compete within any area, with some densely populated urban areas particularly prone to intensifying competition. This competition is, obviously, mostly experienced *between* clubs, rather than *within* clubs. In many European countries, the situation is quite different. In Spain, for example, the local state is often the dominant provider of football coaching and competition, managing competitive situations for younger players within municipal sports clubs. In the Netherlands, meanwhile, the voluntary sector predominates but with an emphasis on large clubs accommodating many teams and players.

Despite the valiant efforts of the FA's National Game Division to influence this culture through its *Charter Standard* initiatives, competitive children's football in England is now characterized by a high density of smaller clubs associated with particular estates, areas or towns. This heightens the potential for the sport to foster confrontations and to exacerbate the competitive tendencies of the adults involved, including the parents of the participating children. Furthermore, this density and complexity presents a range of problems for those seeking to regulate both competition and the management of clubs. In the Netherlands, football's national governing body owns and manages leagues at all levels. However, in our research, we found only two examples of county Football Associations running youth leagues. In both cases this appeared to enhance strategic and disciplinary interventions, and encourage widespread adoption of appropriate child protection policies and procedures. In all other cases, leagues were run by volunteers, leading to considerable variations in practice.

Understanding how children experience football is therefore a problem of some complexity. Agencies with different objectives and histories are likely to deal with children in very different ways, and the potential for children to feel valued and empowered will vary as a result. In the chapters that follow, we consider the views and experiences of a range of stakeholders in children's football, including the participants themselves, in an attempt to shed some light on these issues. Before we embark on this journey, however, we need to consider the challenges and difficulties of our research, and examine how researchers in the future might best investigate the machinations of the complex network of agencies that make up the football family.

Notes

1   The lyrics of the songs of the former Leicester-based, independent band, Jumpers for Goalposts, are available at www.jumpers.dabsol.co.uk.
2   Consider the common Potteries expression from the 1950s and 1960s, 'Chuck a bow aggen a woe, yed it, kick it an bost it.'
3   These are the key characteristics of play first, as first portrayed by Huizinga (1938).
4   *Sport in the Community, the Report of the Wolfenden Committee on Sport*, was published by the CCPR in 1960. The Albermarle Report on *The Youth Service in England and Wales* was published by HMSO earlier in the same year.
5   The latest reconfiguration, in December 2005, is an Equality and Child Protection Department based at the Soho Square offices of the FA in London.
6   The Football Association estimates that there are 4,360,000 children participating in affiliated football in England (FA 2003). This figure incorporates a growth of fourteen per cent for mini-soccer; thirty-eight per cent for boys' youth football and forty-nine per cent for girls' football since 2001 (FA 2005b).

Chapter 4

Researching the football family

Celia Brackenridge

In Chapter 2 questions were raised about the ownership and control of children and young people, and in Chapter 3 assumptions about the needs and interests of young footballers were reiterated. The first purpose of the current chapter is to explain how our research team attempted to design a study of the FA's child protection work in football that would do justice to the width and depth of young people's involvement in the game. The second purpose here is to introduce the reader to the 'football family', as understood in this research.

As the Independent Football Commission notes (IFC 2005: 8), 'No one knows how many people play football in England.' It estimated that around four million children, 700,000 adults and 250,000 volunteers are involved in football, mainly outside the ranks of the Professional Game. The Premier League (PL) and Football League (FL) include ninety-two clubs, thirty-eight of which had academies in 2004, with perhaps as many as 130 young players in each. The Football in the Community (FITC) scheme estimated reaching over one million people each year, the majority of whom are legally defined as children, i.e. below eighteen years old.

As we have already seen, the structure of the children's game is diverse, fragmented and heterogeneous. It also impinges on the 'adult' game in ways that stretch the cultural if not the legal definition of 'child', since footballers of sixteen and seventeen years of age sometimes play at the very highest professional level, albeit it rarely. Knowing that our project could never hope to be representative of the large numbers of children and young people engaged in affiliated football, we opted to sample in a very targeted way.

The chapter opens with an examination of the organizational precursors to the FA's Child Protection Strategy, which, as with child protection work in many other governing bodies of sport, was instigated after a number of child abuse scandals. It moves on to describe the research design, to introduce each of the main stakeholder groups that were involved and to explain how we prepared to address the insider/outsider tensions that often trip up researchers of sensitive themes.

The emergence of child protection in football

The FA Board approved its first Child Protection (CP) policy, strategy, action plan and roll-out programme in December 2000. It is interesting to speculate on the reason why the FA chose this point to commence its formal CP programme. During the 1990s, along with many other governing bodies of sport, it had become increasingly aware of CP as an issue both beyond and within sport. High profile publicity from cases in other sports such as swimming (Brackenridge 2001a, Myers and Barrett 2002), together with the experience of managing the FA National School for talented boy players, and occasional cases of abuse within football, led the FA to seek advice about child protection from the NSPCC. What followed was the development and launch of a comprehensive CP strategy for football (brand named GOAL), across a range of policy and operational areas such as education and training, communication and case management (FA 2000a).

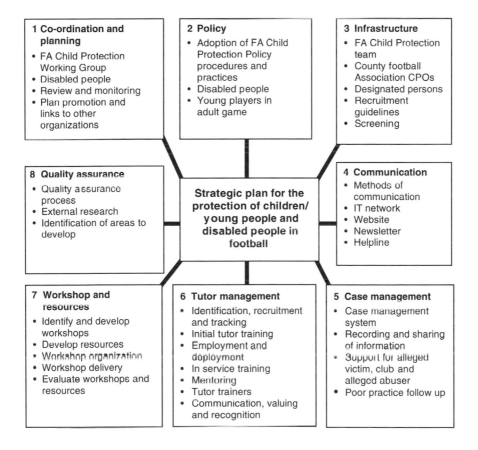

Figure 4.1 Overview of FA Strategic Plan

The FA clearly benefited from the experiences of other organizations in developing its own CP Strategy. However, it would be misleading to suggest that CP work began in football only as a result of the reaction to cases in swimming and other sports. CP and welfare work more generally was in evidence in the FA for some years prior to this project, through initiatives such as the *Charter for Quality* (FA 1997) and innovations within individual clubs. Charlton Athletic FC, for example, developed and promoted CP procedures long before most other professional clubs. The Academy and Centre of Excellence system also took forward child welfare work but it was not until the advent of the CP Strategy that an integrated approach to CP became possible throughout the professional and national games.

The FA made a commitment through its *Child Protection Policy*, published in May 2000 (FA 2000b), and the *Procedures and Practices Handbook* (FA 2000c), published in October 2000, to develop a comprehensive child protection system (Figure 4.1) through the affiliated game. Provision for disabled players was subsequently removed from this strategy and placed under the FA's overall Ethics and Equity Strategy.

The FA plans for CP were consolidated into service level agreements for the development and implementation of *The FA Child Protection Policy, Procedures and Strategy* (2000b, c and d), the management of an FA Child Protection Helpline by the NSPCC, the appointment of a named consultant to the FA from within the staff of the NSPCC, and the commissioning of the research project.

The FA made it clear that CP and welfare would become embedded in all parts of the organization's activity as part of its drive to 'use the power of football to build a better future' (FA 2000a). The FA's aims for education, delivered with and through strategic partners, included ending any cruelty to children. Child protection specifically, and player welfare more generally, permeated the work set out for all sections of the revised FA structure. Together, these initiatives were intended to help assure quality in the experience and, ultimately, in the performance of soccer players at all levels of the game.

The FA *Strategic Plan for the Protection of Children/Young People and Disabled People in Football* (2000d) set out the rationale for CP in youth (i.e. under-eighteen) football. It specifically included referees of 16–18 years old who may referee within the adult game and highlighted the fact that some players as young as fourteen were playing in the adult game. Indeed, the women's game, further discussed in Chapter 12, operates open-age football where adult women and girls often play together. The FA Strategy also explained the legal context of the FA's CP work at that time; this is something that clearly changes constantly as new legislation is introduced or existing legislation revised.

The key principles of the FA's *Child Protection Policy* were:

- The child's welfare is paramount
- All children have a right to be protected from abuse regardless of their age, gender, disability, culture, language, racial origin, religious beliefs or sexual identity

- All suspicions and allegations of abuse will be taken seriously and responded to swiftly and appropriately.

The aims of the FA *Child Protection Policy* were:

- To develop a positive proactive policy to protect all children and young people, who play or participate in football, enabling them to do so in an enjoyable and safe environment
- To deliver quality assured Child Protection Training and build a network of accredited Child Protection tutors to facilitate this delivery, supported (where appropriate) by the National Coaching Foundation (NCF)
- To demonstrate best practice in Child Protection
- To promote ethics and high standards in football.

The research project – design and staffing

In line with local and national government approaches to evidence-based policy, the FA made a commitment in December 2000 to invest in longitudinal research into its CP work. The Quality Assessment Sub-Group of the FA's CP Working Group sought an independent research project to monitor and evaluate the effectiveness of the CP programme. Many other governing bodies in the UK had set up policies and procedures for CP but, at that time, few had successfully implemented these or collected evidence of their impact or effectiveness. Also, while there were examples of evaluation and monitoring work on anti-racism in some other sport organizations (for example, in Australia), the FA was, to our knowledge, the first sport organization in the world to commission such research on CP. This was, then, an initiative congruent with the FA's strategic aim to 'be seen as the leading sports governing body in the world' (FA 2000a).

Although the FA *Child Protection Policy* was formally launched in May 2000, the research project took as its start point the period following the 2001 National Child Protection Conference at Derby. As researchers, we worked closely with the FA's CP staff in these intervening months to shape and refine the project brief. In order to achieve successful implementation of the new CP system in football, it was agreed that it would first be necessary to map the current situation, that is to audit existing CP provision, welfare problems, numbers of CP-trained and non-trained personnel, levels of awareness and concern, and so on. Only then could progress towards CP targets be measured in any meaningful way. Second, for monitoring and evaluation to be specific, and to provide reliable quantitative and qualitative data, targets for CP would need to be specified very tightly in terms of both outputs (quantifiable data) and outcomes (experiential data). The former would give the FA a platform for specifying and respecifying annual targets over time. The latter would assist with a programme of cultural change in the organization that would have to be confronted if child cruelty and

Table 4.1 Overview of research design

	Quantitative research	Qualitative research
Phase I: audit (2002)	Mapping of current CP facts and figures in football through questionnaire surveys of key stakeholders, analysis of head office data and existing football archives and records	Mapping of views and experiences of CP from key stakeholders through interviews, focus groups and online media
Phase 2: review (2003–2006)	Collection of evidence about changes in facts and figures as the CP strategy rolls out, through repeat questionnaire surveys, tracking of helpline data, case records, etc.	Collection of evidence of personal and cultural changes in football as the CP strategy rolls out, using case studies, interviews, focus groups, e-mail diaries, etc. with individuals and groups of key stakeholders

abuse were to be eradicated from the sport. Up to that point, the only evidence for such cruelty lay in the unanalysed case reports held on file by the Association. As so often happens with grand plans, achieving tightly specified targets was problematic right from the start. It was not difficult to identify broad areas of concern and intervention, but it was extremely difficult to couch these in measurable ways.

In summary, the research brief was to measure the impact of GOAL on the game of football (see Table 4.1). The project comprised two major stages:

Phase 1 (audit): An independent audit of current CP provision throughout English football, from the Premier League down to local leagues (excluding non-FA affiliates) during 2002.

Phase 2 (review): A longitudinal study to monitor and review the impact of the FA's CP strategy as it rolled out from 2003–2006 inclusive.

Together, the FA CP staff and I, as Project Director, agreed a set of key research questions that would drive the project (see Table 4.2). Following these, a framework for analysing the data was adopted that focused on:

- Voices (what people say about CP in football)
- Knowledge and experience (what people know through experience – their awareness, interest or understanding
- Feelings (what people feel – their attitudes and emotions
- Action (what people do/have done – their achievements and behaviour).

A wide range of methods was adopted during the audit phase in order to tap sources of information as completely as possible and to supplement the survey data. These included:

- Self-completion 'bracketing' interviews with the research team and key FA Ethics and Equity staff to set out expectations and to predict concerns and outcomes (discussed more fully in Chapter 14)
- Selected literature reviews to place the work of the FA within the context of CP provision in world sport and to identify relevant sources
- Internet surveys of eleven key constituencies (see Table 4.3), hosted by the internet survey company Mercator, based at Thornbury in South Gloucestershire, and using its SNAP survey software. These were first pilot tested across two FA counties[1]
- Case studies of thirty-three clubs in six different counties (see Table 4.4)
- E-mail diaries from CP officers and workshop tutors
- Analysis of existing CP-related case management files[2]
- An audit of progress against the 2002 Action Plan
- Spot-checks of CP content on the FA website[3]
- Individual and group interviews with key stakeholders (see Appendix 2 for schedule of questions).

Table 4.2 Research questions

What are the facts?
What CP provision is already in place at the different levels of the sport? Policies, procedures, numbers already trained, system for dealing with disclosures, level of current reporting to the FA, how cases are dealt with, numbers of disciplinary hearings, suspensions, dismissals, etc., involvement by police. In other words, all tangible elements of CP provision/non-provision.
What are the feelings?
What do the different stakeholders/people feel about the issues? i.e. positive/negative experiences, barriers, fears, concerns, anxieties, attitudes? What are the value-added/value-subtracted elements or intangibles associated with the programme roll out? What are the perceived cultural changes within different stakeholder groups and the FA overall? How is the FA's CP programme perceived by those inside and outside the stakeholder system, including government, NSPCC, Sports Councils, overseas football organizations?
What are the actions required?
What do the various stakeholders want done, achieved, changed, improved? How can this be fed back into the annual CP action planning process? How can examples of best practice be disseminated throughout the game?
What voices or discourses are heard?
What is said by the different stakeholders? What consistent messages are given out? Who agrees or disagrees with the FA's CP initiative?
What is the impact of the FA's CP strategy on football?
How does all of the above change quantitatively and qualitatively over the five year span? What type and extent of cultural change is achieved in the organization, attributable to the CP programme roll out, in relation to the FA's overall strategic vision?

The second year of the research, 2003, included repeat surveys, interviews and focus groups and a repeat audit of data from year one. Research ethics procedures, which are discussed in Chapter 14, were extremely important to this project because of the very sensitive nature of the subject matter and because minors were involved. Particular care was taken not to include the under-twelves in the internet survey method (although some slipped through the net – literally!). Approaches to very young children were informed by advice from teachers and from the government document *Children are Service Users Too – Consulting Children* (Fajerman and Treseder 2002). Pilots were conducted in the early spring of 2002 and the instruments (surveys, interview and focus group schedules) were then revised prior to the major phases of data collection.

Finding a suitably qualified and available research team might have presented difficulties for such large project over such a wide geographic area. In the event, a committed and hard-working team was brought together fairly quickly that blended experience of research methods, sports management and development and football coaching, scouting and refereeing. We also had a disability specialist in the group.

All researchers adhered to a set of Research Team Guidelines, setting out protocols that had been agreed with the FA, and gave detailed information about the design, methods and data collection procedures to be adopted. Incident forms and ethics procedures were likewise made available through the guidelines booklet, which was revised and reissued in the second year.

Where necessary, staff attended specialist training sessions in research methods or data analysis. General training was conducted by the Project Director to bring everyone up to a similar baseline and was supplemented by periodic team meetings. All of us conducting fieldwork, who had not already done so, also attended the FA's own workshop on Good Practice in Working with Children and each member of the team submitted to a Criminal Records Bureau background check via the FA.

In keeping with the reflexive nature of modern sociological writing, I encouraged everyone working on the project to keep a research diary, charting not just the facts of the project but also their feelings as the work developed. Some of us chose to keep this confidential and others were happy to share the contents. This is something I now do as a matter of course with all research students and that I have found particularly helpful in the past with long-term projects (Brackenridge 1999). The usefulness of these diaries is discussed in Chapter 14. Overall progress of the project was monitored by a Steering Group, comprising a mix of FA and research staff. A virtual Advisory Group team, comprising senior researchers from the University of Gloucestershire, supported the research team (see Figure 4.2).

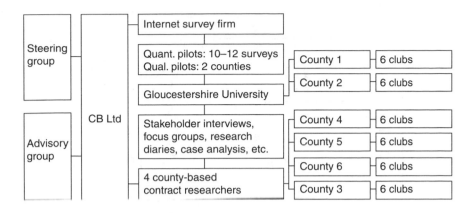

Figure 4.2 Research management structure

Researching the 'football family' – signifiers and safety nets

Stakeholders can be grouped in many ways. One typical division is between internal and external. Internal stakeholders are more than simply those on the payroll. In the case of a governing body of sport the size of the FA, huge numbers of volunteers work for the game beyond those in remunerated roles. Consumers and producers of a product or service are other common stakeholder divisions. For example, parents and young people themselves 'consume' football, whereas coaches, administrators and referees are part of the production chain in the game.

The FA provided a stakeholder map that gave us a good indication of those who it thought should be consulted for the research audit but it was daunting in its scope (Figure 4.3). The criteria we eventually applied to the selection of stakeholders for the research were that they should be:

- affiliated
- close to children, and
- potential change agents.

This allowed us to narrow down our sample to a manageable group (Table 4.5).

We spent a great deal of time considering the sample and arguing back and forth about how to achieve optimum representativeness in such a huge sport. In the end, our sample sizes were dictated by the number of researcher days provided for in the budget. The balance of samples across the different research methods was juggled repeatedly in order to make it fit the funding frame without

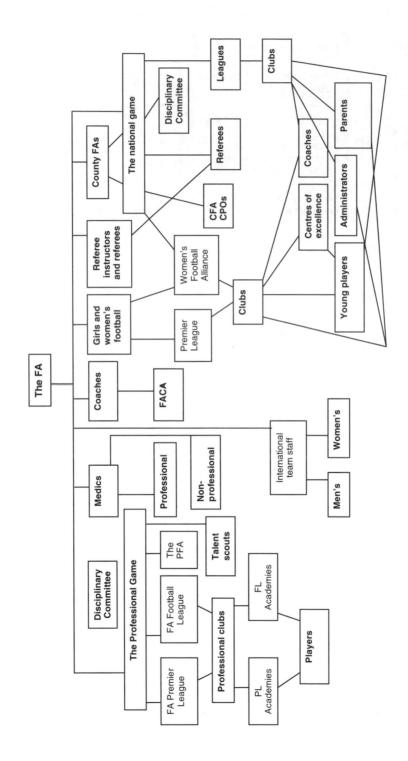

Figure 4.3 Stakeholder map (provided by the FA)

Table 4.3 Internet survey groups 2002

1	Young players (12–17 years)
2	Referees
3	Coaches, managers and teachers
4	Scouts and agents
5	Medics and sport scientists including physios
6	Welfare/Child Protection Officers
7	Administrators
8	Parents
9	School-based helpers
10	Football Development Officers
11	Players over 18

compromising representativeness too far. It would be impossible to claim that we necessarily reached into every corner of the affiliated game, yet the results from the surveys indicated that we achieved an acceptable geographic and demographic spread (Brackenridge *et al.* 2002).

Table 4.4 Distribution and type of football club case studies

County FA area	Types of club approached	Number of clubs responding from those approached
North East	Professional, under-18s (boys), under-9s (mixed), under-16s, under-8s, disability	6/6
North West	Professional, school-based, junior solo, junior in large club, women's	3/5
Midlands 1	Professional, 2 juniors in bigger clubs, solo, Charter Standard, multi-team junior	6/6
Midlands 2	Professional, school/college, mixed, girls', junior solo	5/5
East	Professional, school, girls' and women's (in youth club), junior in senior set up, junior solo, disability	6/6
South	Professional, junior, disability (deaf), girls', mixed large, small	6/6
	Total	32/34

Table 4.5 Target stakeholder groups for individual interviews

Children and young people	FA Coaches Association
Parents	County Secretaries
Directors of Academies	Football Development Officers
CP/WOs of Academies	Other Leagues
Premier League/Football League	Women's Premier League
(Youth Development or CP)	Women's International Player
Professional footballers	Development Centre
Scouts	Schools
Agents	Women's Centres of Excellence
Medics/GPs/sport scientists	Disability football
Referees Association	Chaplains
Football in the Community schemes	ESFA
Commercial providers	

Similarly, in choosing the stakeholder interviews, we wanted to achieve a fair spread from the top to the bottom of the game and across all key sectors (see Table 4.4). The choice of the 'elites' (Odendahl and Shaw 2002) in this sample was always going to be especially contentious because of power dynamics within football (see Conn 1997 and Bower 2003 for a full explication of these in England, and Sugden and Tomlinson 2003 for a wider international view). Luckily, our highest selected contact in the FA hierarchy turned out to be both accessible and very forthcoming in his views. We may have been less fortunate with other individuals.

Our choice of which six counties to approach was determined by considerations of geographic spread, researcher access and, to some extent, the co-operativeness of our FA county secretary and professional club gatekeepers. Attempts to access clubs through these gatekeepers gave us some of our most testing times in the research process but we finally secured entry to clubs at all levels and in disparate areas (see Table 4.5).

We have chosen in this book to focus in Part II on those stakeholder groups that we consider to be priorities in terms of both the research findings and the implications for future child protection policy in the sport, viz:

- children and young people
- parents and carers
- referees
- coaches, managers and teachers
- the Professional Game, Academies and Centres of Excellence
- disability football and vulnerable people
- the women's game
- scouts and agents

... with material on Football Development Officers (FDOs) and Child Protection Officers (CPOs) embedded.[4]

Some historical background to each of these groups is given within their own chapters (and in Chapter 3 in the case of youth football) in order to situate them within wider considerations of the FA's child protection and welfare work.

As already pointed out in Chapter 1, football is fond of its 'family' label, which is used at every level of the game from FIFA down (Sugden and Tomlinson 2003). But we know all too well that families reflect both good and bad in terms of relationships, nurturing, rivalries and support. The football family is no exception, based as it is on very traditional patriarchal structures, authoritarian leadership and close-knit, almost collusive secrecy and suspicion of 'outsiders'. As researchers, we predicted that our access into the various stakeholder groups would be mediated by suspicion, fear, indifference or plain hostility, and that it might also be affected by our own football credentials (or lack of them). Such insider/outsider issues confront many researchers of sensitive topics (Fleming 1997) from drug running, to fraud and sexuality. One way for researchers to address the problem is to adopt a scrupulously objective stance, as Kinsey's researchers did in their interviews with ordinary American citizens about their sexual habits (Gathorne-Hardy 1998). Another is to use credible intermediaries or gatekeepers to collect data on one's behalf or to ease one's passage into the research site, as Foot Whyte did in his studies of street gangs in Boston (Foot Whyte 1984). Yet another is to make strenuous preparatory efforts to become an insider and then to lay out one's credentials as such to the research participants, as Pollert did in her studies of factory women (1981).

In order to help us anticipate and manage potential access difficulties, we adopted a technique that we called 'bracketing interviews' (see Chapter 14). We also wore photo-identity badges bearing the FA logo and carried official letters of introduction from the FA, along with specially manufactured business cards depicting the FA and GOAL campaign logos and our personal contact details. These accoutrements were intended to signify our FA credibility and thus, we hoped, ease our access to interviews with any senior and/or reluctant participants. We also gave tokens such as FA pens and badges to the children and young people as a form of thank you for their help, and offered a prize draw with official England 2002 World Cup shirts as incentives to respond to the internet surveys.

Summary

This chapter has outlined the origins of child protection and welfare work within the FA and describes how it has become embedded within contemporary FA management systems. It also describes how we designed and delivered the research project in order to assess the impact of this work and explains some of ways in which we tried to pre-empt difficulties with research access. We prepared for the daunting task of examining responses to child protection at close quarters within the family of football by adopting a number of signifiers of credibility and protocols or safety nets to deal with anticipated problems. As the following chapters will demonstrate, some of these proved invaluable.

Notes

1   All those approached to participate in the qualitative research completed written, voluntary, informed consent forms that were separately coded and stored securely. Internet survey respondents were informed that responses would be anonymous and that, by continuing with completion of the survey, they were opting into the consent process. However, those who chose to enter the associated prize draw for an England World Cup shirt were asked to give an e-mail contact, held by Mercator (the internet survey host).

2   The results of this analysis are available in Brackenridge et al. (2005).

3   The research project examined progress in the delivery of 299 actions in the FA's 2002 *Child Protection Action Plan* across all seven sections, viz:
   • policy, procedures and practices
   • workshops and resources
   • tutor management
   • communication
   • infrastructure
   • quality assurance
   • case management.

4   The terminology associated with the role of CPO has changed over the years: at the time of our research it referred to individuals who acted as club or county welfare officers in a mainly voluntary capacity. Since our research, club level officers have been named 'designated persons' and the term CPO has been applied more specifically to officers at county FA level. At the time of writing, the recommendation of the Independent Football Commission (IFC 2005) to institute full-time paid CPOs in each county FA was deemed by the FA to be 'not a viable proposition' (IFC 2006: 50) on cost grounds.

Part II

Findings

Chapter 5

Children and young people

Andy Pitchford

For those of a certain age, the quality and organization of youth football in England can come as something of a shock. If your memory of football as a child revolves around either schools matches or parks, playgrounds, gardens and jumpers for goalposts, then the shiny new world of mini-soccer and youth leagues may represent something of a dream come true.

Gone are the ill-fitting school stripes, the nets with rather too many holes, the over-the-bar/under-the-bar disputes, the over-sized footballs and unmarked pitches. Instead, young players of today can enjoy appropriately sized and branded equipment, qualified referees, sponsored kits, tactical team talks, corner flags, technical training and, most impressively of all, crowds. The results of today's mini-soccer and youth matches may still lodge themselves in the memories of the players but they also appear in newspapers and on websites, alongside detailed match reports and league tables.

At a time when professional football is under criticism for its apparent lack of authenticity, the creation of this new world at youth level fills a void for those adults frustrated by the cynicism and commercialism of the elite levels of the sport. As we will see in later chapters, mini-soccer and youth football have something of an addictive quality for many of the adults involved, and offer a source of meaning, belonging and aspiration. The extent to which these feelings are shared by the children involved is, clearly, a question of some importance.

In previous chapters, we have argued for policies and practices that give a voice to the experiences of children and young people. This chapter is therefore devoted to the views of the players in our sample, their experiences, their motivations and aspirations. Before we present these findings, however, we identify the methods used to engage with our respondents, primarily to enable readers to consider how we, as adults with our own ideologies and assumptions, may have interpreted the data and, perhaps, imposed meanings on the subjects of our research.

Researching the field

With the benefit of hindsight, it is possible to characterize our research strategy for engaging with young people as a rather conventional, solid but unspectacular '4–4–2' style approach. We did engage in some experimentation but with a typically English, 'only in safe areas of the pitch' mentality. Since the completion of the second of the two FA CP Research Project Reports in 2003 (Brackenridge *et al.* 2003), a number of academic and consultancy sources have responded to the call by Mayall (2000) for the generation of innovation in research methods which can empower young people, and for approaches which can articulate life and experience 'looking up' from the position of the child. Green and Hogan's (2005) text, for example, captures evaluation of a range of possible methodological strategies, from anthropology and ethnography to narrative and discourse analysis. Similarly, Allen Collinson *et al.* (2005) argue for the deployment of a range of participatory methodologies in the analysis of young people and sport. While some of these approaches may well have offered attractive alternatives for us, we were restricted by the costs of some of these more intensive methods and also by the need to secure a way of working which our clients, the FA, could both recognize and embrace.

As a consequence, our engagement with young people was managed primarily through individual or group interviews. As we outlined in Chapter 4, the context for our sample was a range of football club settings, specifically thirty-two in six counties. It was a requirement of our contract with the FA that subjects should be participants in 'affiliated' football, where the governing body had responsibility and some ability to regulate. As a consequence, we did not interview participants in the National Curriculum, nor players engaged in commercial coaching contexts, outreach or sports development programmes. Our focus was on the organized, structured, competitive sporting realm, not on free play or self-regulated games.

Furthermore, it is important to emphasize at this point that our respondents represented the 'included', rather than the 'excluded'. In a variety of ways, children in our sample had been selected for participation in competitive club environments. Their parents or carers usually make the initial decision to support their entry to this realm but, once engaged, the demands of competitive clubs require children to be subjected to a range of selection procedures. Even clubs with an explicit commitment to social inclusion and equity will find it difficult to avoid some element of selection because the demands of the 'sport' – the meritocratic world of outcomes and league tables – require management and closure. In most geographic areas, participation in competitive leagues is restricted to registered and affiliated players to ensure fair play and transparency. However, the majority of leagues also impose a limit on the number of players who can be registered for a competitive 'squad'. Clubs are therefore forced into selection processes as soon as they enter the competitive realm.

In most counties, leagues manage competitions so that the first formal competition takes place for the under-9 age group. However, there are leagues across the country for under-8s and even under-7s. This means that the opportunities for clubs to manage more informal 'turn up and play', open access environments are continually squeezed. The norm is for more inclusive, 'casual' practices to dominate until leagues beckon, at which point clubs mutate into more performance-oriented, selective environments. Clearly, while these processes may well assist the development of many players, enabling them to enjoy more and more challenging environments, they can also create more opportunities for 'drop-out' than is strictly necessary.

None of our respondents was younger than eight years of age, and the vast majority were in competitive league teams or squads. The exceptions were associated with a disability club, for whom a competitive structure was not in existence at the time of the research.

We interviewed 189 children during the two years of the project, and parent/carer consent was established for all participants. A semi-structured approach was supported, on occasions, by some 'participatory' devices which enabled subjects to shape the agenda and generate discussion. We carried out semi-inductive content analysis on the data, and managed this process with the assistance of the QSR NU-DIST software, Version N6.

Children's motivations

As we will discover in Chapter 6, parents and carers bring with them a range of motivations to children's football. Given that these adults may allow their own interests to override those of their children, it is entirely possible that some of the children in our sample actually attend football clubs against their own will, or at least might prefer to be doing something else more interesting instead. Although none of our participants raised this as an issue, it is worth noting that the club environment is rather more structured than other 'play' settings. Most clubs are structured around a system of adult authority that makes it difficult, for example, for a child to refuse to comply with the request of a coach or manager. Once a child enters the power relations of the club, they are subject to the organization until their parent or carer returns. Walking off to play on the swings because the game is unsatisfactory is, therefore, rarely an option in such environments.

Despite these potential restrictions, the children in our sample were very clear about those aspects of football that they value and enjoy. For a large proportion of our interviewees, the skills and sheer physicality of the game were particularly appealing. A twelve-year-old female player, for example, felt that with football '... you can just run around and be mental', while a colleague from the same team felt that 'Football's the best thing ever in the world ... I couldn't live without football'.

When asked about their experiences and preferences in the game, young people interviewed in club settings tended to emphasize intrinsic rather than extrinsic motivations. Many identified particular skills or game aspects in this context. These often related to their own abilities, playing position or experiences, so frequent references were made in interviews to 'scoring goals', 'making saves', 'good passing and movement', and – repeatedly – 'slide tackles'.

Respondents tended to prefer game situations to training. To an extent this was related to the ability of coaches and volunteers to sustain interesting and varied coaching programmes. Children objected to 'hours and hours of warm ups' and 'just doing boring drills'. One fourteen-year-old female player observed: 'They've basically been doing the same thing for four weeks now and, well, we're bored'. However, the desire to engage in the games and matches also appears to relate to a perception among the children that they can express themselves more freely, and with less intense adult supervision, in game situations. For example, they enjoyed 'playing matches, having fun, doing what you like', and liked 'playing matches more than training – it's the real thing'. This has implications for the extent to which adults, as parents, coaches, referees or spectators, intervene in organized matches and, indeed, the nature and character of those interventions.

The desire of children and young people to engage in the 'real thing' is often interpreted by adults as an instrumental motivation, reflecting their desire to win and achieve. However, while the game itself was of great importance to the children in our sample, winning was less so. The response of a fourteen-year-old female player was typical: 'I'm not really bothered about winning. As long as everybody is improving and doing well, it doesn't really matter if we don't win'. Competitive, 'well balanced' games were seen as the most enjoyable settings, with a number of children keen to reflect on the unsatisfactory nature of repeated wins and repeated defeats:

> In the under-12s, when I was with the younger people, we used to lose quite a lot. Like every game. Because we've done that a lot I'm just not really bothered by it anymore. We just keep on going and try and improve for the next game, and try and have a defeat by less each time … It got a bit depressing but it was OK. Training helps because they didn't bring the games into training. They didn't mention the games in training at all, so you didn't think about it too much – they were always focused ahead on what was going to happen next week, in the next match.

These kinds of preferences were often reflected in a participatory exercise that we employed as a 'prompt' at a small number of the sample clubs. Table 5.1 shows typical responses to this exercise, details of which are presented in Appendix 3.

For many respondents in our sample, amateur children's football appears to be an effective base for sustainable community connections and friendships. Many of them spoke about friendship and sociality and saw this as central to their enjoyment of the sport. A partially hearing fifteen-year-old claimed that 'it

Table 5.1 Footballing likes/dislikes of young people at one sample club

Like most about playing football	Like least about playing football
• Meeting new people/playing against different teams (4)	• Racism and abuse (racial, physical) (3)
• The challenge ('I like the opposition to be a challenge') (2)	• 'Dodgy' refs/more qualified refs [needed] (2)
• Playing with mates/friends (2)	• Injuries (2)
• Scoring/making goals (2)	• Parents shouting/being shouted at (2)
• Getting outside (1)	• Bad coaches (1)
• Seeing new things (1)	• Checks on refs, especially at high standard (1)
• Fitness (1)	• Losing (1)
• Ambition (1)	• Bullying (1)
• Winning (1)	• Playing badly (1)
• Tackling (1)	• When the opposition isn't a good challenge (1)
• Performing (1)	• 'I hate it when people mess about with you for fun' (1)
• The 'rush' (1)	• Warm ups (1)
• A good game (1)	• When you make mistakes (1)
• The 'competition' (1)	• 'People gobbing off at you' (1)
• It's fun (1)	
• You learn stuff (1)	

doesn't matter if we win or lose, the main thing is that we enjoy it, that's all ... We have fun ... making friends'. When asked to identify the best thing about her club, a seventeen-year-old female player said:

> That we've known each other for quite a long time ... and you're used to everyone ... used to the manager and used to the players. We all live in the same area and got the same kind of experiences from playing.

Adult interventions

Left to their own devices, it appears that the children in our sample would prefer to emphasize the inclusive rather than meritocratic aspects of football. However, the majority of them had concerns about the ways in which adults intervened in their sport. While many were clearly grateful for the enthusiasm and expertise of their club coaches and officials, others found adult expectations and demands to be problematic. The confusion of a nine-year-old boy was indicative:

> The adults ... the parents ... they interrupt and stuff. And they tell the kids what to do and the kids won't listen to the manager ... You get confused and don't know what to do.

Where adults openly criticized players, children raised objections about both the language used and the setting in which such criticism took place. Many raised concerns about their own coaches:

I listen to the good things but I just ignore it when he shouts at me.

When we lost 12–0 ... I got blamed for that. I was captain and the coach blamed it all on me ... Football is a team effort, and he can't just stand there and blame it all on me. So I just stood there and we had a big argument, and I just walked off. He shouldn't blame something on me that is a team effort, and football is a team game. It isn't to be played individually. I think my team mates kind of agreed with me, I think. He shouldn't have blamed it all on me if other people didn't play as well as they could, either ... Coaches need to be more aware of what they say, and think about what they say before they say it.

Others, meanwhile, experienced difficulties with spectators associated with other clubs. While on some occasions criticism would be open and explicit, in other instances children were aware of subtle distinctions in the use of language that served to label or discriminate:

Yeah, you get that at (rival club) a lot. Sometimes the parents get a bit out of order too, swearing and shouting.

I made a tackle which wasn't a foul but their guy didn't get up for a while. Their supporters started booing me ... I didn't like it. Why do you think they did that?

When we play (rival club) they give the opposing team abuse ... If they're shouting about us they won't go 'Hey, pick up number five', they shout 'Pick up the lanky one in the middle'. They can see your number but they just want to have a go.

The desire of adults to intervene in match situations was the cause of particular stress for our children. It seems that many parents, coaches and spectators place heavy expectations on children playing the sport, and that these expectations can create a highly pressurized environment. Sometimes, this kind of pressure led to what was perceived as an overly competitive environment and then children expressed particular resentment and concern. Tales of confrontational behaviour by adults were frequently recounted, leading to discomfort for the young people involved:

There was a foul and one of the men from the other club came running on the pitch and whacked the referee, and I ran on the pitch and shouted at him. Then my mum told me off for sticking up for the referee. I was crying because my mum had a go at me.

The problem is that when they have a match they are fighting ... and all the young people see them ... That happened last Monday. The coach thought somebody was chatting up his girlfriend and he had a fight with him and beat him up in front of all the children, but really the man was just talking to her about football.

The children in our sample were anxious about this kind of behaviour but also demonstrated concern for the adults involved. While they were, on occasions, embarrassed by the actions of adults, they also demonstrated a desire for those adults to enjoy the sport in a safe environment, free of confrontation. They were also clear about how they wanted those adults to behave. Respondents valued 'being listened to', and were willing to identify the qualities of coaches who supported them. A ten-year-old boy commented: 'My coach makes it fair for all the players, he makes sure you get a game'; and another observed: 'My coach is encouraging and honest but not angry.'

The behaviour of team mates and opponents was also raised as a concern by our respondents. For some children, racist taunting was an extremely uncomfortable but frequent experience. Although team mates had intervened to calm players down when this had happened, the players involved had become almost resigned to accepting racial abuse as part of the fabric of the game: 'You can't stop it, can you?' observed one twelve-year-old player.

Some girls complained that boys did not take them seriously as players. This was reinforced by comments from club coaches, for example:

> they can't play with the boys because of the way the boys behave ... and the way the parents behave ... 'Don't let her tackle you, she's a girl' ... and that is really sad because sport should be for everybody.

Another female player recalled:

> When I used to play for the under-10s the boys in the other teams wouldn't shake my hand at the end of the game ... It was because I was a girl. I thought it was just a bit stupid but it could upset some people, especially if they weren't used to it.

These attitudes appear to be prevalent despite the widespread use of codes of conduct and behavioural policies. However, our respondents suggested that such measures were effectively imposed by adults, and that children have few opportunities to influence them. The following comment was typical:

> Yeah, we've got a code of conduct. They told us that when we started. Sometimes (player) gets told off and he has to go and read it! (Laughter) ... It's not up to us though, it's to make sure we're good.

Similarly, where other club systems had been designed in order to protect young people, but without the input of the youngsters concerned, respondents expressed some confusion over adult roles and effectiveness. Many were, for example, aware of behavioural policies or CP strategies but few had been given the chance to shape or contribute to these documents. Young people were equally unsure about CP procedures, and few were aware of an adult in their club with a specific responsibility for this. When asked who they would turn to if there was a problem or concern, the young people repeatedly identified a specific adult who they thought they could trust. This was usually a parent or their immediate coach and, as a result, only a very small minority identified the CP officer by person or role. It appears that, even in Charter Standard clubs, where CP responsibilities and policies are clear and explicit, young people are not as fully informed about their own welfare as might be expected.

The extent to which children have opportunities to influence aspects of club policy and operation more generally is considered in the following section.

Clubs and empowerment

Our first attempt at analysis of data from the initial year of the project suggested that the voices of children were, effectively, marginalized across all areas of the sport. Few of our respondents were able to identify examples of how they had been involved in decision-making processes, or when they had been consulted. However, further consideration of the interaction between adults and children in these settings enabled us to distinguish between potential empowerment in three aspects of the club experience. First, a degree of empowerment is possible at the immediate 'practice' level, where interaction might lead to adults responding to children's desires to run matches or training in a particular way. Second, it is possible for children of all ages to be involved in policy development through, for example, the development of codes of conduct or even the club ethos and constitution. This might, typically, be managed through democratic processes where club committees include player delegates or representatives. Third, it is possible in a variety of ways for children to take ownership of club operations, from the level of strategic management to specific functions, from team selection and coaching to fixture organization and administration. These distinctions mirror Kirby et al.'s (2003) models of participatory practice, outlined in Chapter 2, which characterized organizations as potentially 'consultation focused', 'participation focused' or 'child/youth focused'.

Many young people in our sample were able to identify examples of empowerment at the first level. For example, they were able to distinguish between different coaching styles:

> I prefer (coach A) because he listens to us. We can ask questions and he'll change things ... makes training more fun. (Coach B) just tells us what to do. It's boring a lot of the time.

We're encouraged to ask questions all the time ... He (coach) says we learn more if we ask about things we're not sure about.

Similarly, respondents pointed to an 'open' club culture that allowed them to engage with other aspects of practice. When asked about CP responsibilities, a twelve-year-old player observed:

I don't know who that is but we can ask about everything. They always say for us to say something if we're not happy. It's easy to speak to (coach) or (chairman) because they're always really nice.

However, our respondents were rather less forthcoming in relation to empowerment at the second level. As we have seen, engagement in the development of codes of conduct and CP policies was limited, and this appeared to be reflected in other areas of strategy formulation. Interestingly, though, some of the adult respondents from the same clubs were able to articulate a number of practices at this level. Those at several Charter Standard clubs, for example, identified the use of 'open meetings' or 'amnesty meetings' where players were invited to contribute to discussions on club policies. At other clubs in the sample, democratic processes for young players have been instigated, with players electing team representatives to sit on club committees. One administrator noted:

We have player representatives to the under-14s and under-12 girls who sit on the committee. They have voting rights. They have as much say as any committee member.

In some older age group teams, this empowerment extends to the week-to-week management of training and fixtures. Another administrator said:

The under-16s practically run themselves now because they've had experience of it at fourteen and fifteen ... One of them goes to the league meetings once a month. One does fixtures and one (they take it in turns) does all the phone calls to players the night before each game. Two of them attend the management committee meetings once a month and there's a standing agenda item to ask them 'under-16s, what's happening?' I haven't managed to get them to wash their kit yet ...

According to our respondents, innovative consultative processes are also in evidence at professional Academies and Centres of Excellence, primarily in relation to coaching styles and parental input (see Chapter 6, Parents and Carers, and Chapter 8, The Professional Game).

Whether the inability of young people in our sample to identify these kinds of approaches was caused by the communication systems within the clubs concerned, or by some fault in our research strategy, is open to question. Awareness of these possibilities certainly appeared to be low but if we were to return to the same clubs now it may be that the message has been more effectively articulated.

However, other adult coaches in the sample were blithely happy to demonstrate the levels of resistance to consultative and empowering processes that appear still to dominate the sport. For example:

> You can listen but you have to, sometimes, as a manager, you just have to make your own decisions and listen but not really include what the players are saying ... tactics, because you might consider it and think about it but, I mean, if he thinks that's the best idea then that's how we have to play. You can't have everyone saying 'I want this formation' or 'I want that formation'. It would just get really silly and the manager, he needs to stand up and say 'No, we're doing it this way and that's it'.

> They're probably not so much involved in the running of the club ... we've got a committee and they deal with that side of things for them. Not many of the players like to get involved ... they like to have it all on a plate.

> Basically it's all parents really. We don't have any youngsters. I have had when I've been coaching ... My son, he used to come down and he used to come and help but basically we don't have any young people as far as the committee is concerned.

> No, not formally, no. They're a bit young really to give them that kind of a role, I think.

Despite the reluctance of many adult stakeholders to engage in empowering practices, there are examples from our sample of clubs where some consultation or devolution is evident. That these examples are in comparatively short supply is perhaps because of the relative immaturity of this segment of the voluntary sector. Many clubs will be new or in the first few years of their operation and probably led by a small number of adult volunteers, already stretched by the weighty administrative burden that has fallen on their shoulders. Equally, however, it may be that the prevailing ideology of adult-centred decision-making in sport forces alternative, child-centred approaches to the sidelines.

In relation to Kirby *et al.*'s distinctions, the majority of clubs in our sample would, at best, be characterized as consultation-focused organizations. Children are, in these settings, encouraged to ask questions, to contribute ideas and to 'speak up'. They do not necessarily enjoy power or authority in return for this input. These children, then, are listened to but not always heard. A small number of clubs in our sample could be characterized as participation-focused organizations, offering as they do opportunities for children and young people to gain membership of committees and other decision-making groups. None of our respondents was able to identify their club as sharing the characteristics of a 'child/youth focused' organization.

Again, we should point out that the position of children in football more generally is rather more complicated than the picture we have painted here. We are looking for the most part at clubs that are essentially (though not always in practice) voluntary sector democracies. The possibilities for empowering measures are clear in these contexts. In other settings, the possibilities are rather less clear. The increasing range of agencies involved in the delivery of football for children means that, while some players will be the recipients of free or subsidized coaching in a professional club, others will be engaged in a market exchange with a commercial provider. At the same time, other players will be receiving 'welfare' from state or quasi-state agencies in the form of football coaching or competition, while others will be subjected to the demands of educational institutions. The ownership and decision-making processes in each of these settings will necessarily differ, affording children more or less opportunity to influence football policy and practice.

Summary

The children in our sample had many positive things to say about their experience of football. Many were highly committed to the sport and found it to be a largely enjoyable and consuming pursuit; indeed, for many it appeared to be a central life interest. However, many others found themselves caught up in the interplay of competing adult motives which, from time to time, restricted their enjoyment and threatened their future participation.

Reconciling these motives can be very challenging. Selecting a team that can compete and win matches for a club may be in direct conflict with any attempt to 'include' all participants equally in playing opportunities. Allowing players to 'own' tactical decisions and strategies may endanger the ability of the team to 'compete'. Finding a balance between the performance requirements of competitive teams and democracy, or between meritocracy and inclusion, may not always be possible. It seems clear from our respondents that children can often be subjected to these tensions, and that many of these conflicts will have been created by the aspirations of the adults concerned.

We have argued elsewhere (Pitchford et al. 2004) that the concerns of the sociology of childhood, outlined in Chapter 1, raise many important issues for the agencies and individuals who manage football for children. These issues are reflected in the experiences of the children in our sample. It seems clear that much of the delivery of football in England is based on a range of adult assumptions about the motives and development of the children concerned, and that many of these assumptions may be misplaced.

If our sample is at all representative, the needs and demands of children in football are not quite at the centre of decision-making processes. Our respondents provide evidence that children can and do articulate views that should be taken into account. They demonstrate a high level of concern and responsibility for the experiences of the adults who have helped them, and for the welfare of their fellow players. A sixteen-year-old male player, for example, when asked if he had anything further to add at the end of an interview, simply said: 'No, I just hope you make it safer for young children.'

Alternative models for football, and for football clubs, are both possible and, arguably, preferable. We look forward to a time when these models can be more fully embraced, and when we can say that children's voices occupy the centre ground in decision-making and policy formulation.

Chapter 6

Parents and carers

Andy Pitchford

We have seen in previous chapters that children's football has been reborn. Gone is the informality of free play in the street or the park. Instead, the new incarnation of football is characterized by regulation, organization, and a determination to create 'safe', 'structured' and 'child-friendly' environments. Given the apparent expansion of the junior version of the sport that took place during the 1990s, following the publication of the FA's *Charter for Quality*, it seems safe to say that this growing activity is well into its adolescence. However, just like many other teenagers, children's football is discovering that parents can be the source of all manner of problems. Despite being essential, they are also frequently embarrassing. Despite providing in all sorts of ways, they are invariably both pushy and provocative.

Stakeholders from all realms of football spoke to us about this parental paradox. The growth of the contemporary form of children's football since the 1980s owes everything to the efforts of parents but, ironically, parental behaviour is overwhelmingly depicted as the main threat to children's experiences and their future participation in the sport. Indeed, in Chapter 5 we have already noted the concerns of many young people about the behaviour of parents and other adults at their clubs.

In order to explore these issues in further depth, this chapter is focused primarily on the views of the parents and carers in our sample. It also draws on observations from other stakeholders where they engage with parents in this apparently contradictory position. The chapter is also written, predictably enough, by a soccer dad infected with the mini-soccer bug, a malaise for which the processes of academic reflection and researcher neutrality appear to be no certain remedy.

Parents and the football family

As we noted in Chapter 1, the family has long enjoyed a high profile in the upper echelons of association football. Two factors have contributed to this. First, the biological and cultural impact of football-playing parents on their children has given some individuals a head start in the talent stakes. Second, the closure and nepotism of professional football has, for many years, given family members something of an advantage. Although this benefit is, at times, a double-edged sword, the lack of governing body regulation of working practices within the sport has enabled empires to grow and reproduce, with the family often inescapably entwined within. Fathers as agents, wives running the club shop, daughters working in promotions, sons as apprentices – extensive opportunities have been available to those men able to gain a foothold in professional clubs.

Managers who employ their children as professional players are common at the highest levels of the sport. However, aside from the difficulties of managing family relationships in the workplace, the individuals involved can often be undermined by football's increasing insecurity. In the highly unstable environment of professional football, the limited tenure of most managers and coaches means that personal relationships often become pressurized and intensified. Managers who attempt to engage with their offspring in these settings are faced with enormous challenges if they are to do so in an equitable and transparent manner. Given the potential financial rewards now prevalent in the higher echelons of the sport, it would be unsurprising to find that favouritism is a continuing concern among professional players. Although the term 'gaffer's son' is often used in such settings as a form of gentle abuse or banter, aimed at those perceived to be in favour, it reflects an enduring concern about the power of familial relationships in football.

Families may well create advantage in professional football but they also carry with them a host of uncomfortable tensions. Add to the potential for favouritism the probable incidence of unrealized expectations, unfulfilled potential and the desires of individuals to settle disputes along family lines, and professional football becomes a source of emotional conflict rather than prosperity. These tensions are most eloquently depicted in Colin Schindler's (2001) account of the Summerbees, in which three generations of the family tangle with the pains and pressures of professional sport.

Thirty years ago the impact of these issues on the junior game would have been limited. Children in competitive football would be coached predominantly by teachers in primary and secondary schools, and by voluntary or professional coaches in the comparatively undeveloped youth sector. Although some of these individuals may well have been parents of the children concerned, in general, families would have been more distanced from the sport. School matches would frequently take place during the week, restricting the ability of fathers and mothers to gain an interest and a stake in the teams concerned. Clearly, parents will have both helped and hindered the development of their children in the sport in a variety of ways but their involvement in the organization and operation of the sport at this level was undeniably limited.

The situation today is very different. A cursory glance at the sports pages of any local newspaper will reveal the extent to which the family is now firmly embedded in youth sport. Fathers, particularly, have facilitated the growth of mini-soccer in the past fifteen years. Managers and coaches will frequently oversee their child's development in competitive mini-soccer teams, with the promotion of the child concerned to the position of 'captain' not uncommon. Parents are also actively involved as administrators and volunteers and now have a demonstrable stake in the clubs concerned. In contrast to previous generations, they are also now active spectators. In its new location in the voluntary sector, junior football is organized around the working days of both children and adults. Consequently, it is possible for members of children's immediate and extended families to attend and support them. This has implications for the character of the sport at this level, and for the children who play.

As a result of these changes, the familial tensions characterized above are now just as likely to be prevalent in the local park as in the professional game. In some respects, these difficulties are likely to be more intense at the elite level, but the ability of parents to access junior football, and the sheer scale of the sport in this country, means that it has become a potential venue for the manifestation of the parental anxieties and pressures that we identified in Chapter 1.

The FA CP Research Project brought us into contact with ninety-four respondents who we classified as parents or carers of children at our sample clubs. However, among the other 425 respondents representing various stakeholder groups, there were many more who were parents of children engaged with the national game. Although our interviews were focused on parental interpretation of child protection measures adopted by clubs and the national football authorities, they also afforded us the opportunity to explore with respondents their roles and motives, and their broad relationships with the range of agencies. Our interpretation of these findings follows, focusing on the impact of the new environment for junior football, the motives and behaviours of the adults concerned, and the attempts by clubs to manage – and in some cases empower – parents and carers in these settings.

Parents and the quest for silverware

As we noted in Chapter 4, our research has engaged primarily with the affiliated game. The parents in our sample were therefore most familiar with the mini-soccer or youth league environment that involved their children in competitive matches which, in various ways, influenced the ethos and structure of the clubs concerned. Training, for example, would be organized to support progress and development in the leagues and, in all cases, competitive matches would be prioritized over 'friendlies' or other less formalized interactions. The clubs also competed in tournaments, some of which were organized around different value sets. At one club, for example, parents reported participation in a 'Fair Play' Tournament, in which player and parental behaviour had contributed to a points system.

However, because of their connection to the affiliated game, few parents were familiar with alternative, open access interpretations of the sport. All of our club environments could therefore be contrasted to such programmes as *Strikes!* or *Soccervation* (see examples in Chapter 3) where parental input is generally more restricted. In part, this is because of the geographic location of these initiatives, but it is also because the outcomes of matches in these settings are not emphasized, as there are no published results or league tables. For our respondents, the norm was for parents to be in attendance at matches with a specified and meaningful outcome. This means that all of these events would be presided over by a qualified referee or, on occasions, by a willing coach or parent. The outcome would be recorded in writing, agreed by both 'managers', and forwarded to a league or tournament organization for processing. Varying levels of bureaucracy exist around the country for these processes but, increasingly, the major leagues use central FA information technology resources to collate, calculate and publish league tables.[1]

Parents and carers at these matches therefore have more than just the performance of their child to consider. The outcome of the match has currency, too. As a result, those watching mini-soccer and junior soccer differ in two key respects from those who stood on the sidelines in the past. First, they have a more meaningful stake in the activity and, second, the arrival of mini-soccer has actually increased their physical proximity to the action. As a Football Development Officer observed:

> ... the junior Sunday set up, with the advent of mini-soccer, probably hasn't changed the philosophy of a lot of parents. Probably the problem now is that the parents are just a bit closer to the kids than they were, and the kids can't hide quite so much.

Given the initial objective of the FA to use mini-soccer as a method of enhancing skill levels and increasing enjoyment, the notion that it may actually increase the pressure on children was a cause for concern among many of our respondents. The following comment, from a junior club's CP officer, was typical in this respect:

> When young children come into football they play on a very small pitch with a lot of adults, just like a boxing ring, where parents are shouting their encouragement and their kids are in the middle and they become very stressed ... you can see why some finish football very early because they are fed up with all the taunting and lack of encouragement on the pitch.

High levels of adult attendance at competitive matches appear to be prominent at mini-soccer across the clubs in our sample. As children get older, however, it appears that these attendance levels subside. Whilst, in some areas, this may reduce the potential for clashes or confrontations, it also reduces the potential pool of volunteers and helpers, as two parents in our sample noted:

> I think in the early stages it can be quite funny because you get mum, dad, grandma, grandpa all turning up for little Johnny ... but as they start to progress, the parent input starts to drop away, really. And by the time they're 14 you're lucky if you get a car pull up, drop off and drive away, really. They don't want to run the line or get involved.

> You do get more parents at mini-soccer, and as they grow up the parents drop off. You might get 50 parents around the pitch at mini-soccer, but then only 20 for the 11-a-side game.

At their most intense, mini-soccer and junior matches create an environment in which parents can emulate the spectating practices of those who attend professional matches. Respondents spoke of encouraging and enthusiastic spectators, but also of those whose chanting, 'booing', cheering, posturing and gesticulating had created difficulties. Mini-soccer can be an exciting game for players and spectators, involving high skill levels and fast changes of emphasis and dominance. As a result, it appears that many spectators can become rather lost in the event. So, too, can the reality that this spectacle is being created by children, whose own love of the activity may well be challenged if the adults on the touchline do not consider the impact of their actions. A coach from one of our sample clubs observed:

> Parents have got to realize that it's the children who are playing, and not them. People tend to think that they're playing football from the sidelines. You've got to remember it's the children on the pitch that are playing. You're there for them, you're not there to live out your fantasies through your child. A lot of people do that.

Will the parents please behave themselves?

The challenges created by committed, assertive parents in competitive scenarios were constant themes in both years of our research. The following excerpts, from a range of respondents, typified these concerns:

> There's nothing wrong with youth football that dismissing parents away wouldn't rectify overnight, and I say that as someone who's been a parent standing on the line as well.
>
> (Parent)

> The abuse that they get ... from people shouting at them ... other parents ... there's people that you don't even hear in the week, you don't even know

what their voice is like until Sunday. They come down to let steam off. They shout at their own kids, critically. The kid's eleven and he's not allowed to develop ... to understand the game of 11-a-side. It's all win, win, win ... They haven't enjoyed it this year.

(Coach)

I think some adults try to live what they haven't achieved through their sons. I've actually seen children crying with cold and things, and adults shouting at them 'Shut up, are you a man or a mouse?' And I find it very, very sad to be honest with you. I think it's parents, particularly dads, not wanting to lose face. They don't see it as their children having a game of football, they see that it's them who's going to lose face if they lose this game of football. It's the adults that need to be closely looked at, and the people who misbehave should not be allowed to participate in the game.

(Coach)

At mini-soccer sometimes you've got eight managers on the sideline as well as myself, and you could scream with frustration because you're telling them to go to one position and the parents are screaming at them to do something else. And it's just trying to find that fine line between not wanting to upset the parents but making sure the kids are OK.

(Coach)

For me the big issue is around the pressure that's put on them, particularly by parents and by those involved in managing and training young people, regardless of the level. And I see a lot of that with my own children. Parents who are aggressive and who are very critical of their own and other children's performance. And there are occasions when I don't think it's a pleasant environment for young people to be playing sport in.

(Parent)

Nobody, at grass roots level, to my knowledge, has a mortgage that depends on the outcome of the game. But to see them, you would think that they did.

(Coach)

I would love to see a fly on the wall sort of thing, for the BBC to come down to catch a few matches over the season, because I think if they did that it would open people's eyes to what really happens in children's football ... and it would open the eyes of the FA and people across the country to what actually goes on, and it might make some people realize that this is a sport for bringing the children on.

(Coach)

The key factor in this behaviour, for our respondents, was the *over-involvement* of parents. In Chapter 1 we noted Hellestedt's (1987, 1990) concerns about parents whose desire to see their son or daughter develop successfully was manifested through an instrumental approach to sports participation. Certainly, many respondents in our sample claimed that parents were indeed too focused on competitive matches and their outcomes and, in some cases, became too vociferous, argumentative and confrontational as a result.

> I think it's a shame because at the mini-soccer I don't think the parents allow the children to enjoy it. They're screaming and shouting from the side, and bellowing across the pitch. Mini-soccer is designed to give the lads the space and to give them more touches of the ball, but with some parents shouting across the pitch at them I don't think it gives them the opportunity to play the game in the way that it's meant.
>
> (Coach)

> Parents can be so vociferous at times, and you're thinking every kid on there has got two parents who've turned up. If it's seven-a-side, that's 14 kids – that's at least 28 parents on the sidelines. Most weeks you've got both parents there, sometimes you've gran and grandad, and you've literally got sidelines along the back full of spectators. That's where the pressure is.
>
> (Coach)

In most cases, this pressure was associated with mini-soccer and 11-a-side provision for those of primary school age. However, despite the apparently lower levels of spectators for the age groups beyond twelve and thirteen, some respondents felt that in their areas the full game created more difficulties. One parent observed:

> I've heard accounts of quite appalling behaviour at mini-soccer but in my experience it's been good. The sidelines are worse in the 11-a-side game.

It may be that the characteristics of the 11-a-side game (for example the heightened physicality, the absence of roll-on, roll-off substitutes) combined with the increase in adult expectations of good performance leads, on occasions, to greater difficulties and more confrontations. It may also be that these variations can be accounted for, to an extent, by regional and urban/rural distinctions. For example, it appears that in more densely populated, urban areas, mini-soccer more easily creates localized confrontations. In more rural areas, with greater physical distance between competing clubs, these kinds of tensions appear to be more manageable.

While these responses all relate to the over involvement of parents, some of our sample also raised concerns about what Hellestedt described as the *under-involvement* of particular families and carers. One coach observed:

> I have a concern at times with parents and the way they often behave. For example we did a session yesterday and there were a number of kids just

rolling up, virtually on their own. So we were asking them about who was picking them up and they were saying 'Well, nobody, I'm making my own way' ... To me that doesn't seem quite right. You get kids turning up for sessions with no kit if it's freezing cold, they'd just have a pair of shorts and pumps and stuff, and things like that often concern me. Sometimes parents drop off kids at sessions that we run and don't seem to care who they're dropping them off with. Our staff are fine, obviously, but we could be anybody.

Respondents from a range of backgrounds, meanwhile, noted the desires of many parents to use the football sessions as a form of childcare. Some parents at junior clubs objected to 'looking after other people's kids while they disappeared to the shops for three hours', while one coach noted the relative costs of different forms of childcare:

> We charge two pounds per hour, basically. So compare that to a nursery or an after school club. Of course they're going to come to us because we're childcare on the cheap. But that then causes more problems for us because the kid may not want to be with us, and may be disruptive or just not want to do the stuff.

Our focus so far on Hellestedt's concepts of over-involvement and under-involvement needs to be considered in context. Our interpretation of the data has been influenced by the overwhelming number of research respondents who identified parental behaviour as a key concern. However, it should also be noted that our research project was neither an incidence nor a prevalence study (measuring, respectively, the number of parent behaviour problems annually or the proportion of young footballers who experienced them). We were not able to access prevalence data from any county FAs nor, at that time, did the FA record centrally incidents of touchline misdemeanours or indiscretions in ways that would have provided meaningful data. We cannot therefore say with any certainty whether these issues are as pressing as our particular respondents perceive them to be, although, at the very least, they appear to be worthy of further consideration.

Furthermore, our respondents found it easy to speak about the positive benefits that parents could experience from their engagement with mini-soccer and youth football. Many were clearly highly motivated, engaged in coach education programmes run by the FA and – in one instance – sponsored by their club to visit youth football clubs in the Netherlands in order to audit good practice and share ideas on player development. Many, therefore, were eager to share their views about those aspects of coaching and volunteering that they had enjoyed:

> When it goes well, it's lovely. When you have a good game. You watch them and you think yeah, they've got it. You see them getting the passes right and

really enjoying it. You think to yourself, 'Yes, you've actually listened in training and you've put it into practice'. And that is lovely to watch, when it all comes together. Even if they don't win the game, you can still think 'Bloody hell, you're passing it and it's going to feet'. The kids love it.

(Coach)

You can see it in their faces. When it goes dum-dum-dum-dum-dum [mimes a passing movement with hands] and the ball's in the back of the net, you know and they know they've done well.

(Coach)

Because you enjoy your kids doing it, you enjoy it too. The vast majority of the kids in my team have been together since they were eight, so to have actually watched them progress in the way that they have has been great. They're such a nice team and there's a very, very nice club atmosphere. It's nice to be part of it, and that's how the kids feel as well. Certainly my team, they do. Because they have been together for so long, they're close ... It's not just about your team either, is it? You care about the other teams too and that's what's important to our club. Our club is a small community; we're all going camping together this weekend, as a club. It isn't just about your team winning their league.

(Coach)

Many parents spoke of their clubs having a shared vision or philosophy, which supported a progressive and supportive culture for the players. While some clubs were able to encourage players to share in this vision or philosophy, we occasionally noted distinctions between the expectations of adults and those of children. At one club, for example, the young players spoke of their enjoyment of close, competitive matches, while the parents reflected on the emotional difficulties of such encounters:

Emotions run high with cup games and what have you, and occasionally the team you're playing – well, you'll beat them 15–0 or something and it will be fairly straightforward – but if it's closer people will be quite on edge. People are very emotional about their kids, aren't they? They want them to win and to do well, and they always want their kids to score the goals. Life's not like that.

Clearly, for clubs to be successful in creating safe and positive environments for children and young people, it is crucial for them to find ways of overcoming the tensions created by varying parental motives and behaviours.

Managing conflict and managing parents

The most obvious examples of the need for effective conflict management occur on match days, when the pressures of children's football reach such a level that some kind of intervention is unavoidable, leading to confrontations and unwanted repercussions. Typically, the catalyst for such interactions will be an incident on the pitch that reflects either a clash of philosophies or the apparent importance of the outcome of a match. A number of coaches noted:

> You will get incidents in games like that where the parents from another team will be cheering when one of ours misses a penalty. It was important, that penalty could have won them the league. But it's so sad, like. You might, as a parent, feel the pressure inside, but you don't have to act like that.

> I had to pull people this season. There was one time when about six blokes were telling the other kids to kick my player, who was the smallest on the pitch. I had to go out there to the parents and tell them, and half of them ended up looking at the floor. When the game's finished, reality kicks back in again, but it's such a shame that they had to act like that in the first place.

> I ran a mini-soccer centre at a facility for under-8s, under-9s and under-10s. Some of the language there ... I had to dive between two parents in the centre circle, and the referee sort of stood back ... People were trying to coach children's football the way they would coach adults' football. You'd get people pulling shirts, the elbows would start to come up ...

> There are a lot of clubs out there who are very, very heavy handed. They're quite aggressive, and I would definitely say that we're not at all aggressive. We had a game last season when our lads were playing really well, and as the game wore on all you could hear was the sound of shin pads being kicked, because their lads weren't as good as ours and they version was 'Right, you boot the ball down there, and when you get a chance you kick them'. And that's all you heard, all game, the sound of shin pads being kicked. And you will get that.

In facing these problems, a number of our respondents found themselves in more severe situations, with the threat or presence of violence an unsettling and recurrent theme. Approaching a spectator from an opposing team can, on occasions, be a way of successfully countering problematic behaviour: but it can also lead to more hazardous confrontations.

> Last season one of our teams had a major problem at a game. There was [sic] arguments, threats and physical abuse from the sideline. I had to go to the police afterwards and sort out an accusation of assault. They threw it out there and then but, in a corresponding fixture, we'd gone through the league and the

referees' association to sort it out, but we had to get a police presence down there to make sure that the game went ahead. And this was for the under-15s.

(Coach)

Last season I was actually put out of work for five weeks when I was attacked. I was attacked at a football game, and it's been dealt with by the police. I was kicked to the ground from behind, simply for celebrating, clapping my son scoring at the end of the game. I was just proud ... next thing I know I've just hit the floor. The guy did a runner from the game but somebody got his registration number on his car ... I was put out of work through damaged shoulder and ribs ... I did consider, for a short time, if that's what people can do to you then is it a good thing? Is it worth it? But what I decided to do was not let a mindless thug take away the good things that you can try to do with the children, and walk away from it.

(Parent)

While the temptation to leave the sport must be great for many who have experienced these kinds of situations, others have discovered alternative strategies that allow them to stay involved. Some clubs, as we will see in Chapter 9, have attempted to restrict fixtures so that they only come into contact with other Charter Standard clubs, who are perceived as more likely to adopt child-centred approaches. Others, meanwhile, attempt to focus on progressive policies for their own clubs in order to, in the words of one respondent: 'At least get our own house in order, so if we end up in arguments with other clubs we've got something to point to'.

The management of parents within club settings takes on a variety of forms. To an extent, it is driven by the ownership and constitution of the club in question. As we will again see in Chapter 8, the membership of many junior football clubs is effectively restricted to adult team managers and coaches. Children themselves are not necessarily members of these organizations and, even where they do enjoy club membership, this status does not necessarily confer any power or voting rights. Parents are even more distanced from decision-making processes, unless the team managers and coaches happen to be parents of the children in their teams. Where the level of parental involvement on committees is limited, where there is no formal representation for parents, there is a tendency for clubs to deal with problematic behaviour on an *ad hoc*, case-by-case basis. These clubs tend to lack codes of conduct, behavioural management guidelines or spectator management strategies, and it is in these scenarios that touchline confrontations appear to be most likely.

In more proactive clubs, meanwhile, parent management strategies vary considerably. In some more extreme cases, individual managers and coaches appear to have taken rather draconian stances towards parents who they perceive as problematic. One coach claimed that he simply discouraged parents from attending matches:

> I don't have any problem with my parents because my parents don't turn up.
> I give a statutory fine if parents turn up. It can be detrimental at times ...

Others attempt to manage parental involvement through a 'metre line', distancing spectators from the field of play, a tactic borrowed from professional Academies and Centres of Excellence, where parents are given designated areas from which to view the game. These settings are also increasingly identified by parents as locations where touchline behaviour is positively influenced by codes of conduct. Increasingly, and often at the behest of the relevant league, such codes are employed by grass roots clubs, although their impact again appears to be dependent on the overall level of parental involvement and empowerment at the club in question.

In some clubs, codes of conduct are effectively imposed upon parents, with other opportunities to influence club policy limited by committee structures that exclude parental representation:

> We don't really involve the parents much at all. Parents can offer opinions and give advice but at the end of the day the coaching staff and the club's committee make the decisions. Parents are consulted through letters, and parents are able to talk to their coach who then goes on to a management committee once a month – so any things they have can be expressed with their coach and the club management committee.
>
> (Administrator)

Other clubs, however, take a more democratic stance. A number in our sample were bound by their constitutions to ensure that each team had a parent representative with a place on the club committee. In others, there was a single parent representative who sought the views of parents across the club and fed these into committee meetings. In some Charter Standard clubs, where many parents had already accessed the *Soccer Parent* training described in Chapter 1, team managers negotiated 'playing agreements' on a season-by-season basis. For example:

> This year, although we'll be playing competitively, we'll be setting out agreements with parents before we start where there will be player rotation, and players – including the best players – will play in different positions, so they will be left out something like 1 in every 10 matches in order to give everyone a chance ... It's tough with over 80 parents to deal with but you can either communicate or not, and when you don't communicate, well that's where you'll get a problem.

So, it appears that a range of good practice mechanisms are already in place in many clubs. Although these mechanisms appear to be welcomed by parents, the most effective approaches seem to be where parent management policies are supported by democratic structures, enabling parents to have a voice in the running of the club with which they associate. Just as children appear to thrive and prosper most in those settings where involvement and empowerment are prominent features of the club culture, the energies of parents are likely to be most effectively harnessed by similar approaches.

Summary

Without the considerable efforts of parents, acting in a variety of roles, football for children and young people would be in disarray. Parents lead, manage, coach, referee, administer, volunteer and travel in order to ensure that the sport in its current guise is maintained and developed.

Equally, these same efforts have helped to create a new form of the sport and, whether by accident or design, it seems that this new arena is one in which parents – and fathers in particular – can find the kind of certainty, security and identity which eludes them elsewhere. Football is now organized into a range of exciting new formats that benefit from the time and energies of parents and that can also provide returns on these investments in terms of their children's enjoyment, development, and results. It is these potential returns that are the source of many of the problems that currently blight the sport at this level, as many of these same parents exert pressure on their children, and the clubs they play for, to deliver the benefits that they expect to accrue.

This pressure is intensified by the particular structure of children's football that has been allowed to develop in England. In mainland Europe, much of the angst described in this chapter is alleviated by the ways in which junior clubs are organized. In England, we have a high density of small, competing clubs, each with particular vested interests and a following of potentially troublesome parents. As we have seen in previous chapters, the norm in Europe is for single clubs to dominate geographic areas, to benefit from a range of economies of scale, and to manage competition within club boundaries. Confrontations between parents, clubs and children are therefore minimized. The idea of a 'big local derby' in mini-soccer for under-8s and 9s, common in many densely populated urban areas in England, would be regarded as faintly ridiculous by many of our European counterparts.

Despite the many challenges they face, our respondents have provided evidence that some clubs in England have found effective ways of engaging parents and connecting them to their club structures. While we have also been able to identify a range of parental management strategies, it seems that approaches that involve and empower stakeholders stand the best chance of long-term success.

Note

1   The success of the Football Association's 'Full-Time' service (http://full-time.thefa.com) was alluded to in Chapter 5. In June 2006 there were over 400 leagues listed on the site.

Chapter 7

Referees

Gareth Nutt

Who would be a referee? After all, who as a player, coach, official or spectator cannot claim to have attributed the result of a game (generally a defeat) or individual shortcomings in a performance to the decisions of the match officials (the referee or his/her assistants)? As a former player and coach, I have to confess my guilt but, as a teacher who has refereed many games at schools level, I also have some empathy with these beleaguered officials.

It seems that, whatever level of football attracts your interest, the role and performance of the referee has always been 'fair game', open to public scrutiny and, in some cases, held in contempt by players, managers, coaches and spectators alike. Traditionally, the role of referee has been treated with some scepticism by 'football folk'. During the rise of professionalism in the late nineteenth century, the amateur lobby regularly protested about professional instrumentality, with ungentlemanly players intimidating referees and venting their concerns about an increase in foul and violent play. Later, in his seminal football text, *The Football Man*, Hopcraft (1968/2006: 241) suggested, 'it is increasingly obvious that the standard of handling top-class football has got to be raised'.

Since the 1990s, however, a hardening of attitudes appears to have accompanied the rise in the game's profile. At a professional level, post-match interviews with managers, phone-ins on national and local radio stations from 'you the fans' and the frenzy created by the competition between the printed and broadcast media are often allowed to exaggerate, distort or fuel controversial decisions with little room for balance and redress by the officials themselves. Never mind that the impartiality of referees is the cornerstone of the game's integrity, that they are only 'human' or that players themselves may make mistakes: debates and rants about referees are rarely conducted in a rational and considered manner. All this only serves to illustrate the rather ambiguous position that referees occupy within the game. For, while they are at the 'heart of the action', they often appear resolute in retaining a degree of detachment as if to protect their impartiality.

It is not difficult to conclude that many of the problems facing referees, at all levels of the game, have been generated by the 'harsh glare of the ever extending and more sophisticated TV coverage of top level football'[1] that, at times, presents a 'skewed' view of referees' roles within games. The Sir Norman Chester Centre for Football Research team (2002) concurred by pointing out:

> It must be said that most refereeing occurs in a routine and unobtrusive manner; the vast majority of matches at local and national level do little to direct public attention to the match officials or to the behaviour of players. In fact, in some ways it is the referee's lot to be in the public eye only when routine is interrupted by malpractise by players or misjudgement by officials. 'Good' refereeing is, regrettably, but predictably, hardly news.[1]

So what do we know about referees? Despite the recurring criticisms over a relatively long period of time, referees and refereeing have yet to be thoroughly researched (Colwell 1999). Thomson (1998) has traced the development of referees from their role as 'gentleman arbiter' to their current high profile position by drawing on a variety of perspectives from the grass roots to the top of the game. His account of personal testimonies and anecdotal evidence from leading players, managers, pundits and fans is illustrative of the reshaping of football's 'literary landscape' and of the ways in which our insight into the culture of the game is being extended. However, despite the broadening of the game's appeal, which has accommodated a wider range of material, including that on refereeing, there remains a deeply entrenched favouritism regarding the celebrity status of high profile footballers and managers in the form of their life stories and reflections on their experiences within the game. While this genre may lack literary depth and be vulnerable to claims that it is cliché-ridden and formulaic, at its best it does offer some genuine insights into the lives and culture of the game at the professional level. As Seddon points out:

> Against the background of the time in which they are written, these works can serve as a useful measure of the changes which have taken place in association football over the years.
>
> (Seddon 1995: 137)

All in all, then, the recent autobiographies of leading referees (Collina 2003, Elleray 2004 and Winter 2006) should be welcomed. However, while each book attempts to offer something different, there is considerable uniformity in style, presentation and content. They amount to little more than a career chronology in which readers are invited to share the experiences and meanings that referees attach to their time in the game. Some attention is given to the problems of players' poor behaviour and the abuse referees receive from spectators, but there is a strong sense that lip service is being paid to these crucial issues and presented more as a testimony of their single-mindedness and resilience to make it 'to the top'. There is an almost indecent haste to gloss over the refereeing experiences gained during their formative years so that discussions can turn instead to high profile events and incidents in Premiership, FA Cup Final and international matches.

Not surprisingly, there are no explicit references to Child Protection (CP) although some consideration is given to the creation and management of the playing environment, the physical and social welfare of young referees and their part in protecting the interests of the players. Collina (2003), for example, outlines the supportive role of his local referees' association and the role that mentoring can play in the development of young referees. Evans and Bellion (2005) also recognize the pivotal role that mentoring can play in the development of referees while continuing to ignore CP as a vital ingredient of any training programme. Contributions such as Entwhistle's (1999) offer a more realistic account of the realities faced by 'grass roots' referees. Reflecting on thirty years of experience in Manchester's amateur leagues, he is inevitably drawn to a range of matters, again including the actions and behaviour of players, managers, supporters and spectators. He concludes by offering some thoughts on the growing need to address the referee shortage and strategies for future referee recruitment and retention.

The remainder of this chapter arises from reflections on the FA CP research project, as outlined in earlier chapters. Identified as one of the key stakeholders in the provision of football for young people, particular attention is given to the role of referees in the implementation of the FA's CP policy. Although the analysis draws principally upon data generated from an internet survey and semi-structured interviews with referees, additional information was also gained from the 425 interviews with other stakeholder groups. The study focused on CP issues but the data also revealed significant information about the prevailing culture of refereeing today, particularly at grass roots level.

Recruitment and retention

A perception exists that there is a crisis in the recruitment and retention of referees throughout England. Moreover, there is little evidence that young people are being attracted to remain in the game as officials for, although the 14–18 age band generally records the highest level of referee recruitment, one FA Regional Manager of Referees reported that it also registers the highest levels of drop-out. Evidently, at a time when there are in excess of 28,000 registered referees, recruiting and retaining young officials in the game is proving to be very difficult. Some even assert that the referee shortage is the biggest challenge facing grass roots football in England (Coote and Folwell 2005):

> The biggest problem in the county is the lack of qualified refs. There aren't many ex-players prepared to take it on. It's not a very enviable job; I mean I hate it when I have to ref.
>
> (Junior club official)

The problem of turnover among the nation's active referees appears to be considerable. As the Sir Norman Chester Football Research team at the University of Leicester (2002) noted:

> It is routinely asserted that the more than 5,000 local referees who are recruited annually only replace the number who gives up the game each season either through work, injury or retirement ... Of the new recruits, reportedly one quarter last only a matter of weeks; some of these are, simply, quite unsuited to the task in hand, or give up because of work or other commitments.[1]

For many, the abuse from players and parents on the sidelines explains exactly why there is a shortage of football referees across youth football in England. However, the Sir Norman Chester Centre for Football Research (2002) offers a contradictory view by challenging the extent to which the problems of violence and abuse are endemic within the game:

> even at the local level, player violence and abuse aimed at referees is hardly an overwhelming issue, especially given, on the one hand, the amount of football played locally in England and, on the other, the unusually high level of informality which characterises the lowest level of organised football in this country ... It is a simple matter, of course, to focus on a small number of highly publicised incidents in local football and suggest they represent the 'routine' experience of referees in the modern era. This is not the case.[1]

A survey inviting referees in England to reflect upon their experiences of training and development concurred. Pitchford (2005: 16) reported:

> Although respondents reported a range of concerns about player and spectator behaviour, there appeared to be only a limited connection between these concerns and referees' intention to leave the role. The apparent 'exodus' of referees suffering abuse and violence, much heralded by the media, is not reflected in the views of those who have responded to this survey.

It may be true that the reasons for giving up are far more complex than single causes, but our research confirmed that one of the principal reasons offered for the high and stubbornly resistant rate of drop-out remains the reactions and abuse that referees receive from players, spectators and officials.

The nature of referee abuse

Like their adult counterparts, young referees are not immune from the excesses of poor behaviour. Indeed, we have seen in other chapters that the excessive demands placed on children by their parents are a particular feature of youth football. In a number of instances, the attitude of some parents towards young officials showed a total lack of respect. In fact, some referees we interviewed cited harassment and intimidation from parents on the touchline as the principal reasons for 'dropping out'. One former referee claimed that, in some cases, bad language, remonstrating and generally bad attitudes occasionally continued after a match:

> They really ought to sort out the parents on the touchline. That's the real problem. I know one referee who has given up this year because he was getting so much stick. He said that he worked every week and just went out to give the kids a game and all he got was parents on his back so he said, 'Why should I bother?'
>
> (Referees' Association official)

The problems confronting young referees were most acutely experienced in mini-soccer and the younger competitive age groups. These age groups were more likely to attract larger groups of relatively committed spectators. For many, it was thought that the introduction of mini-soccer for the younger children would provide an ideal context for players to develop their technical ability within a competitive setting and an opportunity for younger referees to gain some experience of game management in a more supportive environment than the perceived challenges posed by refereeing under-15 and under-16 fixtures. But, as one experienced referee of youth football reported, the attendance at younger age group fixtures can pose more of a problem to the younger referee:

> I've been told that it's worst at the under-11 and under-12 sort of age groups. When you get to the under-15s and under-16s, I find that the crowds are pretty sparse unless it is a big game because 'Johnny' doesn't want his dad watching when he is 15 or 16. When he is 11 or 12 he hasn't got much choice ... unfortunately when a young man makes a mistake he takes two paces forward and is confronted by a line of angry parents on one side; he takes two paces back and he is confronted by another line of parents on the other side. So he has very little protection. That, to me, is a key problem. It is parental pressure and harassment by team benches especially when they get older experienced people running the clubs.

On the other hand, a parent we interviewed pointed out that poor referees themselves could initiate poor behaviour by the players and spectators. His view was that young players were particularly vulnerable when unqualified officials from competing clubs were forced to officiate in the absence of an appointed association referee. He claimed:

It is the poor standard of refereeing which leads to problems on the pitch. That's usually brought about by referees not turning up for matches or not having been arranged and one of the managers or coaches taking over responsibility. Sometimes they are good and sometimes they are bad. In the last three matches this has led to violence on the pitch between players which has only been brought about because referees were either biased or weren't observant enough to see when fouls and things were happening off the ball.

Awareness of CP issues and the approach of coaches, team managers and club officials to the behaviour of their players and spectators are evidently seen as important ingredients for creating a supportive playing environment for young players. A number of referees asserted that young players needed firmer direction from their managers and coaches and that the attitude and behaviour of players towards the officials was often related to the way in which the coaches communicated with the players and officials. Where club officials and spectators showed the officials respect, it was generally accepted that the players' behaviour was less of a problem. Some referees identified Charter Standard club officials as excellent role models for their teams adding that, where clearly defined codes of conduct had been implemented and enforced, there was a much better atmosphere at games (see also Chapter 6). As one referee remarked: 'The parents are much more restrained and I'm able to referee with a smile on my face.' But, even in such a supportive environment, creating opportunities for young referees can present problems.

While advocates of socially inclusive practices accept the benefits to be accrued by the young referees, a number of club officials expressed their concerns about the duty of care to their players. In particular, they questioned the extent of the responsibilities conferred upon junior referees appointed to officiate at junior club fixtures. One team manager we interviewed described an incident involving a junior referee and a player with special educational needs (SEN). His view was that the referee's lack of experience and 'inability to communicate effectively with the player' had resulted in an incident that was ultimately referred to the county FA Disciplinary Committee. Similarly, a club chairman reported that he had gone to see the county FA's CP officer to discuss the issue of who retains the duty of care when a game is officiated by a junior referee:

> I brought up my fears that when you have got junior football and you have got a junior referee who is a minor himself, who does the responsibility lie with if, for example, the pitch is unfit to play ... Last year a young junior referee said the pitch was fit but myself and another member of the committee said it wasn't and we wouldn't let them play. The local league fined us. So I have actually been asked to see the county Child Protection Officer ... If that game was played and a young lad falls over on the hard pitch and gets

himself injured who is responsible? Can you say that the referee is? He's a minor. Is it the league? Is it the club? Is it the FA? Is it me as chairman of the football club?

There was a sense among these club officials that some referees and Referees' Associations had failed to grasp fully the significance of CP issues with their role as match officials. In fact, one FA Regional Manager of Referees suggested that there are still some referees who do not think it concerns them at all. To illustrate, he gave examples of adult referees failing to recognize their responsibilities to junior assistants while others were slow to acknowledge that, even in open age football, there are likely to be under-18 players. It also emerged that some referees take an over-zealous approach towards younger players playing in adult football, causing some young people to become upset or even to leave the sport. On one occasion, it was claimed that referees adopted different 'man management' techniques for adult and youth players. Commenting on their transition from youth to adult football, a group of young players noted the differences of approach:

> To us, they were like teacher style, lecturing us. But, when they were speaking to an adult they had their hands behind their back. They were having a right go at us. If we looked like we were going to walk away he would threaten us with a booking but if an adult went to walk away he would just leave it.

The relationship between officials and young players is not always better at youth level. As these club officials commented:

> I think referees at youth level are big time Charlies ... who are full of authority ... Half are too strict and take the law into their own hands and far, far too over the top with the way they treat kids.

> I do think the referees for local children are just not with it at all. I think they try to take it too serious. They treat them like adults. You always get the odd bombastic referee. They need to get younger people in. The coaches up here are so keen that they make sure the kiddies are protected.

Significantly, some club officials expressed their concern about an apparent discrepancy between referees' understanding of CP issues and those of the clubs. A designated officer for CP at a Charter Standard club expressed the view that it was essential for referees to understand how importantly the club viewed CP and what her role within the club entailed. As she pointed out:

> we are not messing about; we are doing a job because we are taking it seriously and, at least, listen to our concerns. I know they can't see everything when they are refereeing a game but things they should see quite plainly. But, if there is an issue of child protection that needs to be pointed out, at

least give us the time of day. It is very frustrating, it does make you wonder 'Why am I bothering?'

These views contrast with evidence from our internet survey suggesting that referees perceive that other referees treat children and young people very well. The implications for raising referees' awareness of CP issues and the implementation of a training programme are self-evident. Changes that require referees to review and modify their practice have been slow to emerge, however, as one FA Regional Manager for Referees conceded:

> It's something that, I think, we have to admit in the refereeing department we need to get on board much more quickly than we have done. It's been talked about time and time again and I know the issue of finances comes in to it and how we are going to provide training for all the referees we have got but I know it is something that has to happen ... It's something that throughout this season and beyond needs to improve dramatically because refereeing is a key part of football and therefore needs to be involved.

Awareness of child protection and the GOAL campaign

Overall, there was little evidence that referees were aware of the FA's CP policy and GOAL campaign. This was supported by the internet survey that recorded only 13.8 per cent of referees knowing anything about GOAL. Significantly, even some of those who had been on the three-hour training workshop (Child Protection and Best Practice) accepted that CP was a much bigger area than they had initially thought and that their knowledge continued to remain partial.

To address this concern, the FA's policy now requires all referees to be CRB checked as a condition of their re-registration; furthermmore, all existing referees have been asked both to complete the home-based guide version of the Child Protection and Best Practice course and to submit a questionnaire about it for assessment and approval. New referees are required to complete the CP workshop. Implementing these requirements was not without difficulty. Indeed, the Independent Football Commission report (IFC 2005: 21) confirmed that resentment and even hostility to these measures among the refereeing community had been 'pretty widespread'. The IFC (2005: 22) noted:

> a real sense of grievance amongst referees that they do a difficult job for little reward in usually hostile circumstances; they are not appreciated; they feel undervalued.

According to the same report, the FA, in partnership with some proactive county FAs, has taken a number of corrective steps to 'ease the tensions', thereby creating a climate that is now more receptive to training initiatives and the sharing of good practice.

Training referees – making progress?

We found the provision of CP training for referees variable with little uniformity in delivery (Brackenridge *et al.* 2002). Importantly, the IFC (2005) noted that some counties had since recognized the shortfall and were putting on referee-specific CP workshops while others had put all their instructors through workshops at cost to the county FA or local Referees' Association. The production and distribution of the distance-learning package for existing referees also helped, particularly as some with referee training responsibilities accepted that they needed better knowledge of CP issues. A review of Referees' Association websites confirmed an awareness of the pivotal role that referees have to play in creating and managing a safe environment for young players and officials. The Referees' Association website (www.footballreferee.org), for instance, contains a section dealing with the 'Frequently Asked Questions (FAQs)' about CP and CRB clearance. This commitment to supporting the FA's CP policies is supported further at county association level where positive messages of compliance and training are conveyed. One county FA states:

> Referees play a vital role in making sure best practice happens in football. The key role you can play cannot be overestimated and we've been working for some time on a programme that means all referees will complete some form of child protection training.
>
> (www.sussexfa.com/referees/links)

In some cases, counties are exploring integrative approaches to bring key stakeholders together in a more strategic manner. But, as this county official concedes, tensions remained:

> I have spoken to the chairman for referees at the county FA and asked them that part of the budget for instructors should be used, not just on first aid for the managers and coaches but to actually get all the referees in the county through a child protection course whether it is set up for referees or the same one that coaches and instructors have to do. Then, perhaps, we are singing from the same hymn sheet. Also, the good thing that has happened during the last few months is the directive from the technical committee to get a coaches' association going so we have people like the development officer that can give information about educational courses ... We are inviting referees to these sorts of things so that coaches and referees can get together and maybe discuss the situations with child protection and the problems they have. So maybe the coaches might understand the referees' point of view, and vice versa, as long as it makes sure that it's a safer place for children then we are trying to move in the right direction ... The sad thing with referees is that they won't go on courses unless they are free even though they are the only people who get paid on match days, which is an irony.

Within such a volatile climate, it is perhaps unsurprising to find that young referees are unlikely to be any better informed than their adult peers. Raising the profile of refereeing and accepting it as a core ingredient of the game is seen as essential to any strategy designed to address the shortfall. Additionally, a range of incentives and support mechanisms designed to help young officials develop in an atmosphere 'where they are not going to get beaten up by "dug-outs", parents or other people who are slightly unsavoury in football' was also advocated. As one FA Regional Manager for Referees remarked:

> They must get some satisfaction out of it. So we have to raise the profile to attract people into the game in the first place. And then, once we have attracted them how we are going to keep them. We need to look at implementing support mechanisms such as young referees going into Academy football, Centres of Excellence, ESFA competitions and 'semi-cosseted' environments.

Mentoring

There is increasing evidence of a commitment by county FAs and Referees' Associations to protect and retain young officials by implementing mentoring schemes.

> New referees now are being given the opportunity to have a mentor allocated to them in their early stages to help them to progress and to keep them in the game because we have had a large drop-out.
>
> (Referees' Association official)

An experienced local referee also supported a mentoring scheme for young officials:

> I certainly know that the FA in our area takes it very seriously ... I think it is a marvellous idea. It's about having a process and following that process. For too long, football has got away with people just doing it; I think it was long overdue. I'd like to see it expanded as much as possible. I honestly think they should be mentored for half a season at the very least ... A mentoring system would be good for them ... You need someone with experience there to say, 'You can deal with this; you'll be OK'.

Mentoring is generally offered during the early stages of a young referee's training but, at the time or writing, there is little evidence of any uniformity of practice throughout the country. For instance, in one region 'refereeing academies' benefit from the support received from very experienced ex-referees and instructors including ex-PL officials and licensed instructors. In another instance, mentoring was an altogether more *ad hoc* arrangement borne out of a supportive relationship between a young referee and a more experienced colleague who took him 'under his wing'. We found no evidence of a structured programme of support and little indication that the mentor's qualification to undertake the role was any more than that accrued from seventeen years of refereeing experience. While acknowledging the benefits of mentoring, the need to consider the systematic and structured nature of support for young officials was highlighted by one club official, who reported:

> the good thing that has happened in this area is that there are a lot more mentors to go with younger referees so they are assessed on a much more regular basis and they are advised much better ... I suppose it will be down to the quality of mentoring and who actually is the mentor ... at the end of the day, they are only as good as the trainer they get.

The case for structured mentoring programmes is compelling, with support for schemes of this sort coming from national, regional and local managers, club officials and referees themselves. To that end, we could turn to some of the initiatives associated with professional football clubs' Centres of Excellence and Academies for guidance (see Chapter 8).

Refereeing in Academies and Centres of Excellence

Our findings revealed that mentoring schemes appear to be at their most effective in association with FA Academies and Centres of Excellence. We were informed that young referees in one association were introduced to the local professional club and invited to officiate at Centre of Excellence fixtures covering the under-15, 14, 13, 12 and 11 age groups.

The referees soon realized that they were likely to benefit from the codes of conduct that are applied within the Centre of Excellence and that they could go out and referee the game without worrying about the behaviour of players, parents, coaches and spectators. This allowed them to concentrate on their refereeing since they were less likely to be subjected to dissent and verbal abuse, although one young Academy referee described some of the subtle forms of pressure applied to his refereeing by the coaches of some visiting clubs:

> When you get a bigger club ... the atmosphere changes because it's them controlling everything ... They bring along quite a lot of coaches and they sit there and 'bore' on you. If they are not happy about something they will just shout it out and they won't mind. They mumble and grumble; it puts a bit of a thing on you like, 'I've got to get this decision right, I've got to be 100 per cent sure'. It's little things that just play on your mind.

As part of the process, the referees received feedback from their appointed mentor on their progress and were given points to consider for future games.

What we are doing in arranging with these academies is protecting the younger future referees in their early stages. What we hope is that they will develop and become better referees at a younger age ... Either through the mentor scheme or schools of excellence, we need to provide them with support early on because when your confidence is up you can deal with things.

(Referee mentor)

At the end of the season, a review is conducted to determine whether sufficient progress has been made for them to move into a different playing environment such as those of the Charter Standard clubs. In such clubs it was acknowledged that there is a climate more conducive to supporting the development of young referees. The concern of all officials was that a referee's development proceeds at a pace that maintains interest and the motivation to 'move on' to more challenging environments. Thus, the timing of transitions between the various levels of football is crucial.

One FA Regional Manager for Referees offered a vision of the potential that Academy football had for the development of young referees:

We have to look at the whole Academy set-up and obviously academies run under-9s and under-10s up to under-19s. We are looking at the professional environment where they have a controlled environment with codes of conduct and parents not being allowed to be too close to touchlines, of minimum entry requirements, etc. We have actually written the guidelines which says that since these referees are part of the Academies we have an expectation of them. They will get extra training, more targeted training to suit their needs, they will get training on diet, fitness and nutrition. They will be in a semi-cosseted environment where they will have a mentor on the touchline throughout their games in the Academies that will give them instant feedback just as coaches give instant feedback to the players. We are trying to mirror the player environment in Academies and trying to bring referees into the same environment.

The view is that Academy football can protect younger referees during the early stages of their development. The expectation is that they will then develop the confidence to become better referees at a younger age. One of the spin-offs to emerge from the work with Academies and Centres of Excellence is an initiative to develop the pool of women referees. Regional managers are very conscious about trying to recruit more female officials because the statistics reveal that the percentage of women and girls in refereeing is not commensurate with the increasing numbers who are playing the game. Moreover, it seems that many of the current CP measures employed to accommodate and protect the increasing numbers of female officials tend to be reactive rather than the consequence of long-term strategic planning. An exception to this rule described developments in one of the counties that run an Academy for girls' football. Steps are currently being taken to incorporate a course for refereeing within the education and training programme because Academy officials recognize that not all of the girls will go on to play at the standard that they currently aspire to reach as players. Following the successful completion of the course, the young referees are given opportunities to extend their experience in local authority competitions like county youth games, ESFA competitions, Academy football and at Charter Standard clubs.

The fact that there is somebody for a young referee to talk to and to guide them through their training and the early stages of their development was recognized as an important for both recruitment and retention. Despite the disparities throughout the country, there are examples of good practice in mentoring which need to be shared if the experiences of this young Academy referee are to become the norm:

> It was absolutely fantastic the support I received. From all these people at the Referees' Association. I was taken under the wing of, mainly, the training instructors to start with and since then I've had help from other quarters from the Academy referee mentor and other mentors that have come in to help.

Regrettably, not all young referees experience such positive support. Indeed a number of young referees complained that there were few opportunities for their views to be considered. During the project there was a sense that they feel intimidated about sharing their concerns and expressing their training needs with older colleagues and mentors. This was most acutely experienced at disciplinary meetings during which their decisions were interrogated by a panel of mature, well-educated and experienced ex-referees. To overcome any feelings of anxiety, one association convened separate meetings for young referees to attend while still encouraging them to attend the main meetings. But, although he pointed out that twenty per cent of the membership of the local association was under eighteen years of age, that association representative confirmed that very few chose to attend meetings largely because they thought them to be boring and of little relevance. He complained:

> They just don't turn up. We have one, maybe two who turn up but they probably think that their thoughts are trivial but they are not. They are very important.

Effective mentoring might go some way to ensuring that barriers to meaningful communication are broken down and that support structures are put in place. These combined measures would allow young officials to deal with some of the emotive issues surrounding their role with far greater confidence than, hitherto, has been the case.

Summary

Until such time as young referees are the beneficiaries of some of the initiatives described here, it is difficult to see how the respective referees' associations will overcome the current shortfall in numbers and apparent ambivalence towards refereeing by young people. One Regional Manager expressed his frustration thus: 'There has probably never been a better time to come into refereeing. It's just getting that message across'.

There are signs that the message is getting across, but, while there are pockets of good practice around the country, there is still a need for more consistency in the recognition of CP and in the view that CP issues should be at the heart of the training and development process. In this way, the relatively low levels of awareness of CP issues among referees can start to be addressed. Moreover, where good practice in supporting referees against abuse exists, mechanisms should be established to ensure that ideas are more readily shared. To that end, referees should be drawn in 'from the margins' to establish greater links with the National Game's Strategic Plan. Mentoring has clearly emerged as a major initiative but mentoring schemes need to be extended, with clear distinctions drawn between mentoring and assessment. The training of mentors is also an issue that has yet to be resolved. The fact that someone has many years of refereeing experience does not always guarantee that they are the best equipped to provide effective mentoring. Our research project revealed that county FAs are committed to supporting young referees and that mentors may be able to mediate and support their development. But, as one club chairman pointed out, the shortage of trained mentors does not always allow this. Where it is seen to be working, the results of mentoring are clearly encouraging. One young Academy referee confirmed:

> My experiences as a young referee have been brilliant. I'm sure there are other people who haven't had such a great time in refereeing as myself. I'm happy that I am enjoying myself.

Note

1   Visit: http://www.le.ac.uk/so/css/resources/factsheets/fs15.html

Chapter 8

The Professional Game

Andy Pitchford

For the majority of the twentieth century, most children experienced professional football from what might be considered a safe distance. Watching from the sidelines would have been as close as most ever got, though a lucky few would have acted as ball boys or girls, and an even more select band eventually signed on as schoolboys to the youth sections of those clubs with an eye on future talent.

Today, the situation is rather more complex. Though still a significant minority, many more children, at increasingly early ages, are being exposed to the talent development process of professional level clubs. Meanwhile, those without the talent to progress to elite training are catered for by 'participation' initiatives, typified by the Football in the Community programme[1] offering professional coaching within and beyond the National Curriculum. Children who find it difficult to engage with aspects of the National Curriculum may well experience *Playing for Success*[2], or other related social inclusion programmes. Those who simply wish to watch matches may be tempted by the attractions of junior supporter and family membership schemes and will, inevitably, be subjected to some kind of interaction with the ubiquitous furry club mascot. A select number of these spectators will, in turn, be put forward to be match day mascots themselves, to go 'behind the scenes' and experience first hand the glamour of our national sport.

The commercialization and commodification of football at the highest levels in the past twenty years has dramatically increased the range of opportunities for children to connect with professional clubs. On one level, this can be interpreted as a welcome advance for an industry long derided for its casual approach to present and future customers. On another, it presents a host of challenges for those seeking to ensure the safety and welfare of children and young people in these settings. At the same time, the 'professional' game has extended hugely. In the years since 2000, for example, clubs as far down the pyramid as the Southern and Isthmian Leagues[3] have operated with full-time playing squads, outreach schemes and performance programmes for young players.

For the sake of simplicity, however, our focus has been on the Professional Game in its traditional incarnation at the levels of the FA Premiership, the

Football League Championship and the Football Leagues 1 and 2. Initially, our attention was focused on children as players attached to clubs in these leagues. As we will discover, however, these organizations are increasingly concerned with the variety of ways in which young people can interact with the sport and the adults who manage these processes.

Out of our league

Until the late 1990s, the position of children in professional clubs had been largely unexamined. Although many ex-professionals have commented in their autobiographies on their times as schoolboys and trainees associated with clubs, any suggestion that these experiences were negative or problematic in some way would be swept aside by a nostalgic, uncritical apology for the 'school of hard knocks'. While the apparently regimented nature of training in these settings may have been tough for the young people involved, those who survived claimed that it never 'did them any harm', and that it aided the development of their character. Even such independent and widely respected literary contributions as Hopcraft's (1968/2006) *The Football Man* paid scant attention to the challenges and dilemmas of young people in the game.

For those men who gained some benefit from the system, this acceptance of the status quo was understandable. For much of the twentieth century, professional football evaded any external regulation and resisted attempts to bring the industry into line with other sectors of the economy. The battles over the abolition of the maximum wage in the 1960s are testimony to the reluctance of the sport to acknowledge and recognize norms and conventions held elsewhere. During this time, the key technical roles in professional football clubs – coach, manager, trainer, youth coach – had been reserved for those with a playing history in the sport. This occupational closure enabled the reproduction of a militaristic culture derived in part from the legacy of men's physical training in the armed forces and national service, and in part from a suspicion of techniques associated with more intellectual or middle-class fractions of society.

In this chapter we note the shifting relationship between the professional clubs and the FA's coaching departments. Although this helps to explain some of the innovations in coaching and applied sport science in the post-war period, the relative closure of the professional sport remained until the late 1990s. At this point, a number of separate but interrelated developments began to undermine the stability of the youth development systems owned by the professional clubs. First, the success of the FA's National School at Lilleshall, which since 1984 had successfully developed the careers of a series of high profile England internationals, posed difficult questions for the professional clubs. Their Youth Trainee systems failed to engage successfully with educational institutions and to create alternative exit routes for the many who failed to make it to the top. Second, the new owners of football clubs, ushered in with the establishment of the FA

Premiership, began to demand more value for money from the various departments of their newly acquired organizations (see Hamil *et al.* 2000, King 1998).
Third, insider accounts of the established Youth Trainee programme began to
expose the abuses and neglect inherent within the system (consider the work of
Parker 2000, 2001 in particular).

Against this backdrop of increasing disquiet, the professional clubs eventually
accepted the recommendations of the FA's (1997) *Charter for Quality*, which led
to the establishment of new Academies and Centres of Excellence, to be regulated and monitored by the FA, in conjunction with the FA Premiership and the
Football League. These new training agencies, while still housed within the professional clubs, were structured and funded in order to attend more closely to
welfare, child protection and educational concerns. At the time of our study,
there were forty-two FA Academies in receipt of funding that allows them to
develop a greater range of services than the fifty FA Centres of Excellence, most
of which are associated with clubs in the Football League. The majority of these
organizations offer development programmes for boys and girls from the ages of
8–18, with scholarships or Modern Apprenticeships offered to those aged sixteen
and over as the most significant stepping stone towards a professional contract.

The financial volatility of the Professional Game means that the future of the
Academies and Centres is constantly under review by club owners, although the
system has yet to be subjected to any rigorous external scrutiny. Instead, a limited
range of academic sources have attempted to evaluate the success of the new system. Monk and Russell's (2000) critique of educational attainment, and Daniel's
(2004) assessment of recruitment and retention strategies, are typical of the scepticism that abounds in the external environment.

Given this history, it is perhaps unsurprising that we, as a research team, found
it difficult to gain immediate access to the Professional Game. Only one of our
team had any previous contact with professional clubs and, as noted in Chapter
4, we all experienced repeated avoidance tactics from some of those we
attempted to engage. Eventually, the use of gatekeepers from our own networks
secured access, enabling us to interview players and staff at six professional clubs
in our respective regions. In addition to this, among our stakeholder sample were
a further four directors of FA Academies, seven FA Academy Child Protection or
Welfare officers, a chaplain working at a Premiership club, and six sport scientists, working for or with professional clubs. Furthermore, many more of our
respondents, whose primary interest was in the National Game, had experienced
the Professional Game as an employee, partner, customer, parent or player. The
views of all of these stakeholders are incorporated in what follows but we begin
by focusing on those who sit outside the confines of the club, as customers or
users of club services.

External perceptions: teacups and tantrums

For many of our respondents, it seems that the mud that has been thrown in the past still clings to the image of the professional game. Concerns about the coaching culture in FA Academies and Centres of Excellence were commonly expressed, as were complaints about recruitment and release procedures. The attitude of a Football Development Officer (FDO) indicates the levels of anxiety that we frequently encountered:

> I think at the professional level, we need to change the whole culture of how they look at children, how they treat minors. It has been in the past, to use a football expression, a case of bawl, bark and bollock.

Another FDO suggested that the historic culture described by Parker (op. cit.) had changed little in recent years, claiming that 'bad language, threatening behaviour, verbal abuse ... feature very highly because that's the way the coaches coach'. Similarly, a junior club coach objected to the anti-intellectual culture that seemed to dominate at his local professional club:

> At [an FA Academy] for example, we had a very talented young boy who was actually ridiculed by the coaching staff because he wanted some help with his homework ... And they're supposed to help with his education! And he got like 'Oh, here comes brainbox' in front of everyone! If it happens at that level can you imagine at a Sunday club level?

Others, meanwhile, claimed that the closure, nepotism and political manoeuvrings that characterized the old system were being perpetuated. A physiotherapist, with experience of both FA Academies and Centres of Excellence meanwhile, argued:

> The coach or the manager is king. He does fitness, he does nutrition, he does the football practices, he does the buying and selling ... Football is a very insular game and people feel threatened by other members of staff coming in and taking away part of their little empire. They feel vulnerable even to the point that you may have two people working in the same club who may work against each other because they are guarding their little empire.

Some respondents argued that this continuing insecurity made the Professional Game reluctant to engage with external expertise, and restricted the opportunities to promote and share good practice with people representing other sections of the sport. Others, meanwhile, claimed that the particular demands of the Professional Game made it unlikely that clubs would prioritize the needs of children above the requirements of their particular organization. Many pointed to the Academy and Centre of Excellence recruitment process, or the 'trawl', as it was frequently described by respondents, as evidence of this:

> And the Academies don't help neither because what they do, the youngsters that they take on ... 7, 8, 9, whatever and they've got their squad of 16 ... the moment they see somebody else, somebody better, one of the boys that was already there is out. Professional clubs don't help either because they sign up 16 lads and then when they discover somebody new, one's got to be dropped. It's shocking. Mental abuse – raising their expectations. This has implications for their education and so forth.
>
> (Coach)

The dynamics of the trawl can extend to parents entering the marketplace in order to secure particular financial terms for their child and for other young people with whom they are associated. A county FA officer claimed that a number of parents in his area had begun to operate as agents for children in their dealings with professional clubs, representing their own offspring as well as particular ethnic communities:

> The most sought after person in our region last year by clubs wasn't a coach, he was somebody who was basically a salesman. He wanted to sell two things: number 1, his son, who was the best player in the region. Number 2, he said that he would get access to all the kids that no-one else could, because of the colour of his skin. He said that to me, and the saddest thing is that the clubs started to bid against each other to sign this guy up. If they told him to go away, that he couldn't make a living out of it, then fine. But he's now being paid a retainer and he is given the title of a scout. That's the sort of people that these clubs deal with.

We consider scouts in more detail in Chapter 13 but the fact that such representatives were generally viewed with some suspicion is indicative of the attitude held by many of our respondents towards professional clubs. We did find examples of Charter Standard clubs who reported positive relationships with their local Academies or Centres but they were in the minority. More common was a sceptical and at times hostile attitude towards top-flight clubs. This may well be hard to stomach for those within the Professional Game who are working hard to ensure that the sport deals effectively with its responsibilities for children and young people.

The inside stories

Twenty years ago, the youth departments of professional football clubs were limited in a number of ways. Most obviously, staff members were thin on the ground, as clubs tended to operate with just one full time youth team coach and a physiotherapist, who would often be a volunteer. In some instances, Youth Development Officers were paid employees, but their roles were vulnerable to shifts in policy and related budget cuts. The focus of their activity would be on the youth team, through which contracted youth trainees would compete in regional leagues or the FA Youth Cup.

By the late 1980s, some clubs had started to run coaching centres for younger players. In some instances, these were responses to the demise of district schoolboy football. In others, they reflected the efforts of the FA to create county-based Centres of Excellence. Some of these initiatives operated codes of conduct but few had effective Child Protection (CP) procedures in place. Few, if any, of the staff working in these settings would have been police checked. Some would have held FA coaching qualifications but this was not a mandatory requirement given the absence of an effective regulator. Many of the clubs maintained fractious relationships with local education providers underscored, in part, by ongoing turf wars with Schools Football Associations, and also by the clubs' limited tolerance of individuals who wished to pursue career options outside football. The role of the Professional Footballers' Association (PFA), which remains a key partner in the new Academy system, grew from both concerns about the fragility of playing careers and recognition of the need to develop skills to support young players in other vocations beyond football.

Recruitment to this network was normally from within the football family. First team managers would tend to appoint friends or close associates – people they could trust – to key roles within their clubs. Unfortunately, this nepotism tended to create houses of cards, which would come crashing down upon the dismissal of the manager in question. A new man would come in and with him would come new friends and associates. On occasions, the youth team coach would find himself, in moments of crisis or upheaval, promoted to the temporary position of first team manager, only then to have his employment terminated on the introduction of a new leader.

The impact of the *Charter for Quality* on this unstable, ineffective and incoherent system appears to be unquestionable. Our respondents within the game spoke at length of the benefits of improved facilities and medical care; enhanced job security; rationalized CP and welfare procedures; educational support and systematized, accredited coaching. The minimum requirements for FA Academies and Centres of Excellence mean that there are now simply more staff in place at clubs with a focus on delivery of football coaching to children and young people. Academies typically employ separate coaches and physiotherapists for each of the age groups that they operate. These groups are then supported by individuals in full-time support positions such as Education and Welfare Officer and sport scientist. These operations are then overseen by academy directors, with assistant directors often effectively assuming positions that are the equivalent of youth team coach. Some Academies employ officers on a full- and part-time basis beyond this norm. While the infrastructures of Centres of Excellence are necessarily more limited, they still support coaches and medical staff in a range of player age groups.

Arguably, this increase in staff, and the associated demands on service delivery, have created a new set of challenges for the protection of children and young people. It could also be noted in some instances that the overall increase in operations has left some individuals facing difficult and sometimes untenable workloads. However, we can be sure that this influx of new staff into professional football clubs has helped to facilitate the beginnings of a cultural shift towards more child-centred practice. Many of these individuals are from backgrounds outside professional football, and bring with them an awareness of legal requirements and propriety that was not always evident in the old system.

For some who spoke to us, the key moment in this shift in recruitment was the appointment, in 1998, of the first wave of Education and Welfare Officers to the Academies. Among these were a number of highly experienced teaching professionals. They not only helped to create a more progressive culture in their clubs but also committed themselves to the sharing of good practice and a range of co-operative mechanisms that shattered the secrecy and closure of the previous system. One senior football administrator argued:

> This all started six years ago with the influx of 38 head teachers into professional football, into the clubs … That's where it all began, when the Academies were created. Qualified teachers coming into football and saying 'OK, what are we doing about child protection?' We owe all the advances to that process really.

This co-operative approach was supported by both the FA Premier League and the Football League. In both of these umbrella organizations, specific CP functions were developed and overseen by designated officers. They began to compile examples of good practice and to lead programmes of monitoring and training events. Evidence of such good practice emerged from the clubs in our sample, with Academies and Centres of Excellence managing a range of innovations – beyond enhanced vetting and recruitment – that reflected child-centred principles. These included an apparent commitment to more democratic coaching styles, the development and implementation of codes of conduct for players, coaches and parents; the use of reflective diaries as a way of tracking personal and professional development, and the progressive management of players' conduct on the pitch. Furthermore, some research participants reported procedures having been put into place to protect young people from the dangers of an over-emphasis on results. An Academy Education and Welfare Officer observed:

> I think the professional game is leading the way. I think there are a lot of deep thinkers in the Academies, particularly, and I think they're becoming

more influential. It's the professional game that's taking a holistic approach to the development of young people, and it's going to take some time for the rest to catch up.

A director of an Academy at another club in our sample argued:

> We owe it to them. We've got a duty of care, we've got more contact time with them than ever before, and we've got to ensure that we've got a safe place to play ... at the end of the day that is what your product is, working in the best interests of the players, not your own best interests.

We have already noted in Chapter 6 that Academies and Centres also operate match day mechanisms to limit the ability of parents to interrupt or interfere with the interaction between coaches and players. This reflects an ongoing concern from staff in these settings about the relationship between the host institutions and the players and their families. The following excerpt, from an Academy physiotherapist, reflects this anxiety, and suggests that clubs are not simply ploughing on with their search for the next Wayne Rooney, regardless of the impact on individuals and their support networks:

> There are some families that are ruled by the Academies in the sense that everything the family does revolves around the particular child who is with the Academy. When young players are rejected sometimes the family takes it worse than the player, they invest all of their hopes in the idea that this person will create a lot of wealth for them ... If you've got a kid that's being put under a lot of pressure by their parents, they will turn their ankle or get a kick, and not cope very well and come and see the physio, and from there you can start to pick things up. Then we can start to say that the player will see the doctor and maybe I will talk to the family ... I have seen many families where the whole extended family is committed to the idea of this one kid making it as a professional footballer.

A number of clubs in our sample attempted to reduce the tensions created in such settings by developing more open and transparent selection and release procedures, supported by communication strategies which included regular newsletters, briefing and debriefing meetings for parents, and individual contact. Some players who had been released from their contracts with clubs were still engaged in discussions with Education and Welfare Officers. These officers were committed to enhanced career planning for those unable to make the grade at professional level. This reflected the desire of clubs to retain open and effective dialogue with a range of other institutions, including educational providers at Further Education (FE) and Higher Education (HE) levels, as well as football clubs at lower levels of the English football pyramid or even abroad.

This openness even extended, in some instances, to a progressive relationship with referees, with one institution in our sample housing a development centre for officials. As we noted in Chapter 7, this centre allowed trainee referees to officiate in the relatively controlled environments managed by professional clubs, while benefiting from further training and mentoring opportunities. This ability to work with a range of stakeholders reflects a desire to share their good practice but also, as the contribution of one Academy director testified, to disseminate this further:

> I think a football club is a central point of the local community, and I think that the football club has had the potential to be a leader in the field, if you like. I think the football club should be more aware that the local community will take your lead. So through running courses [such as coach development days and child protection workshops], we can affect the clubs as the senior club. Anyone connected with football in the locality should look to us for the lead. We've talked about doing workshops for welfare, child protection, physiotherapy for local football clubs.

This view was shared by a director of another Academy who argued, with similar confidence:

> I think there's a big opportunity for us to communicate good practice to the junior game, I think it's crucial that we get the opportunity to talk with people and show them how to cope with certain situations. I think if we were encouraged to talk to the junior game about child protection and about good practice, I think we'd have quite an influence. OK, I know that people go through the child protection course but I think there is an opportunity to talk people through how to cope with different scenarios, and I think we – as the professional clubs – would be respected and listened to.

The people we spoke to, therefore, helped us to create a picture of professional clubs as the hosts of a range of good practices, offering children and young people increasingly safe and effective environments for the development of their talents. This suggests a significant shift in both practice and discourse, away from the closed, dismissive militarism of the past. This picture is, though, at odds with the perception of those outside the system, who appear to remain sceptical about the motives of those employed in the sport to develop young talent. At one level this divergence appears to be puzzling. The likelihood, however, is that the kinds of changes we are reporting are gradual. Just as there may well be clubs with progressive recruitment and welfare policies, there may well also be clubs that fulfil their minimum requirements but allow aspects of the historic culture to be perpetuated. Our sample was skewed in the sense that we were only able to access those clubs who opened their doors to us. Others, who might perhaps have revealed a more reactionary picture, refused us access or simply ignored our requests.

Images of football perpetuated by the media have a lasting impact in the minds of the game's consumers and participants. Many respondents claimed that the behaviour of professional players had a genuine impact on the behaviour of children in grass roots football. Television pictures of 'snarling, gesticulating players surrounding referees' were identified by them as particularly problematic and were encouraging young players to enter into their own confrontations and arguments. Regardless of the validity of this view, the external image of professional football does seem to be influenced by this kind of coverage, in a way that perhaps discourages more sympathetic interpretations of current or changing practice at a local level. Representatives of the professional sport, on the other hand, were reluctant to acknowledge any such relationship. One senior administrator with a lead agency, for example, argued that this was:

> ... sensationalism ... to sell newspapers. I think there's an amplification of what's going on in the professional game but there are some bad boys who continue to behave badly, just like there are some naughty vicars. That don't [sic] make religion bad, does it?

In summary, it seems clear that there is an opportunity for the Professional Game to communicate its strengths much more effectively. Concerted strategies to relay good practice are likely to encourage more appropriate emulation by those engaged in the youth game. They would also, perhaps, help to moderate and qualify the otherwise confusing messages sent out by the media about prevailing values and approaches within the game. If professional clubs are to build trust with others in the sport, and convince them of their commitment to good practice, overcoming these kinds of tensions will be crucial.

Power play

A truism often sprinkled casually into conversations about football is that the sport is pretty much the same at every level. It is said that there are as many great games, dramatic incidents, last-minute winners and last-ditch escapes from relegation in junior football as in the Premiership. Perhaps, because of this, adults can gain benefits from associating with the sport at all levels. Mini-soccer, for example, may not carry with it any potential for financial reward, but it offers the potential for enhancing social status through the performance of one's own children, or through association with successful clubs or individuals.

Activities that offer adults the opportunity to accrue status are likely to become highly contested. The markers of status in football – trophies, championships, blazers, tickets, trips, badges – are by definition in limited supply. Getting hold of them, and then hanging on to them, requires both co-operation with supportive networks and also some strategic thinking in order to deny access to competitors. It was therefore no surprise to hear many of our respondents claim that grass roots football is intensely political, mirroring the kinds of intrigue and skulduggery with which the Professional Game is often associated. What was surprising to us, however, was the claim that CP services were equally mired in the politics of status and ownership, and that progress in delivering CP policies was sometimes slowed by the posturing and positioning of the agencies concerned, particularly at the highest levels of the sport.

The client for our research project was of course the FA, which, as the sport's national governing body, had over time assumed the lead role in CP. However, as we have already seen, other major agencies had operated formal CP policies and procedures for some time before the establishment of the FA's CP team and, as a consequence, felt some sense of ownership over the field. Our perception of the FA as the primary motor of cultural change was often challenged by respondents who represented these other organizations. For example, when questioned about the apparent downgrading and demise of the FA's Child Protection functions, one senior executive responded:

> The downgrading of the Child Protection team will give them a major problem, so I think the FA need to get a major handle on that ... the FA provided a fantastic resource, a fantastic back up which we will all miss. But it won't be the be all and end all because it didn't start – let me tell you this – with the FA. Remember this! It didn't start with the FA ... It started with the Academies and the [professional] clubs.

In some cases, this sense of ownership extended to the idea that the Professional Game might be more effective in relation to CP if it was allowed to 'go it alone':

> they [the FA] need to look at giving the professional clubs some autonomy really, because I think the real issues lie at present around the grass roots area. The professional clubs have made great leaps ... But down at grass roots level very little is there and very little money is there. I know from going round tutoring that they don't have money and that a resource in that area would be more useful than trying to work with professional clubs when they may have some cash to put forward and they're way ahead of the game anyway.
>
> (Administrator)

A number of clubs gave the impression that they would rather liaise directly with social services departments in their areas than go, in the first instance, to the FA CP team, or that they would go to the FA about referrals only after having reported them to the local statutory authorities. Indeed, the professional clubs felt that this was imperative because of their legal responsibilities as employers.

This distancing from the FA was exacerbated by the apparent disenfranchizing of some individuals with particular CP expertise:

> There's a Child Protection Officer at a blank League club who has a huge background in child protection and social services, and they [the FA] won't let her deliver any courses. It just seems really messy; we should be far more flexible.
>
> (Administrator)

As I noted earlier, the FA Premier League and the Football League also operated their own CP functions, with some success. Representatives of the Leagues pointed to initiatives that extended CP responsibilities beyond the immediate realms of Academies and Centres:

> The Academies are up and running, and have been looking at child protection for four years now. I think though that in all the other aspects of the game we're not OK. We're getting there but there's a lot to do. Good practice for match day mascots, what about stewarding and what about match day co-ordinators? What about community staff and how can we mesh it together? There's not enough there at the moment. We're now getting all our community staff to wear identification badges for when they're out in the park doing coaching. That's just one example but there's a lot to do. By December of this year, [our] League clubs should have a Child Protection Officer in place whose job it will be to monitor all of the club's activities.
>
> (Administrator)

This acknowledgement of the complexity of the Professional Game, and its interactions with children and young people, should clearly be welcomed. We were unable to measure the success of these intentions beyond the first year (when there were five such officers in place) but, again, the implication is that the Professional Game is not just aware of but in many cases leading good practice. It also, however, reflects a reluctance by the Professional Game to allow the FA total responsibility – and total authority – for CP. The underpinning view appeared to be that the agencies representing the Professional Game were best placed to manage CP in their own backyards, and that the FA should focus only on the 'National Game'.

This division can be explained in part by debates over policy and procedure, and by the shifting and apparently vulnerable position of the FA's CP team over the course of the research project. It also, however, took place against the backdrop of broader power plays between the FA and the FA Premier League particularly. A senior FA executive argued:

> They [the Professional Game] would want to run everything, because power and control are two extremely potent drugs. The third member of

that triumvirate is money ... there could well be occasions where people's views are that the FA get in the way ... the privateers do not look upon themselves as being administrative, and certainly not committee-led and bureaucratic. They see themselves as entrepreneurial and decision-led ... so there's a bit of a culture clash there and sometimes when the cultures clash ... they'll turn round and say ... 'We could do without that lot'. Really I don't think they could ... because sometimes you do need to just step back and look at the big picture before you go steaming on. You can make big mistakes in this game.

As a research team, we are not in a position to resolve the rights and wrongs of this debate, nor to come to any genuine conclusion on who would be best placed to lead CP developments in the Professional Game. But it is clear to us that these divisions have led at times to unseemly tugs of war over credit and responsibility. At a time when many external observers hope that the FA would be able to talk with 'one voice' on CP matters, these battles could be especially problematic.

Summary

For those attempting to improve the treatment of children in football, the domain of the Professional Game appears to be particularly challenging. The FA's CP team, and their colleagues in professional clubs, have been trying to improve the treatment of young people in these settings while, at the same time, coping with the political reverberations of regular collisions between the lead agencies. Successful partnership working has been undermined by the force of these collisions and, despite the best intentions of many of the officers concerned, advancing the interests of children in professional football clubs has often been slowed as a result. Power games between the FA and its senior partners have not been helpful in this context.

As a research team we, too, found this territory challenging. It was difficult for us to gain access to the Professional Game, and our initial experiences did not suggest a realm in which openness and transparency were commonplace. However, those professional clubs that did permit us entry frequently demonstrated good practice and considerable innovation with regard to CP. The picture we created as a result was at odds with our first impressions, and with the perceptions of many external stakeholders, who continue to view the Professional Game with great scepticism.

These rather contradictory signs suggest that more effective communication within the game is essential if CP is to be further enhanced in the professional sector. Clubs must communicate more effectively with their local communities if they are to overcome the impression that they are driven mainly by self-interest, while the major footballing and CP agencies involved must find better ways of co-operating if they are to avoid the accusations of political wrangling and turf wars that were raised by many of our respondents.

Notes

1   *Football in the Community* (FITC) is a national campaign managed by the Footballers' Further Education and Vocational Training Society (FFEVTS), an arm of the Professional Footballers' Association. In all cases, FITC programmes are run from, or in association with, professional clubs.
2   Playing for Success, an educational inclusion initiative funded by the Department for Education and Skills, has technology-rich classrooms at most clubs in the FA Premiership and the Football League.
3   These leagues represent the regional level beneath the Conference, itself now divided into a national top tier and two regional feeders.

Chapter 9

Coaches

Andy Pitchford

It is easy to laugh and dismiss the antics of Mr Sudgen, the PE teacher in the 1969 Ken Loach film *Kes*, as he cuts a humiliating swathe through the defensive ranks of his pupils before unleashing a Bobby Charlton-style finish past a hapless keeper. In truth, however, there is probably an element of Mr Sugden in many if not most of those who have coached, managed or taught children to play football. I say this at the outset not to cause controversy or belittle the efforts of those people who toil for hours every week to create football opportunities for young people but because of my own involvement in the sport. Much as I would like to defend my contributions to children's football, and demonstrate how I have consistently put young people first, it would be inappropriate for me to pretend that I have not been tempted at some stage to demonstrate my own, albeit limited, prowess on the pitch. Or to pretend that I haven't enjoyed the 'glory' that the sport provides in various ways for those adults who lead or coach teams to league or cup successes. In other words, my own experience suggests that coaches operate with a range of motives. Some of these may well be altruistic but others may be more to do with the ego or status interests of the coaches concerned.

The coaching career in question here has been relatively short. I have been a recent beneficiary of the FA's new regime of coaching awards and, as a result, have been involved as a parent and coach of mini-soccer camps and teams for the past four years. Other members of our research team have rather more impressive pedigrees. One, for example, has taught and coached for over twenty years in schools, clubs, Centres of Excellence and with representative and county sides. The coaches in our sample represent a similar spectrum of experience. Among the fifty-nine coaches we interviewed were representatives of FA Academies and Centres of Excellence, the English Schools Football Association (ESFA), the Football in the Community programme (FITC) and commercial coaching companies. Most, however, were volunteer coaches associated with our sample clubs, whose primary interest was the grass roots level of the national game.

In earlier chapters, we have considered the role of leadership and coaching in school settings and in the Professional Game. This chapter is therefore focused on the experiences of the adults who are attempting to lead and develop practice at the level of the local community or neighbourhood, most of whom operate within the affiliated game through junior football clubs.

Let the coaches 'coach'!

Footage of Mr Sugden on the ball is often used in teacher training scenarios to open up discussion on the nature and purpose of physical education. Although the focus of this chapter is away from schools and the curriculum, we have borrowed him for roughly the same purpose. Throughout our interviews with coaches, we repeatedly came across diverging opinions about the fundamental purpose of adult leadership in children's football. While this could be expressed in relation to a division between those with a 'performance' orientation, for whom results and league tables were of some importance, and those with a 'participation' orientation, for whom fun and continued involvement were greater priorities, there were also respondents who questioned the need for adults to even 'coach' at all. Proponents of this position claimed that an overemphasis on organization and adult leadership was leading to practices which restricted children's independence and their ability to play and develop.

These three positions effectively mirror three of the key approaches adopted by those adults in children's football who regard or describe themselves as 'coaches'. The first of these can be described as 'team management', and incorporates adults assuming responsibility in competitive scenarios for team selection, preparations and warm-ups, substitution management, tactics and motivation. Depending on the ethos of the club and the attitude of the adult concerned, this can also extend to implementing codes of conduct and other club policies. The second approach can be described as 'training', and entails the management of sessions aimed at developing fitness, individual technique and team play. Adults take responsibility for designing and leading practices, exercises and – most commonly – 'drills', for motivation and for discipline where necessary. Again, this may also embrace the implementation of club codes and policies. The third approach, which could be subsumed under training but which can equally demonstrate a quite different character and emphasis, relates to the provision of game opportunities. Here, adults merely facilitate game situations for children, by providing appropriate kit, equipment and space, and ensuring their safety. This involvement could extend to selecting teams, refereeing and the coaching of 'game situations' but, equally, all of these aspects can be devolved to the children themselves. Some coaches in our sample were openly suspicious of the idea that children should 'just play', without any adult regulation or structure, while others – as we will see – felt that this approach was of great importance.

As we outlined in Chapter 5, the structure of the affiliated game in this country means that most coaches will be connected in some way to competitive leagues. Most in our sample, therefore, tended to prioritize the first two of the approaches outlined above. For all of these respondents, two key issues were ongoing priorities. First, coaches had to decide who was to play in matches, and, second, they had to determine how those matches – and their outcomes – were to be managed.

In terms of selection, some coaches were clear that the competitive domain compelled them to select teams on the basis of ability:

> We're in a league so we're in it to win it. If we didn't want to compete we wouldn't be in a league, it's as simple as that. If we want to win, we have to select the best players. It's not rocket science.

> I know the arguments about the kids who don't play on a regular basis, but you ask any kid whether they want to play for the best teams or the worst teams? They don't mind whether they play regularly if they're involved with a winning team. Some do go but the majority of ours stay because we've won a lot over the years.

This clear emphasis on a performance orientation led to coaches being reluctant to rotate players in order to guarantee equal playing opportunities, or to rotate players in different positions in order to develop their play. One mini-soccer coach argued:

> Rotation causes two problems. First, the team can't get settled because you've got people coming in and out. Second, people don't get used to their positions so they don't learn about discipline and the importance of team shape. I have some sympathy with the idea but I think putting it into practice is very, very difficult.

For these coaches, encouraging commitment and good organization were a key route to success:

> I would say that for mini-soccer, the two issues we have to manage most are positional sense and the whole idea of being 'switched on'. If they can understand where they've got to play, and if they can concentrate, you've got a good chance ... If they drift, that's where you end up in trouble.

Disciplining and motivating teams is therefore a key feature of coaching from the first stages of competition. Given the emphasis on positional sense and concentration, it is unsurprising that many respondents described mini-soccer and youth football as a noisy and boisterous environment, with coaches and spectators constantly shouting directions and encouragement. One coach observed:

> 'Get back!', that's my favourite. That and 'Pass!' and 'Go on!' You can hear it through the whole game. For some people that sort of shouting is the

whole sum of their coaching ... You can call it motivation if you like but often I think it borders on intimidation.

We have noted in several previous chapters how stakeholders have raised concerns about the atmosphere that prevails at many mini-soccer or youth football matches. Clearly, where coaches set an assertive tone in order to encourage concentration and 'commitment', some confrontation or escalation is a possibility. It seems equally clear, however, that alternative approaches to team management are available, and that the kind of vociferous, command style characterized here is not necessarily appropriate for all settings.

One alternative approach is centred on rotation policies that are established as part of club codes of conduct. A number of our respondents claimed to operate such policies in relation to both playing appearances and playing position. Some ensured that every player in a squad played some part of every match; some even operated with a stopwatch to ensure equal opportunities. While these measures appear to have been consistently welcomed by the children concerned, some resistance was evident from other sources:

> There's three of us running the team. I'm the fair play man – I don't really know anything about football – the other guys are the soccer nuts. There will be two minutes to go in an important match and I'll be saying 'Hang on, Johnny hasn't had a game today', and they'll be saying 'Leave it out, we're 2–1 up, we can't make a change now!'

One coach recalled a series of parents raising objections to such policies:

> I've always run rotation but I get hell for it. Parents just want to win ... The kids would love it because they'd learn all sorts of new stuff – like understanding overlapping and covering – but the parents would complain because sometimes it affected the result.

Where coaches persist with such policies, they often also appear to embrace a more democratic team management style. Additionally, these same coaches had experienced some success with parental codes of conduct:

> We have removed some parents from the sidelines, which coincides with what they've read and signed. We usually get rampant apologies from them and allow them to return.

This combination of democratic team management, the use of progressive codes of conduct and rotation policies tends to characterize those coaches who we would associate with a participation ethos. Many of these were also part of Charter Standard clubs, suggesting that the FA's *Charter for Quality* (FA 1997) has had some success in identifying those clubs with a more inclusive emphasis. However, some of our respondents felt that even Charter Standard clubs were helping to sustain a system that was failing children and forcing them into over-competitive, over-coached, scenarios. In some cases, according to one coach, the system even worked to exclude some young people:

> I think the whole set up is just plain wrong. You get one extra kid and they can't fit him in the team or the squad so they just drop him ... and this will be at the age of 8 or 9. But it goes deeper than that ... Even the titles of these organizations are a problem. I don't want to get into semantics too much but I won't use the term 'club', I think it's just too exclusive. I've started to set up 'centres' instead, where people can share good practice and various communities can come and enjoy the sport. 'Club' says keep out, not welcome.

Respondents with these kinds of concerns tended to favour the third of our 'coaching' approaches, where adults facilitate matches and encourage children to learn through game situations. Encouraging contemporary versions of 'street football' was therefore a priority. One coach, who now runs coaching courses that encourage parents to help their children play football at an introductory level, recalled his own formative experiences:

> When we first played, when we played in the streets, we didn't need referees. Part of playing the game was about self-discipline, fairness, working, accepting challenges, how to win and how to lose, all those things. We go back to all this on our parents' courses. What we're trying to do is say that we want to work properly, we want to get good standards out there. Are you honest? Do you help each other? Are you resourceful? We think personal qualities must be linked with the playing of the game, and this citizenship, if you want to call it that, is a major part of our courses.

Two other coaches contrasted street football with current approaches to coaching in club football:

> Street football made you quick, made you busy, made you good. What's replaced it is practices led by coaches, especially at the early level, that just aren't relevant. They are organizational practices – receive the ball here, pass there, follow your pass – so it's an organizational thing. Whereas in the street, you pass and make a move and come and show for something and that's where you get your understanding.

> I often look at those [football] computer games and think some of today's kids are like that. They can be coached to do every skill in the book. They can do Garrincha turns, Cruyff turns, whatever ... but they're like automatons ... But

they haven't learned to use them for themselves. They haven't learnt to play properly and find solutions and develop their own tricks. They've just been force fed stuff.

These kinds of respondents appear to favour more relaxed, open access play environments in which children take more responsibility for learning. Adults in these settings do coach but prefer to emphasize learning through matches between equal ability teams. We noted the success of *Soccervation* and *Strikes!*, both of which operate in broad terms on this basis, in Chapter 3. However, these agencies tend not to engage in competition against clubs or other similar organizations, preferring instead to manage matches within their own domain. They tend, therefore, to sit outside the affiliated game, even though the FA's own executives and officers are increasingly supportive of such playful, child-centred approaches.

Coaches and child protection practices

Coaches occupy a hugely significant position in the new world of children's football. They are the adults with whom children have most contact, and are the adults with most authority in club settings. Not only do the coaches in the voluntary sector take responsibility for team management but they also dictate training and, ultimately, decide who plays and, in many cases, who drops out.

Coaches are also, constitutionally, the most powerful individuals in many clubs. Although the constitutions of junior clubs often identify children and their parents as club members, the norm is for committee positions to be allocated to the coaches for particular age groups. These positions are not necessarily subject to voting, and only in a minority of examples do constitutions appear to allow for the election of parent/guardian or player representatives. Rather than coaches being subject to the will of the club's democratically elected committee, in many cases the coaches *are* the committee. While often this will be an inevitable feature of voluntary work in the sports sector, in others it represents an opportunity for individuals to develop small but not inconsiderable empires.

In some cases, these empires can obviously be benign, caring networks, but in others they may protect and enhance the status of particular individuals. Change will not always be welcomed by such groups, and it is unsurprising that some of our respondents were rather suspicious of the FA's Child Protection policy, seeing it as an unnecessary and threatening burden. This was especially the case with interview respondents in Year 1 of our research project, from both established clubs and 'one-team-club' scenarios:

> There are those coaches and clubs out there, and within any county, that have been doing the same thing for 30 years and it's worked for them ... so 'We don't need the FA' ... that sort of attitude.
>
> (Coach)

One bloke said 'Look, I'm a one man band. I run one team. I only run it 'cos my son's involved and once he stops I ain't going to be involved any more. Why should I go on a child protection course? Why should I go for Charter Standard? It's going to cost me money and I really ain't that interested'.

(FDO)

Coaches in these settings demonstrated reluctance to engage with CP training and vetting procedures, and were sceptical of their likely impact:

There's just so much paperwork. Even if you're a linesman on a Sunday and you're a dad ... you've got to be police checked. It's ridiculous. I turned up to a game to referee it, and this dad says 'I'll referee for you' but I have to say, no, because you haven't been police checked. By the time I can get people checked I will have lost that person or volunteer.

You have to fill in ... whether you have any prior convictions. Now that's only you declaring it, and what they say is that if something happens you can get done for lying as well, but does that really matter to a paedophile? They're going to break the law anyway, so self-disclosure isn't going to make any difference at all.

Another respondent observed a difference between older, established coaches and newer recruits to the sector:

the up and coming new ones love going on courses and you know, they'll do everything won't they but the older ones ... comments like 'Why should I bother with one of them?', 'I don't need to know that side of it'. You know pound to a penny they're the ones taking a child home from training ... I bet they wouldn't think they've put themselves in a vulnerable position taking the child home on their own, you know you just don't do it anymore ... I don't think they see Child Protection, even if they've done the badge the old Junior Team Manager Award that was, the child protection wasn't connected to it ... well all the old JTM members are really not that clued up on the Child Protection side and they're not that bothered about going on a Child Protection course.

(FDO)

Some coaches recognized the legal implications of the new policies and procedures but were still ambivalent about their impact. In other words, some coaches felt that safeguarding was something that they *had* to do, rather than something that *should* be done in order to deliver best practice. One coach, for example, commented on working in pairs and the need to avoid entering changing rooms without another adult:

[It's] just to watch your own backs in one sense ... you feel like you shouldn't have to do it, but legally you've got to.

Similarly, some coaches were content to pay lip service to CP policies but were uncertain about their effectiveness:

It's just a policy ... it's just on a bit of paper ... if you read it, you read it, if you don't, you don't. People are aware of it, but like I said at the league, 'How can you tell?'

Although evidence of these kinds of attitudes persisted in Year 2 of our research, levels of awareness and acceptance of CP issues among our coaches appeared to increase during the project (Brackenridge *et al.* 2005). Coaches were increasingly positive about the content and quality of the FA's CP Workshops and related training initiatives and materials:

I think we get more documentation from the FA. The club seems to get stuff and hand it out at the manager's meetings and you are made aware that it is seen to be taken seriously. It does come up at meetings on a lot more regular basis than perhaps a couple of years ago. It is something on which you get more and more information and certainly the club committee make people aware of it.

Where awareness was high, coaches had made attempts both to engage in best practice and also to counter what they now perceived as poor practice or abuse:

I think we've been successful because our philosophy is about safety, enjoyment, no pressure, no shouting or screaming, and we issue codes of conduct for the kids, and to the parents – especially during tournaments where we do get particular problems.

Several coaches reported their concerns about aggressive style of coaching practised by many 'older' coaches and a clear indication that this should be dealt with head on:

Children, whatever background, love to be encouraged, they love to be praised. You can stand on the sideline and scream and shout at a child and that's never going to help them at all. We've had this issue this year where we've been up against teams this year who are very verbal and quite physical. The girls had an issue at a match with another manager who was actually from a Charter Standard club who was telling his girls to use their elbows and kick ... I was appalled and I went to him at the end ... It was clearly not acceptable. He wasn't very happy but I made my point.

One of the things that I actually saw on the Child Protection course was the video that was shown of this coach doing the things not to do while he's actually coaching the team at training and during the game. And even in this day and age it does go on with certain teams and certain coaches because they just haven't been coached themselves properly. And it's just that negative response that we give to kids playing football, it's just that negative response that's no good. Like even down to basic no proper first aid kits, you know, say the player gets hurt – 'Oh just leave him, he'll be OK in a couple of minutes', things like that. That's just a no no. You know you've got to put the kids first and make sure they're protected.

Many coaches had also attempted to manage the behaviour of their own teams' parents, recognizing that reliance on disciplinary processes was often inadequate:

It's not sufficient to have to fine a parent £60 and suspend them from attendance – let's try and get hold of the problem before it becomes one.

However, some respondents recognized that other sanctions were similarly problematic. In one case, a coach had threatened the exclusion of a child if his parent refused to comply with the club's code of conduct:

I had one instance last season with one of the parents who actually used abusive language towards his own son. I had to have a word with his parent and explain to him and more or less gave him a warning. I sat down with him and told him that his lad wasn't happy about what he had said to him. I explained to him how I felt that if he was to carry on then unfortunately the consequences would end up with his son not being able to play.

In relation to the behaviour of their own players, the majority of coaches reported that they would not tolerate swearing or bullying from players, who would be warned and if necessary pulled off the pitch or verbally warned for such behaviour.

I think we did have a touch of bullying perhaps ... if you could argue it was bullying ... a few snide comments ... and I just give the kid a warning straight away. You see in our policy the kids have three warnings ... so they get one straight away if there's any bullying.

Other advances reported by respondents included coach mentoring programmes, where new coaches were supervised and assisted by more experienced colleagues; democratic approaches where coaches asked for input from players on team management issues; and coaches leading debriefing sessions after matches and tournaments for both players and parents.

However, even among those with a positive attitude towards safeguarding and the FA's general approach, there were some continuing problems. Some of these coaches, it appears, continued to harbour popular myths about child abuse. For example, one coach was only concerned about having a second adult along if he was working with a girls' team. Another coach said he learned from the CP workshop that he was not allowed to touch players. Other coaches indicated a perception that more care should be taken when looking after girls as opposed to boys. The changing room facilities highlighted this issue with a number of coaches reporting that they would never allow a solitary adult to go into a changing room and would always seek a female adult to help manage the situation. This aspect appears to be linked to the fears of false allegations and a need to protect adults as much as children:

> Never put yourself in a vulnerable position ... especially with the girls football ... You know like, walking into the changing rooms, I mean the men don't go in anyway it's normally us women coaches who go in with the girls but even me I don't go in on my own. I make sure there's always someone with me because I wouldn't put myself in a vulnerable position because you just never know, do you?
>
> (Coach)

Awareness of club CP policies and referral procedures was low across our sample of coaches. When asked who the children would go to if they had concerns, coaches generally answered that they hoped the children would feel comfortable approaching the coaching staff or parents. Rarely was a designated person for child protection mentioned. The coaches' responses also indicated weaknesses in the dissemination of information. Very few coaches had received regular CP updates from the FA, with some suggesting that the club secretary might get this information but only passed it on when necessary.

· This sense of distance from the FA was reflected in the comments of several coaches. Some of them felt that the FA's input had been rather faltering, while others felt that football at grass roots level was being overlooked by those in significant positions in the national governing body:

> I can't say that they [the FA] are good. I don't think they are good because we go on a course, we get all our information and we never hear anything else. And that's it ... for like another three years, you get your book to read, you do the course and then that's it. You're having to go on the net and look at Child Protection policies and how to implement them for your club and things.

> My concern is there aren't enough people from the FA who actually come out to the grounds and who witness this sort of thing and report back. You get plenty when it's cup finals etc. but very few come otherwise. It would

certainly benefit the FA by opening their eyes – it would let them see what actually happens at a non-professional level. For example, young lads and parents see professional games televised – witness bad role models (coaches, referees, players, etc.) and think it must be right, it must be like this and think that's how it should be for the Saturday morning junior game. We're trying to improve it here and the FA is allowing it to happen there. That's where the imbalance is.

Summary

Although we have considered observations from coaches in a number of settings, our focus in this chapter has been on volunteer coaches in the rapidly expanding voluntary sector. It is clear that many aspects of this sector are new and challenging. Coaches here are engaged with groups and teams from early ages, with clubs offering organized training for under-7s and even under-6s in some cases. The FA has attempted to regulate this domain through the new structure of its coaching qualifications, with the FA Level 1 Coaching Award designed primarily to support training for children at the grass roots level. The FA's county organizations work with local leagues to promote good practice, and employ Football Development Officers to facilitate coach education programmes and to promote the Association's CP policies.

Where this work is successfully co-ordinated, it seems that the message is getting through. For example, coaches from Charter Standard clubs that compete in progressive leagues, appear to be adopting increasingly child-centred approaches, and to take safeguarding seriously. Such approaches may well be challenging but these clubs are demonstrating that their implementation is possible. However, we have also seen that there are many coaches who are reluctant to engage with these approaches, and whose comfort, status and security may well be threatened by the kind of cultural change that the FA seeks to bring about.

Chapter 10

School teachers

Gareth Nutt

I have very fond memories of my career as a teacher and, I guess, like many PE teachers, some of the most memorable are associated with extra-curricular activities and events. However, for all the pleasure gained from reflection, there are some incidents that, by their unsettling nature, have proved to be pivotal in the development of my professional philosophy. One such incident occurred during the late 1980s to a young male student whom I shall call Alan. Alan was a bright, articulate and popular Year 10 student (16 years of age) who played a full and active part in the school's extra-curricular programme. He was a gifted sportsperson who, as well as playing for the school's football, rugby, basketball, cricket and athletics teams, also played district and county schools football and was a member of a highly successful junior football club.

The incident in question took place during the early weeks of the summer term. This is a period during which PE departments in schools turn their attention to summer activities, although there is an inevitable overlap with the football season as schools and clubs complete their league and cup commitments. On this occasion, Alan had been selected to run for the school in the district schools athletics trials. However, on the following morning, I was confronted by an angry colleague who was demanding that I withdraw him from the district and county schools football squads. Alan had failed to attend the athletics meeting the previous evening and I was asked to 'deal with it'.

Alan's reaction to my enquiries about his non-attendance was astonishing. In floods of tears, he offered no excuses beyond the fact that he was 'exhausted'. It transpired that during the preceding eleven days, Alan had played ten competitive football matches (on some occasions he had played two games a day), attended two athletics meetings and played in two 20-over cricket matches. I was now being asked to punish him by withdrawing the privilege of representative schools football; the problem, it seemed to me, wasn't Alan's. In many respects, Alan was not only a victim of an excess of voluntary goodwill but also a total lack of communication between adults purporting to be offering him the opportunity to participate and develop his interest in a range of sporting activities. While I have no doubt that their efforts, on behalf of young people, were all conducted in good faith, I can't help but conclude that Alan's best interests had been ignored. Worryingly, I don't think Alan's case was untypical for, even then, critics of schools and youth football were expressing serious concerns about overplay and physical 'burn-out' with figures of eighty to ninety games a season for the talented elite being cited to illustrate the problem. In my view, it is incidents such as this that prompted the publication of the FA's *Blueprint for the Future of Football* (FA 1991) and accelerated measures to remove the responsibility of developing the talented elite away from 'well-meaning' amateurs. Not surprisingly, the opposition from the ESFA was resounding.

During the last 100 years, the voluntary efforts of schoolteachers have been the bedrock on which the English Schools Football Association (ESFA) has provided football for thousands of young people. With its ideals rooted firmly in education, the association has consistently claimed to provide football for children rather than children for football. Yet it is clear that, for many, the links with the Professional Game are inextricable. Kerrigan's (2004) centenary publication presents a meticulously detailed account of the ESFA's history during which its relationship with the Professional Game is regularly confirmed. Yet, while the paths from schoolboy football to full international honours followed by players such as Duncan Edwards, Sir Bobby Charlton, Peter Shilton and Michael Owen are regularly plotted, the book also serves to highlight the uneasiness that has existed in the relationship between the ESFA and other settings for youth football, most notably the FA, the burgeoning county FA Youth Leagues and the Professional Game itself. While it is beyond the scope of this chapter to offer a chronology of the spats and tensions that have existed between the ESFA and other stakeholders, there is little doubt that Howard Wilkinson's *Charter for Quality* (FA 1997) accelerated changes to the scope and nature of youth and schools football. The current landscape offers some intriguing features that, more than ever before, demand a more collaborative approach to providing a coherent structure for the provision and development of football for young people of all ages and abilities.

Diverging or converging cultures?

The ESFA unapologetically articulates a philosophy that puts the care of young people first, in the strong belief that teachers are the best people to exploit the educational value of schools and youth football. In writing a brief frontispiece for the association's centenary book (Kerrigan 2004), Philip Harding (ESFA Chairman 2003–2004) argues:

> Today, there is evidence that sport in an educational environment enhances academic achievement. Furthermore, teachers are experts in the care of young people. The young sportsperson has many demands on his or her time and the teacher, cognisant of these, will ensure that one sport does not

become an all-consuming passion. Unfortunately, the same cannot be said of a club environment.

Of course, good teachers will do all that Harding claims but his pejorative view of club football fails to take into consideration the many structural and organizational changes that have taken place during the last ten years for the benefit of young people. In particular, he appears overly dismissive of much of the good work carried out by club and community football schemes where the Charter Standard clubs exemplify many features of good practice. He also fails to acknowledge that many young people experience and enjoy the game in a variety of social settings and that it is the prevailing culture in each of these that does much to determine their long-term affiliation with football. As Richardson and Reilly (2001 cited in Stratton *et al.* 2004: 186) point out:

> The developmental and social consequences of participation in soccer vary from one child to the next. The consequences may be associated with the internal emotions and experiences of children as well as the external societal values and meanings allied with soccer, and the resultant conditions in which participation occurs.

Many young players are exposed to a plethora of formal and informal opportunities to engage with the game (schools football, junior football, community schemes, soccer schools, etc.) during which they will experience a variety of social settings and relationships. The meanings they attach to their experiences will determine the extent to which they will continue to participate. For many, their ability to adapt and to develop socially and psychologically will determine their levels of success. We have already seen the value that young people place on playing for their clubs. As Daniel (2004: 219) reported:

> When they were asked what they particularly liked about playing junior league football, most boys chose to focus less on the football itself and more on the context. The whole experience of being in a team with a shared history – many of the boys had played together since they were 5 or 6 years old – was seen by many as the key attraction. Great shared moments, such as cup final appearances, winning penalty shoot-outs and victories against old rivals, were frequently mentioned.

Given this view, I think it is unwise for schools to presume that they possess a monopoly on good practice. Notwithstanding the fact that our research project revealed some worrying concerns about the experiences of young people in junior club football, can we be absolutely certain that opportunities for all young people to experience high quality teaching and playing are available in all our schools? Moreover, can we be entirely confident that the motives and behaviour of all teachers comply with Harding's assertions?

As Embrey (1986) revealed, there are cultural differences that impact upon the experiences and interpretations that young people attach to their involvement in schools and youth football. Embrey's (1986) study compared the nature and incidence of dissent in school team and junior club football matches and, having followed the experience of nine young players over a period of two years, he revealed that clubs suffer greatly from the influence of spectators, whereas schools are more prone to problems resulting from the players' sense of compulsion and the formality of their relationship with the teacher–coaches. Some of Embrey's analysis of spectator behaviour resonates strongly with our own research findings but, as one senior ESFA official's cautionary tone confirms, not all behavioural problems can be attributed to 'less disciplined' club managers:

> I would also say looking around that the behaviour of some of the teachers in charge of schools are now causing some concern as well ... This particular year we have had two teachers who have been removed by their heads after reports of their behaviour, unsporting behaviour on the touchlines ... There have been others that have been warned and heads have taken them aside.

During interviews with teachers and officials from the ESFA, it emerged that some of the concerns about the deterioration in behaviour by players and teacher–coaches were associated with the increasing importance attached to national competitions for individual schools. One ESFA official commented:

> The more national competitions we run the greater the likelihood of poor practice and poor behaviour ... I think we have to look at the effect that national competitions have on the pupils but also the attitude of the member of staff and the parents ... I think there is a link between poor behaviour, poor practice and this progression towards a national championship ... It certainly is a lot more important now.

So, rather than setting an oppositional tone, perhaps more should be done to bring schools and clubs closer together, both organizationally and philosophically. Perhaps some of the current trends will accelerate this process.

Teachers as coaches and Adults Other than Teachers

It is generally accepted that the industrial action taken by teachers during the mid-1980s precipitated a rapid decline in the extra-curricular provision of most state-maintained schools. Until then, many PE departments were able to draw upon the support of colleagues from other departments to supplement their contribution. However, the increasing levels of accountability that have accelerated changes in the nature of teachers' work during the last twenty years have seriously affected the number of teams schools have been able to field. As one senior ESFA official acknowledged:

> Each school is now producing fewer teams than they used to. Maybe in the past, they would have a year group team right the way through taking part in either local or national competitions ... Now they are struggling to keep the age groups because they don't have enough teachers to take one each ... We are probably reducing the number of entries in the competitions.

In many schools, opportunities to play football depend upon the capacity of PE departments to support a programme that accommodates their commitment to a range of physical activities. The staffing problems in representative football appear even more acute and is this not helped by a perception that younger teachers coming into the profession are less likely to take on the breadth of responsibilities of some of their more experienced colleagues. On this point, one ESFA official noted:

> Many of the young PE teachers now will do the job but come a Saturday, they're usually good footballers, they will go off and play for whoever it might be and it's finance; it's extra money ... What impact there has been is that it is more difficult to get them to volunteer at 30 years of age than it would have been at 22 or 23. If a teacher doesn't take up an extra-curricular activity early they are unlikely to make it up later ... They will have other priorities. As we are losing them at the top end we are not getting them coming through at the bottom end.

With fewer and fewer volunteers from within the school workforce, PE departments and district associations are making greater use of Adults Other than Teachers (AOTTs). In a number of cases, district and county Associations make use of retired teachers to supplement their teams of officials, while some schools also make use of parents and local coaches. Former teachers and AOTTs working with district and county associations operate under the code of conduct set down by the ESFA, while head teachers are advised by the ESFA of their responsibilities in 'employing' AOTTs to work alongside their teachers in the running of school teams. Schools have also been keen to utilize the expertise of a range of youth sport agencies to advance opportunities across a range of sporting activities for their students. School sport co-ordinators and competitions co-ordinators have the explicit brief of offering extra-curricular opportunities for young people, while FDOs will often be invited into schools to conduct sessions with the students of all ages. These agencies make a valuable contribution to the opportunities for young people of all ages to participate in football. However, the lack of co-ordination poses a formidable challenge. As one leading ESFA official commented:

At the end of the day there are 26,000 schools and 8 million kids out there, we can't run that and neither can the counties; together we can. All we say to the counties and the FA [is], involve us in everything that is going on as a partnership. We are as up with that word as the FA are and, as I say, the FA have taken that on board; the counties haven't quite yet. Their Football Development Officers are going into schools without any reference to the local district ESFA man. It only takes a phone call to the local ESFA secretary of that area to say, 'I'm going into this school for this, this and this' ... It is not just the Football Development Officers; it's other sports organizations, as well. The Youth Sport Trust, the school sport co-ordinators are going into schools and organizing competitions without reference to what has already been put in place by the local schools FA.

It would seem that the case for dialogue and partnership is compelling yet there are those who still possess little confidence in the benefits that outside agencies can offer schools football. Harding (2003, cited in Kerrigan 2004) presents a controversial proposal to safeguard the interests of young people in stating his preference for a 'professionalized' school sport system based on an American model of provision. He claims that such an organization would be guided by:

> The desire to put the educational interests of young people at the forefront of its values. Such a system of school sport would be without unnecessary interference from national or local political quangos, adult sporting bodies, academies run by clubs.
>
> (Harding 2003, cited in Kerrigan 2004: 207)

My view is that such a unilateral declaration of independence would be a radical, if not to say, an implausible step to take given the historical roots of both systems of school sport. Neither does it take into consideration the criticisms that assert that the American high school and collegiate system is every bit as vulnerable to those individuals motivated solely by the desire to tempt young people into putative professional sport. At the heart of Harding's thinking appears to be the ESFA's strong opposition to many of the regulations contained in the FA's *Charter for Quality* (1997) that effectively:

> placed the football education of the best young players in the hands of professional clubs' Football Academies and Centres of Excellence, licensed and regulated by the FA.
>
> (Kerrigan 2004: 124)

Academies and Centres of Excellence

In setting out to provide young players with a 'high quality experience' (FA 1997: 1), schools and junior clubs no longer have the first choice of their better players as they might have done in the past. Therefore, to ensure that a young player's educational and personal development is not compromised, the FA's *Charter for Quality* (1997: 3) specifically states:

> A fundamental aspect is the match programme, to be provided by the Football Academies. It is, therefore, proposed that the key individuals in the make-up of the player's match programme should be the parents. Quite properly the players' match programme should be developed in the best interests of the player's educational, technical, academic and social needs, by the parents in conjunction with the player's school and the Football Academy Education and Welfare Officer.

The establishment of the Footballers' Further Education and Vocational Training Society (FFEVTS) by the Professional Footballers' Association (PFA) has ensured that educational initiatives are embedded in youth development programmes at professional clubs and, within these programmes, Education and Welfare Officers (EWO) fulfil a strategic role. Employed to monitor players' educational provision and to provide for the needs of individuals, EWOs play a crucial role in mediating between the player's parents, his school and the club (see also Chapter 8). Many are educational professionals themselves and able to draw upon their experiences of a teaching career in primary, secondary or further education. In many cases, they are also able to point to many years of involvement in the administration, management and coaching of schools and youth football. One EWO we interviewed was able to reflect upon his work as a teacher, a district schools team manager for the local district schools' association and a coach at his local professional football club's Centre of Excellence. However, although one senior football official interviewee described them as a 'tremendous extra resource', and crucial to promoting the FA's attempt to offer young players a more holistic experience, teachers opposed to the regulations fail to see how a young player's preoccupation with football is in the best interests of their physical, intellectual, emotional and social development. Moreover, many remain unconvinced that clubs have adopted a more child-centred approach. Reflecting on the early challenges presented by the introduction of the educational programme, a senior football administrator confirmed their fears:

> football can take some credit for some exceptional performances but it will also have to look at the bottom end of the scale ... There have been some startling failures as well ... The football culture didn't take it on very easily and we had a lot of battles with a few clubs but not many now ... we are still fighting to get the culture we are looking for into the game ... The thing that I misjudged was the strength of the culture and its resistance to change.

At a competitive level, the consequences of the *Charter for Quality* for schools and youth football have been profound. ESFA officials we interviewed for our FA research confirmed that the release of players for their competitions varied from area to area depending on the attitude of the clubs. Some were evidently prepared to release players for Trophy competitions (under-15 age group) while others took a less co-operative stance. The response from some districts and counties was to maintain their loyalty to squad members not restricted by Academy and Centre of Excellence regulations. As one ESFA official commented:

> If you've got squads of 16 players playing matches every Saturday and then suddenly you get a Trophy game and that means you have 'Tom, Dick or Harry' coming back to play that game; it's a bit unfair on the three lads that are going to be dropped out.

Precisely because Academies and Centres of Excellence are not compelled to apply the same policies, beyond meeting the 'best interests' of their players, there is a sense that an uneven playing field has been created for district and county SFA competitions. The following example serves to illustrate the problems for schools officials and for the young players' themselves, many of whom are denied the opportunity to play in the ESFA's 'flagship' competitions:

> One district last year put out the whole of an Academy side. They were all eligible to play for the district, there was nothing untoward about them but they dropped the eleven who played the previous Saturday and put another eleven in to play a Trophy match. Now is that right or wrong? I'm not going to make a judgement on that. They then played a side that didn't have any Academy players because they wouldn't play them; so it was a very uneven playing field.

To most people, the decision to draft in the Academy players was demonstrably unfair to the remaining members of the squad and the team management should have been made accountable for their culpability. Clearly there is a case to answer, but maybe it should also be the responsibility of the ESFA to take a stronger position of its own to ensure that young players are protected from decisions that run counter to the association's inclusive ethos. For some, the only real answer would be not to allow Academy players to play in schools football. Such a decision would take away the extra layer of competition that the clubs do not appear to want while, at the same time, offering another squad of boys and girls the opportunity to play representative football. Even then, what seems to be a pragmatic solution is not without its difficulties. Although initially set up to protect promising young players from the demands of overplay, Academy registration can tip the balance in the opposite direction. One teacher complained to me:

There is also underplay. I had a parent who phoned me up last year whose son had played three matches in a season. He played for his school but outside his school he played in three matches in the whole season. He had either been on the bench or not part of the squad with this club; it was a School of Excellence [sic] and not an Academy. They wanted to know why we didn't support the kid and why he wasn't playing county or district football. I said because that district doesn't take players from the School of Excellence or Academy. That's taking it the other way, isn't it?

An Academy's decision to limit the involvement of any young player is clearly not always in the best interest of the player concerned and can smack of exploitation. As one teacher reported:

They need a squad of 15 or 16 to cope with what they have got to do and certainly the local parents now see that if a club is bringing boys from Ireland, Wales on weekends to play for the club, the local lads are just there making up the numbers ... Kids are beginning to see through it as well now. Young players are beginning to realize that they are missing 'playing with my mates on Saturday'. Certainly the ones that have known district football from eleven.

So, just as the clubs monitor and assess the development of their registered players, many parents and their children are just as likely to actively reassess their involvement with Academy and Centre of Excellence football if their opportunities to play are restricted. However, the lure of professional football remains powerful and, for many, the decision to leave an Academy is very hard one to make. In these circumstances, the role of Academy Education and Welfare Officers (EWO) and Child Protection Officers (CPO) should not be underestimated. Not only do they represent a pivotal support agency for the players but they also occupy a strategic position in promoting the cultural change currently underway in professional clubs.

Promoting cultural change

With the exceptions of those Academies and Centres of Excellence willing to release players for district and county representative football, there is a sense among some teachers that young players are now beyond the reach of professional educators committed to ensuring that the traditional values and attitudes of the association are maintained. Certainly, the majority of coaches and managers who work in professional football have little experience in the 'outside world': over the years, an aggressive masculine culture has emerged in which bad language, threatening behaviour and verbal abuse feature very highly, described here by two officials from the professional game:

That's the way coaches coach. It is a coaching style that has been prevalent in the game for a lot of years particularly in the professional game ... What I would call over-aggressive coaching has been a strong feature.

Coaches now are, and you must remember that a lot of them are seasoned professionals who have had 15 to 20 years in the industry as players and have been used to, I suppose, what would now be classed as bad practice and have grown up with certain standards. What they are finding is that they are having to readjust their mentality, readjust their thinking and readjust the way they are dealing with young people.

Part of that readjustment comes from coach education programmes run within the professional game itself. For example, the Professional Footballers' Association's (PFA) Coach Education department delivers courses to the professional game for scholars registered with club Academies through to current and ex-players interested in getting on the coaching ladder. Because the department is also responsible for the training of coaches who take up positions within the Football in the Community scheme, CP issues are taken very seriously. One of the PFA's coach educators was keen to confirm that coaches were becoming much more aware of their responsibilities for the welfare of the young players they may come to coach. He reported:

One of the things, I think, is that I do find a better relationship between the players and the youth coaches and the coaching staff generally. What I see is that relationships are being developed through an element of openness and individual programmes being put in place ... We need to be very responsible as coach educators to ensure that when they go out into the field they do have the correct practices.

Coach education programmes are now preparing coaches to embrace a more holistic approach with an increasing emphasis given to encouraging the development of the 'whole' individual. However, change is not a rational, linear process and officials within the professional game have conceded that, despite the structural changes and stricter regulatory climate, changes to coaching practices are taking longer to make than was initially anticipated.

Having been identified as key change agents, Education and Welfare Officers (EWOs) and Child Protection Officers (CPOs) have occupied the 'front line' in challenging the prevailing culture but during the early years of the Academy structure many have been forced to confront unanticipated challenges. An official from within the Professional Game confirmed:

Most Education and Welfare Officers are not ex-players so they are the first set of people (outside the game) to go into football and, I think, they have been on a steep learning curve. I think many of them thought it was going to be a lot easier than it is and they've had the culture to fight as well ... Education and Welfare Officers are under a lot of pressure from the culture within the game. It is difficult unless you have been on the inside of professional football.

This is likely to pose more of a problem if the stability of long-term employment has not been established. After four years of the Academy structure, one official within the Professional Game alerted us to a worrying trend:

We started off with 39 four years ago; more than half of them have gone already and what the worrying factor for me is that the majority have gone into coaching which leads me to believe that they have joined the culture rather than fought it and I think that is a major shift. Not all; some of them are very good, don't get me wrong. Some of them have had some awful battles to fight and have stood their ground but many have collapsed under the pressure within the football club.

Perhaps we should not be surprised about this type of comment because, over the years, many teacher–coaches have been employed to work in the Academies, Centres of Excellence and community schemes run by professional football clubs. So, with the Academy system now firmly established and professional football clubs required to provide development programmes that stand in stark contrast to the 'bawl and bollock' culture of the past, maybe it is time to exploit the common ground that actually exists between the ESFA, the FA and the clubs. With the dangers posed by 'enculturation', perhaps there is also a case for employing Education and Welfare Officers and CPOs independently of the clubs. Here, the FA and ESFA, in partnership, might do more to provide explicit guidance and criteria for the role and put into place a monitoring process that addresses the totality of a player's programme; that is, both the educational and footballing sides of their development. Moreover, unless performance criteria are clearly established, the danger is that monitoring will amount to little more than making judgements about how the educational and footballing development programmes are being offered, rather than focusing on the quality of the players' experiences.

Summary

It is my view that the ESFA must also seek to embrace active partnerships with other stakeholders in the provision of football for young people beyond the imperatives of the Academy systems. The portents would appear to be encouraging. Stratton et al. (2004: 194) describe the strategic role of the FA in bringing key stakeholders together:

The Football Association has established an Education and Welfare Committee including representatives from the professional leagues, PFA, English Schools' FA, Secondary Heads Association, Head Teachers' Association and Association of Chief Education Officers. In addition, the Football Association appointed an Education and Welfare Adviser who, in conjunction with staff from the FA Premier League and Football League, ensures the development of good practice, particularly in respect of education, welfare and child protection issues. The Football Association also provides regular in-service training for staff within the Academies to ensure the education of young soccer players in all spheres in order to equip young players for the future.

One senior ESFA official we interviewed also pointed to the encouraging realignment of their relationship with the FA by pointing out that:

In their constitution we are administered as an affiliated member of the FA. We are given equal membership rights with the counties so we are seen by many as one of the counties. We have an FA council member as every other county has. Until recently they tried to treat us as a county. But with the formation of the National Game Board, I think things are changing for the better and we have got over the message to the new people at the National Game Board that we are a national body. In the football development plan from the FA, we have been remitted by the FA to be the National Governing Body for school sport. Now we always have been but it's nice to have that down in writing from the FA as the national governing body and within that our major responsibility is to provide the national competition structure for schools football ... I have to say that relationships are a lot better and I think they are beginning to see us a national governing body.

The FA's National Game Division is committed to improving the quality of opportunities for boys and girls to participate and develop their interest in the game. Clearly, links between the ESFA with the National Game can do much to enrich the playing experiences of young people. As Daniel (2004: 207) agrees, 'there does appear to be a genuine commitment to expanding and improving the quality of children's participation'. A junior club secretary we interviewed described a project between a school and a Charter Standard to illustrate the potential that collaborative approaches may have for young people:

Over the last three weeks I've had meetings with the headteacher, PE department, the local council and properties part of the school as well and our plan to become a community school and community club is linked together. We are hoping to get an all-weather pitch with floodlights, drain two small-sided pitches, new changing facilities and a normal sized pitch, as well ... We are also launching the sports science project for which the school have just got a government grant. While I was there three weeks ago, the school didn't have a girls' side in the secondary schools competition. We actually had our first competition yesterday and they actually got a team together and they won every game. So the answer is yes, but I think the link between ourselves and the school is very, very proactive and the future of having a community club will work ... We are well on our way; it's fantastic.

Is this a glimpse of the future? Here, a school and a Charter Standard club are developing a model of partnership that bears a resemblance to the European model of provision. The head teacher was adamant that opportunities for students could only benefit from such a partnership. For a school serving a largely rural community and with a limited staffing capacity to support an extensive football programme, it was clear to him that the partnership was key to providing a more inclusive and supportive environment.

Too often in the past, the interests of young people have been sidelined by the tensions that have existed between the ESFA, the FA the county FAs and the professional clubs. In seeking to protect their vested interests, these key stakeholders have been guilty of accelerating division rather than maximizing their complementary strengths. The landscape for schools and youth football has changed irrevocably. It is incumbent upon all stakeholders, including the ESFA, to re-evaluate their role. Gordon Taylor (Chief Executive of the PFA) was in no doubt about the strategic role to be played by the ESFA in creating opportunities for boys and girls to benefit from the game. In his foreword for the ESFA's centenary publication (Kerrigan 2004) he commented:

> With the changes over the last decade – the formation of the Premier League and the establishment of Football Academies and Centres of Excellence taking the best young players from the age 8 upwards – it is more imperative than ever that the ESFA continues to make its mark and establish its historical position as an essential base for the development of a football playing nation.

In doing this it is vital that the ESFA explores partnerships with other stakeholder groups to ensure that the rules of provision, at all levels of the game, are enforced and that the entitlements of young people to a safe and supportive learning environment are protected. I wonder what the qualitative differences in experiences would have been for Alan had a more coherent and collegial culture for young players existed? Unfortunately, since leaving teaching, we have lost touch. What a pity; I'd be really interested in his thoughts.

Chapter 11

Disability football and vulnerable people

Kate Russell

This chapter focuses on what the Football Association (FA) calls disability football, which also includes vulnerable people who participate in the game. By this I mean any footballer who does not participate in mainstream or 'regular' football. The chapter begins by describing briefly the history of disability sport in general before investigating the development of disability football within the FA and relating this to plans for its growth in the wider footballing community. Next, data are presented from interviews conducted with thirty-six respondents involved in disability football, based at thirteen different clubs.[1] The data include accounts of players and parents, together with commentaries from coaches, administrators and others within disability football. It is clear from these accounts that football for disabled people is an enjoyable and beneficial experience. Also evident are the pervading frustrations of both players and coaches trying to gain recognition for the footballer first and their dis/ability second.

Vulnerability

I want to spend a moment here to clarify the term 'vulnerable' in order to challenge some of the myths and assumptions that often accompany (sports) people who have a disability. I do this as a way of understanding the construct of disability sport from a non-disabled perspective – to question my own views and to present a clearer picture of what the individuals in the study actually said to us. 'It can be said that society has created a situation in which disabled children and adults have been taught to be good victims' (Kerr 1999: 1) and, as such, the way in which individuals in that society perceive people with disabilities can actually exacerbate their vulnerability. The National Coaching Foundation (now SportsCoach UK) developed *Protecting Disabled Children and Adults in Sport and Recreation* (Kerr 1999), which highlighted a number of reasons why disabled sports people may be more vulnerable to abuse. These include:

- being unable to recognise or understand abusive situations and behaviours by others perhaps linked to limited life experiences and social contacts;

- communication difficulties (which) may make it hard to explain a situation to a third party;
- intrusion of body space for physical and medical care (which) can lead to a disabled person never developing ownership of their bodies;
- the general thought that disabled people are not abused ... so making it difficult to be believed if they report an incident.

(Kerr 1999: 1–2)

It is also worthy of note that not all disabled people are vulnerable, or perceive themselves to be so, and that not all vulnerable people are disabled. As we have seen in Chapter 2, children and adults alike are susceptible to abuse through a combination of lifestyle factors and circumstances – none of which necessarily preclude age or ability. As researchers, we have to be wary of simply aligning an increase in risk of abuse with a person's dis/ability without first considering the context of the situation. With these points clearly in our mind, let us go on to explore the development of disability sport.

History of disability sport

Sport for disabled people has developed largely over the last century from the introduction of competition for wheelchair athletes at Stoke Mandeville Hospital, Aylesbury, in 1948 (Kerr 2000). Sir Ludgwig Guttman, a neurosurgeon, organized the first International Wheelchair Games to coincide with the London Olympics in a deliberate attempt to give it the same status. It was not until 1960 that the Olympics and Paralympics (Parallel Olympics) were coupled again in Rome and, since that time, have been held every four years. The Winter Paralympics joined the four-year cycle of events from their inaugural competition in France in 1990. Initially, the Paralympics were only for wheelchair users but gradually other classes of athletes have been incorporated. Arguably the most important development occurred in 1982 with the creation of the International Co-ordinating Committee of World Sports Organizations for the Disabled (ICC) as a counterpart to the International Olympic Committee (IOC). This organization incorporated the sport associations for people with cerebral palsy, visual impairment, wheelchair users, amputees and other disabled performers under one umbrella movement, becoming the International Paralympic Committee (IPC) in 1992 (Kerr 2000).

History of disability football

National impairment-specific organizations have been involved in football since the early 1980s, although the FA first became involved in 1998 and supported the English Federation of Disability Sports (EFDS) to run the Ability Counts project. In 2001, the FA launched a five-year Disability Football Development strategy, to become the world's leading governing body in the development of disability football. This led to the FA assuming responsibility for disability football in 2003 and, via the Disability Football Strategy in 2004, to commit to the development of disability football from grass roots level through to England squads (the FA 2005a).[2] Progress has been swift, with over 10,000 disabled players and fifty Ability Counts football clubs in operation during the 2005–6 season (the FA 2005a). In addition, forty-two clubs attended the first Ability Counts Festival for disabled people in 2005, organized by the London Sports Forum for Disabled People, the Amateur Football Alliance and the FA. This signalled a clear message to disability football clubs that their activities were valued and supported by the FA, although participation by disabled girls is still far lower than it is for boys. At the time or writing, there are numerous pan- and discrete disability teams throughout England, with six national squads for disabled footballers: amputees, blind, cerebral palsy, deaf, learning disability and partially sighted.[3]

Key findings from the FA CP project

I focus this chapter on the experiences of the many players with a disability we spoke with, in addition to their parents and coaches. In addition to wanting better communication with the FA, the key issues highlighted by our respondents were: vulnerability and integration; opportunities to play football; and, resources.

Vulnerability and integration

During the first year of the project, the perception among many coaches was that Child Protection (CP) had only been taken on board because of a requirement of Charter Standard and then only because of one person's personal initiative.[4] In many ways, this reflected what we observed in non-disabled (mainly male) clubs: CP was only perceived to be an issue as girls' involvement in the game grew (see Chapter 12), since girls were perceived to be at greater risk from abuse and therefore needed more protection. Ironically, this myth has served to prompt action on CP where before little activity took place.

The FA was also regarded by our respondents as comparatively remiss in providing suitable information to guide clubs in their work with disabled football. Many of them felt that specific standards for disabled provision were not spelt out and that, instead, one standard was expected to fit all participants, whether disabled or not. Clubs in our study wanted specific guidelines to deal with abuse – in particular in relation to wheelchair users, vulnerable adults and those with learning disabilities. Many felt that some of the procedures and knowledge that were taken for granted in the mainstream game were simply not there for disability football. Communication and collaboration on future guidelines were seen as essential.

I think it's important that structures that are laid down for protection – and we're taking about child protection and vulnerable adults – should fit people and not people fit structures.

(Administrator)

Many coaches within disability football recognized the value of CP: they expressed the hope that others in the game would not see CP as merely a 'bolt on thing for equal opportunities'. In many ways, this perception lies at the heart of any new social inclusion initiative. The overriding belief among those charged with the responsibility for supporting, implementing and maintaining the CP initiative in disability football was that it was a reactive measure, brought in to accommodate pressure from a particular lobby group. Such individuals had little understanding of the implications of the CP policy, or how to ensure that it was fit for purpose. Interestingly, the same attitude was discernible among many of those involved in running the girls' game.

During the second year of our investigation, we detected a widespread perception that, although there had been some improvement in the situation, disabled children and young people in football were still probably the most vulnerable to potential abuse.[5] If we refer back to many of the points noted by Kerr (1999), it is clear that concerns over communication difficulties between participants, coaches and parents/carers, the intrusion of body space for physical and medical care, and the inability of some participants to recognize abusive situations were all causing apprehension for some organizers.

With reference to the implementation of CP policies, however, some very positive changes in attitudes, policy and practice were detected:

I think it is absolutely fantastic and that it really has changed I think. It is what we need in disability football because it is the right thing. It is just right.

(Assistant coach)

There has been a change of emphasis in the way issues, policies, child protection, rights, wrongs, accidents, you know reporting them, everything. We seem to have leapt forward ... The change of coaches has had an effect, I think it's a lot to do with that. The coaches have a different attitude, a softer approach.

(Parent)

As we will see more clearly in relation to the girls' game (Chapter 12), the adaptation of coaching styles was prominent when discussing the inclusion of female disability participants. There was a pervading belief that coaches should and would have to develop coaching practices that were adaptable. The needs of the participant would drive the style and content of the session rather than providing a one-style-fits-all approach to coaching and practice. Through this, it was thought that coaches would develop better, safer and more enjoyable ways of engaging all footballers.

Views diverged slightly on whether mixed or segregated groups and teams provided better or more appropriate environments for the participation and encouragement of young disabled players. While most respondents involved in disability football sought greater integration into the 'mainstream/regular' game, those working within deaf football expressed alternative views (see below).

In relation to segregation *within* disability clubs, it was clear that political, pragmatic and ethical concerns had to be balanced:

> I am not a big one for segregating people, but sometimes because they are, some of them, disabled, [they are] less likely to enjoy it if they are playing with more able people ... so you do have to split it there. I try and put [a] leveller on group issues ... people all on the same standard but without too much emphasis going on segregation so they don't actually realize that.
>
> (Coach)

Some disability clubs catering for a range of disabilities opted to divide players into groups, but not necessarily on the basis of ability, which was felt to be potentially negative and alienating for the less able members.

> We tend to split them up ... we do the warm-up altogether and then we split them up into groups, not always in abilities otherwise they are going to feel out of it ... but we tend to mix them up and we put probably two staff with that group and one with the other.
>
> (Coach)

The debate about whether different disability groups should work together or separately is yet to be resolved by the FA. Much of this discussion is undertaken by the individual county FAs or the clubs themselves. The development of national teams for specific disabilities is regarded as a positive move but what is of greater concern for many involved in the game is the total number of actual participants engaging in the sport. This has a knock-on effect on how many distinct teams are possible.

Opportunities to play football

The lack of teams run specifically for deaf players was a particular theme in our study. Some respondents stressed the need for clubs actively to recruit deaf juniors via local schools:

> I worry that with deaf children, they are not being brought into sport. There is [sic] not enough deaf role models going out into deaf schools, PHU

(Partially Hearing Units) and mainstream schools that might have just one individual child and encouraging them to join their local team. For the deaf community sport is important because it brings young people into the deaf community, gives them an identity, allows them to learn different ways of communicating with others and finding that there's a bigger deaf world out there.

(Administrator)

The benefits to juniors of playing in clubs designated for deaf people only were noted by some, particularly in relation to effective communication.

It's a different club because they use sign language. There are all deaf people and ... no hearing people ... It's good, it's better ... because they can understand properly. And this club is for deaf people only. It's good because a lot of people come ... it's more popular. It's got a good reputation.

(Player)

This perception often contradicts the belief that playing in a mixed team would enhance a player's chance of success, although it must be acknowledged there are limited professional opportunities for disabled footballers. As noted by one of our researchers, Claudia, in the field, players were keen to know if there were any realistic chances of 'making it' in the professional arena. The following extract comes from her fieldwork diary:

At one point the deaf kid asked my interviewee to ask me if it was possible for deaf people to become famous playing football. It was so touching. I explained that only one in a million hearing people can become famous in football and that deaf people have a disadvantage but that he should go for it as much as he can.

Many coaches of disabled footballers who participated in our research felt that they should recognize the needs of such players and find ways to accommodate them rather than simply letting talented players be passed over. In particular, it was hoped that, by educating hearing players, more deaf players would have an opportunity of success in the mainstream/regular game.

Integration into normal football is really important ... deaf football is not that unlike ordinary football and sometimes better because you have to use your wits a lot more! ... my son's skilled at football and shouldn't be judged on his deafness but on what he's good at ...

(Parent)

Resources

The paucity of facilities for disabled footballers, including basic facilities such as toilets and changing rooms, was a recurrent theme.

> Some of the facilities you go to are dire. One mum is wheelchair-bound and she wants to go to the toilet ... unbelievable. We are not better at our club really. Lack of facilities, it's disgusting.
>
> (Coach)

The lack of funding, particularly travel expenses for tournament participation across the country, meant that young deaf players sometimes had to restrict their attendance. The high cost of interpreters' fees for deaf people undergoing FA coaching courses was also raised as a concern.

The benefits of bringing disabled youngsters into coaching roles were emphasized by many respondents, not only in relation to enhanced communication with disabled players:

> X (coach) is more communicating, not shouting, they understand the new coach and obviously he is like the boys and girls that are there now. He can relate to them on their level. The coach has had speech difficulties so he talks to them the ways he's been taught, nice and slowly, and they understand that and they can take it in.
>
> (Parent)

... but also in terms of providing an 'insider' perspective to more able-bodied colleagues:

> I have my own set things that I plan before and with the other coach, as I mentioned, he is ... at college, he is helping me, he used to go to one of the special schools there ... He's been helping me for three to four months. I introduced him for two reasons. It gave me another insight of [sic] the thinking sometimes.
>
> (Coach)

Appropriate role models are regarded by many in football as the key to future success and increased participation. As we will see in relation to the girls' and women's game in the next chapter, the lack of visible disabled coaches often sends the message that there is, and will always be, a limit to what is achievable in the game for disabled footballers. While the FA does run coaching workshops for coaches to learn how to cater for a wide range of disabilities, there is no indication at present of how many disabled coaches are actually working with disability groups, although in 2006 over 800 coaches had undertaken the FA's Coaching Disabled Footballers course (Davis 2006).

Footballer first and disabled person second?

One of the most important issues to emerge from our research was the conflict exhibited, at times, by coaches, players and parents/carers alike with regard to the capability of disabled footballers. Disability coaches sometimes had difficulty disassociating working with a footballer from working with a footballer with disabilities.

> I try and come from the position that we are footballers first and disabled second and that if I talk to you as a footballer, at times I may ignore that you have a disability. Most of my players respond to that and that is the best way forward. Quite often some of the younger players who have been sheltered will go away feeling aggrieved because they have either been spoken to by a coach or questioned or made suggestion of [sic] how they can improve. Even people around them are saying 'That's not right, you have a disability and need to be treated properly', or they go away and not understand that we are trying to work alongside the able-bodied people and treat them as if, you know, they have footballing intelligence first and the need to play football first and have a disability second. It's a perception thing.
>
> (Coach)

This dilemma between recognizing differing abilities and selecting appropriate coaching behaviours appeared central to many coaches' concerns about CP. The recurring parental perception that we found, of low expectations of 'success' for their disabled children in the football world, makes this a difficult issue to resolve. One coach noted:

> They [parents] don't really expect it [success] and so they don't seek out and demand the best for their kids, which I feel they should do. Because they see their kids as having a disability and they're not going to be able to achieve their dreams and ambitions in life ... just because they have a disability doesn't mean they don't have dreams and ambition and can aspire to good things.

Summary

It is clear that the participants in disability football engage in the game with the same level of enthusiasm and competitive drive as their mainstream counterparts. What is apparent, however, is a lack of cohesiveness among clubs in the make-up of teams (either pan- or discrete disability groups) and the availability of professional opportunities for players. There is a tension between seeing a player as a footballer first and disabled athlete second, for both coaches and parents/carers alike. Absent from the accounts presented to us was an understanding of the disabled player's perspective, which therefore points to scope for further work in this area.

Notes

1   It should be noted that, at the time of the FA CP research project, many of the strategies subsequently put in place were merely under development. The views of respondents presented in this section may not, therefore, reflect the wider view of today's disability footballer.

2   The Disability Football Directory (http://www.disabilityfootball.co.uk)

3   Ability Counts football clubs are part of an initiative to generate more football clubs that focus on players with a variety of ability levels. As such, teams are pan-disability rather than, for example, solely for deaf or partially sighted players.

4   The FA, in conjunction with various other bodies, has drawn up the following set of criteria for clubs wishing to reach Charter Standard: a written constitution; self-certified screening of managers, coaches and officials; all managers to have minimum of FA Junior Team Managers Award; commitment to attend in-service training; acceptance and promotion of codes of conduct; commitment to provide mini-soccer opportunities for under-10s; commitment to promote schools' liaison and equal opportunities for all.

5   Disabled children make up about three per cent of the total child population (Department of Health 2000). Studies into the prevalence of maltreatment among children with disabilities in the US have found that these children are over three times more likely to experience abuse and neglect than non-disabled children. Disabled children in a US study were found to be 3.4 times more likely overall to be abused or neglected than non-disabled children. They were 3.8 times more likely to be neglected; 3.8 times more likely to be physically abused; 3.1 times more likely to be sexually abused; and 3.9 times more likely to be emotionally abused. (Sullivan and Knutson 2000, cited in National Working Group on Child Protection and Disability 2003). Smaller scale UK-based studies have indicated similar levels of maltreatment (Kennedy 1989; Westcott 1993, cited in National Working Group on Child Protection and Disability 2003).

Chapter 12

The women's game

Kate Russell

In this chapter I investigate the experiences of women and young girls in foot-ball. The analysis begins with a brief examination of women's involvement in football in Britain over the last century in an attempt to set a clear context for the struggle behind acceptance of their place within the nation's most popular sport. The main focus of the chapter is on the experiences of the women and girls who took part in the FA Child Protection (CP) research project between 2002 and 2003. Data were gathered from 134 interviews (over two years) with women who either play football, are parents of girls in football, or who coach and admin-ister the women's game. Through examining the voices and behaviour of these women there is a clear sense that what they have experienced covers the spec-trum of joy at playing football, through to frustration at the sexist treatment by some male coaches and the lack of funding and support from the FA organiza-tion. It is also important at this point to highlight that the data are interpreted from a social constructionist perspective which privileges the meanings and actions of the individuals concerned over other forms of interpretation.

History of women's football in Britain

This very brief overview of the history of women's participation in football in Britain is provided in an effort to highlight the critical incidents that led to both positive changes and also to increased hardship for players and organizers alike as the women's game developed.[1]

The first recorded game of women's football in Britain took place in Scotland in 1888 with an association for women being founded in 1894 (Williams 2003). Similar fixtures were held in Scotland and England throughout the 1890s, with a notable match between the English North and South being played at Crouch End in London in 1895 (Williams 2003). As Williams records, 'whether early women players were politically motivated, fashion conscious, or tentative enthu-siast, the authorities viewed their involvement as a nuisance' (2003: 27). In 1902 the FA Council urged all of its (male) members not to play matches against 'lady teams'. This could be considered as an extension of many of the Victorian notions about the dangers of physical activity for the reproductive capability of women (Vertinsky 1988) or, more cynically, an act to separate the women's game from the larger (male) footballing family. In either case, the support given to the women's game in the early years certainly caused some consternation among the FA hierarchy. 1921 saw the FA banning all women from playing on League grounds under the belief that the game of football was: 'quite unsuitable for females and should not be encouraged' (cited in Williams 2003: 33).

It was not until 1969 that the Women's Football Association (WFA) was formed, although beyond the control of the FA itself. It was only in 1971, after action by UEFA, that the FA finally rescinded the 1921 ban on women playing on League pitches. The WFA had to wait until 1983 before it became fully affiliated to the FA and only in 1991 would the FA finally change rule 37 which forbade girls from playing mixed football in mixed sex teams up until 11 years of age (Lopez 1997). Since the FA took over full control of women's and girls' football in 1993, there has been a steady increase in the number of registered players from just over 11,000 to over 61,000 in 2003 (http://www.theFA.com retrieved 10 June 2006).

The growth in female participation during this time reflected a wider expansion of women's sport involvement in general and, specifically, in relation to policy. This involvement is exemplified in the English Sports Council's *Women and Sport: Policy and Frameworks for Action*, published in 1993. This document set in place policies for women, people with disabilities and black and ethnic minorities and was based on the two key principles of sports development and sports equity. At a similar time as the Women's Sport Foundation was becoming increasing active as a lobbying and advocacy group for women in the UK (White 2003), the Sports Council document formed the basis for the Brighton Declaration on Women and Sport in 1994. The Declaration stated as its overriding aim 'to develop a sporting culture that enables and values the full involvement of women in every aspect of sport' (p. 51) including management, organizational responsibility and research. The Declaration, later endorsed by over 250 national and international organizations, is recognized as stating the principles for women's sports development worldwide (UK Sports Council 1998).

Football is now considered to be the fastest growing sport for women in the UK. The 2005 Women's FA Cup Final between Charlton Athletic FC and Everton FC attracted an attendance of over 8,000 spectators and TV viewing figures of around two million, which reflects positive developments in the women's game. Indeed, the Women's European Championships, held in England during June 2005, had attendance records for the opening match of 29,082 and viewing figures of 2.9 million, with an overall attendance of over 100,000 spectators for the two-week tournament and 8.2 million television viewers (http://www.theFA.com retrieved 5 Feb 2006). The FA has implemented a Football Development Strategy (2001–2006) to highlight the needs of a variety of groups, including women and girls, with the aim of becoming the world's leading governing body for the development of the women's game. Essentially, the purpose of the strategy is to foster the work of the fifty-one licensed FA Centres of Excellence, twenty Academies and the International Player Development Centre (IPDC) at Loughborough University, all of which are targeted at growing and improving the women's and girls' game.

Key findings from the FA Child Protection project

What follows below details the key findings from both years of the FA project. In order to make sense of the vast amount of data collected, this chapter focuses on the primary issues of: competitive structures; coaching issues; women acting as change agents; women footballers as role models; and the issue of sexuality. As one of the key tenets of the project is to allow voices to be heard, I present a wide variety of quotes from the participants in order for readers to learn from the actual experiences of the women and girls themselves. My commentary is only included to help the interpretation of the data.

Competitive structures

There was a concern among many respondents that grouping girls' football into under-12 and under-14 categories, as opposed to the boys' set up of under-11, 12, 13 and 14, did not take into consideration the range of physical sizes and maturity of players. This was highlighted further through the inclusion of girls aged fourteen and above in what is called 'open age' football. The concern expressed was that there was no 'in between' for girls that would allow a gentler progression from small pitches to full-sized ones or from playing with younger peers to feeling comfortable playing alongside older girls. A female, junior level coach, for example, noted:

> I would like another league maybe for under-18s; one for under-16s and then one for under-18s and then go open age. There are some women who are like, you know, rugby players and they're quite tough. My girls started training at another club and the women are lovely but they're big and that worries me a bit. Some can take it can't they? But then it might put a lot off, which could be a shame.

Despite these concerns over how the girls' and women's game is currently structured, the popularity of women's football is still growing. At some point in the future, as sufficient numbers are generated, this should allow the separation of teams into more appropriate age groups. It was pointed out to us that some counties have been proactive in increasing the number of opportunities for girls to play football but that this was still at an early stage and the league structures were not able to keep up with demand. The presence of IPDC at Loughborough University has had an impact on the demand for high quality coaching sessions. Even big clubs are unable to provide the financial or structural support for their young female players, so many of our respondents felt that the Centre would provide a clearly defined pathway to footballing success for the young women placed there.

The IPDC is fully funded by the FA and overseen by National Women's Coach. The Centre has been based at Loughborough University since 2001, providing a Football Scholarship Programme for female footballers. Female performers can be part of the Centre of Excellence system until sixteen and then the Academy system to nineteen years of age. To the present time, the Centre has produced many international players, including Amanda Barr and Karen Carney, both of whom played in the 2005 Women's European Championships. While opportunities for girls are growing, it is still clear that a long-term playing career for women footballers is a long way off. Even the girls playing football recognize this situation and it may provide one reason why many coaches do not appear to 'push' girls as hard as boys:

> They [coaches] look after you because they don't push you too far, whereas lads can get pushed because there are more leagues for men when you get older so we get a bit more fairly treated.
>
> (Female player)

This account appears to highlight acceptance by many girls that there is little scope for future professionalism in women's football (at the time of data collection only five clubs out of ten National Division teams had paid players) and the belief that, if there was, they too would be pushed as hard as the boys. Indeed, there might even be a hint of relief in here about this situation.

Open age football became the focus for many concerns about the physical and social development of girls who play in the adult game. While only girls over the age of fourteen played in competitive matches, girls as young as twelve and thirteen were involved in training. The major worry expressed to us was about physical inequalities and the potential for harm that this could cause. But there was also clear reluctance to accept this situation because of current competitive structures:

> You will get 12- and 13-year-olds training with them on a regular basis and ... there are a lot of inappropriate points there: their strength for starters. Are they big enough and strong enough to cope? Some will be, most won't because they are not physically developed. I am not sure they should be put into that environment to learn things at that young age, that, you know, they do.
>
> (Parent)

Potentially you're putting someone who is both physically and mentally less developed on a pitch with someone who has been around for a while who could potentially cause them harm in some way ... but if a player is that talented, if a youth club isn't fulfilling her needs then from my point of view as a coach I'm really happy that she's playing at that level as it will help her development as a player. But until women's football develops where you have elite youth teams as well as elite senior teams this will continue.

(Coach)

Coaching issues

The absence of women in the coaching of football was comparable to the absence of women within the FA as a whole. At the time of our project there were no full-time paid managers in the female game, bar Hope Powell (the England senior coach). Coaching qualifications were regarded as secondary to being able to 'talk the talk' or demonstrate practical knowledge of the game. Women felt they were losing out to men in this area. There was a general perception by many women in our sample that, regardless of having proved themselves through the coach education system, and countless years as working coaches, they would always fare worse than men. Almost any man could be perceived as being a 'better' coach simply by being able to regurgitate the sound bites heard from football pundits on a Saturday, or by being able to kick a ball the length of the pitch. Having demonstrable, credible ability to develop players' skills was seen as a worthy, but less valued, attribute.

One of the biggest concerns in relation to the women's game was the involvement of inappropriate coaching staff. While there were accounts of excellent coaching practice at the IPDC itself, other top level clubs and Academies indicated that many coaches were just not up to the required standard and were taking up coaching positions for the 'wrong' reasons. One director at a top level women's club described these concerns:

If you have crap coaches no one seems to care and that's where stuff like Child Protection comes in, with the legal aspects. As a teacher you would have to be so aware of making sure that you did things in the right way to make sure that you didn't get yourself into any legal difficulties. But with football it's as if you can let anyone do it. With the women coaches that I have here I can rely on every single one, we know how each other works, they're entirely loyal to me and I know what type of people they are. I'm not saying that all the male coaches aren't like that because a couple of the ones I have are excellent ... its just that now I'm not so sure these new coaches know what they're doing in respect to CP. Many of the new ones don't know the procedures or don't have them in place.

The poor quality of coaching and emphasis on an aggressive style of play were considered to be ill-matched with working with women at any level. A top level female coach reported that:

> many men are just jumping on the bandwagon and want to get involved with women's football for the wrong reasons. They are more concerned with being associated to a big Premier club or whatever and so they can get the kudos from that rather than actually being interested in developing these young women and that's what gets me. So they can say that they coach at Fulham or Arsenal etc. without actually doing their job. They are entirely inappropriate people, coaching in an entirely inappropriate way and our players aren't used to that. They shouldn't be off coaching at this level at all, never mind with women. Their level is more the recreational level where they can behave like that if they want to but not here. And all that will happen is that the women will leave because they don't want to be treated like that. There does tend to be an issue around the preference of the aggressive style of coaching and playing and that's not what we want here. It's a bit like they undergo a personality change once they start coaching and think they're like [X] or whoever and turn into bullies.

Another top level female coach reported a lack of support from the FA in mentoring support for good female coaches coming up through the ranks. This led to a sense of disillusionment about working in this area and battling to produce results with few resources. It was clear that many female coaches working at both grass roots and elite level experienced a 'grass ceiling' effect, whereby only a chosen few were allowed to move up the coaching system:

> I did apply to be one of the women's coaches who are mentored by the FA but it seems to be only the chosen few who do actually get this and so I'm not involved in that scheme. And that's the thing you see, that many women coaches are just not supported by the FA and the ones who really need that support are ignored. That's why so many women are leaving the game. The women who have left X [Academy] with all that knowledge about the girls here is terrible and it will mean that they get treated differently by the newer male coaches I've had to employ.
>
> (Academy coach)

Women as change agents

This particular theme is arguably one of the most prominent throughout the entire FA CP project. Not only has the presence of women and girls in the 'football family' been regarded as a nuisance, and something which creates far more problems than it resolves, but it has also brought with it an almost missionary zeal to create a 'female friendly' space. It is this, in both its negative and positive aspects, that creates the most discussion, and hence the most energy to ensure that things get done. Simply speaking, the introduction and inclusion of so many girls and women into the game of football has made the FA sit up and take notice of gender.

As outlined in earlier chapters, it was clear that many coaches and administrators felt that the pursuit of Charter Standard was having a positive impact on the inclusion of CP into clubs. This was secondary, however, to the prominence of girls and women entering the game and the consequent influence this was having. The inclusion of more girls in football appeared to open up the possibility of questioning coaching behaviour and also permitted challenges to previously-accepted ideas. This included when to enter changing rooms, appropriate ratios of adults to juniors and the issue of travel away from the home club. It was evident that boys in football were seen as far safer than their female counterparts:[2]

> With it being female ... being girls, we do like either myself or one or two of the ladies players to be present ... if not mothers have got to be there. We will not allow the coach to carry it on his shoulders – as I've said with it being girls, we wouldn't leave men around with just the girls.
>
> (Female parent)

There was also recognition that the ways in which coaches treat girls would, in turn, challenge the ways in which boys could expect to be treated. It was hoped that the assumed 'better' behaviour of young women could have a positive, civilizing impact on all:

> Boys could learn something from the way the girls are looked after and the way they behave ... one or two of the coaches have said that ... they'd rather coach girls than boys.
>
> (Parent)

The evidence from the interview data suggests that the increased presence of girls and women in football has changed, and continues to change the way some coaches behave in relation to CP. The issue of changing room supervision and administrating first aid clearly caused the most concern among coaches working with girls:

> It [coaching girls] did bring to light a few different new issues as far as the welfare of the girls, I mean mainly changing rooms. We had to make sure that we got parents involved – especially the mothers – so we'd got female attendants in the changing rooms. There were issues like that. We had some quite good discussion as well about things we needed in the girls' medical bag that we didn't need in the boys' medical bag. You know, as the girls get

older, sanitary issues and things like that. I must admit that, maybe, some of the men don't stop and think about; you don't expect the male coaches to.

(Male coach)

I've always thought whenever the girls have got injured that the managers have never had any idea about how they should treat the girl, like bringing her back and playing her.

(Parent)

Even the most mundane of issues, such as changing facilities at pitches, were creating difficulties within the game. One respondent noted this by highlighting a league ruling that requires teams to provide changing facilities. The key factor here is that it would appear that it is *because* of the inclusion of girls' football that the issue has been addressed. This highlights the accepted difference in the way girls and boys should be treated which, in turn, reflects deeply rooted gender assumptions within the game:

Some of the places we go are dire, and it's the difference again between the boys and the girls. You cannot expect a 14-, 15-, 16-year-old girl to be changing on the side of the pitch. You could say the same thing about boys, but this is an issue that's come up at the league, and the league have come up with a rule that says you have to provide changing facilities.

(Coach)

What came across strongly from the accounts of both parents and coaches was that there were disparities between the way coaches should treat girls and boys. Many coaches we talked with felt that girls and boys should be treated differently, both physically and mentally. This perception also helps to identify the way in which boys are socialized to accept poor treatment as part of being a 'footballer':

I think there are a lot of differences [in the way they should be coached] and I would like to say that they shouldn't – they should all be treated equally but that's not the case because girls are socialized completely differently to boys. So you're there trying to encourage them to do things that someone else has said that they shouldn't be doing. Sometimes I think you need to be more encouraging for girls in a group

(Coach)

Working at boy's Academies and at this Centre I have noticed a difference between how people handle boys and how they handle girls. I think girls have to be handled a little bit differently: boys can be spoken to in a different way. Not aggressively but a little bit louder and they'll understand that and probably react to that more than girls would ... it's the emotional side, especially with girls because they do get emotional. And it's knowing how to deal with that.

(Male Academy coach)

We also discerned the belief that coaching girls and women allows a coach to become a better coach. Coaching women makes many coaches change the way they treat their players and, subsequently, they learn that a less aggressive approach can still produce a successful team:

> I think people think that boys can take a lot more and that is changing, I know I've learnt a lot by the way I treat girls and I can take that back and work with boys differently. I mean they have Education and Welfare Officers at the Academies and they are looked after but it just seems that they have more care for the girls than they do for the boys ... here we do have problems with the girls and we do sort it out, whereas with the boys they are expected to get on with it. They [boys] are reluctant to come forward because they perceive it as a sign of being weak, I think that's what it is. They'd rather be told and shouted at than question what's going on.
>
> (Academy coach)

The concern over whether to coach girls and boys differently was also related to the knock-on effect of the expectations of both coaches and players. The difficulty rested on the 'to push or not to push' question that could not be separated from the more aggressive style of coaching most often found in youth football. On the one hand, there was the following perception of the treatment of girls by male coaches:

> I'm not trying to be sexist here or that but I'm finding some of the men forgetting they are with girls. I find that they expect too much of them and do treat them as if, I mean these are under-14s, treat them as if they've got a load of 16- to 18-year-olds. I wouldn't like that treatment of my son to be honest.
>
> (Parent)

... and, on the other hand, there was a feeling that, while changing a coaching style to be 'softer' could be beneficial to the girl's enjoyment of football, it failed to prepare them for competition:

> From what my husband has told me certainly the coach's attitude towards the girls has softened. For example, when we were at a tournament last year he said to them, 'Well you know, we've come along but I don't expect you to win anything so just play whatever'. I thought that was appalling. In fact they won the tournament. To send them off into the tournament with that attitude I didn't think was very good at all.
>
> (Female parent)

The tension displayed here appears to be between developing a coaching style that was more positive (and essentially less about winning) and one that would still encourage competitiveness among players. This perception of the supposed 'feminization' of sport in terms of exalting the ethos of fun over winning is worthy of note. It has been noted elsewhere: for example, Jefferson Lenskyj (1994) argued that some women who play softball play solely based on feminist principles, seeking to reclaim sport in the interests of pleasure. Sometimes, coaches can make inappropriate assumptions concerning the reason for women's participation and their diverse aspirations, from having fun to attaining high level success. In this way, coaches might misjudge the competitive drive and desire to win that the majority of the girls and women who we interviewed indicated that they wanted. The key, of course, is to deliver both and not to privilege one approach over the other.

Women footballers as role models and the sexuality question

We heard a great deal of concern about the apparent absence of relationship boundaries between junior and senior female players. Ensuring strong and identifiable female role models was also high on the agenda. The following account relates specifically to the development and type of relationships between women and girls:

> obviously you've got youngsters who are influenced by role models. Now, that could be just pure influence on playing ability but it could also be a tender age where they're going through a sexuality period and then other senior players can misinterpret that ... there should be a clear understanding about what senior role models 'give out' to younger [players] – I've seen it happen to many youngsters that have been drawn into something that they don't want to ... to be socially approved of.
>
> (Academy coach)

This person is referring obliquely to 'something' but clearly meaning lesbian relationships. Where these involve girls under the age of 18 they are clearly illegal. Those who tried to assert good practice about appropriate relationships between juniors and seniors, however, felt they were being interpreted as 'the enemy' rather than simply fulfilling their CP responsibilities. This indicates that perhaps homosexual relationships between older women and girl footballers are defined and judged differently from those between older men and boys in the game, in other words not readily perceived as child abuse.

Concern was also expressed about open displays of lesbianism in the presence of youngsters, including girls, at social occasions. There was less tolerance of intimate lesbian behaviour at occasions such as tournaments, for example, than there was of hand-holding and kissing among heterosexual couples at the same events. Many parents blamed women's football for the presence of lesbians in the game, indicating perhaps unfounded or misplaced fears and also limiting the individual choices of their own daughters. This issues seemed to be particularly controversial in open age football whereby girls of fourteen were able to participate at senior levels. The following account came from a senior female coach in an Academy:

> [My main concern is] older females developing relationships with younger girls who are confused. They get drawn into situations they don't understand and aren't ready for.

Griffin's (1992) work highlights one of the difficulties for women in terms of observers' wishes to ascertain the number of lesbians within any given sport. For her:

> women in sport must come to understand that it wouldn't matter if there were no lesbians in sport: the lesbian label would still be used to intimidate and control women's athletics.
>
> (Griffin 1992: 260)

For the women in football management roles who we met, the issue of same-sex relationships was focused much more on developing appropriate professional boundaries and helping to guide and support younger players appropriately than it was about sexuality.

Alongside concerns over the physical danger that a young girl may face in training and playing matches, there was some unease about the social and sexual development of these players. One interviewee who worked for the FA identified how a lack of commitment to deal directly with the issue of sexuality was an indication of the general lack of care towards girls exhibited by the FA:

> I don't think we look after them particularly well. I think on the outside we look at basic needs but we don't go deep enough. There are, I find, loads of issues that sit in and around football that we just don't deal with: we turn a blind eye to. I look at men's and women's teams, open age teams that have 14- and 15-year-old young people in them. I look at changing room environments; I look at the high level of gay women in football and how many young girls coming into the game could easily have their head turned. I look at all these issues and think we only ever touch the surface of them.
>
> (Female Academy coach)

Another respondent interpreted the issue of sexuality slightly differently, and rather more positively. She recognized that gay women were present in football but was less concerned about it because of the sensitive and open approach she perceived was taken to tackling any associated difficulties. For her, the issue of developing sexuality was approached more in terms of helping the young woman through this process rather than as a negative response to homosexuality. It was also clear from our evidence that the presence of gay women in football did not impact negatively on the nature or quality of training or on women's competitiveness:

> I don't think it affects the way the girls work with us but I think it's there and I think we've got the mechanism in place to help them deal with it and help them find the answers they need to find.
>
> (Academy coach)

The issue of sexuality was also considered to be something of a taboo topic in football, adding to the notion that it is swept under the carpet by some in the game. A parent we interviewed highlighted this omission and the need to address the issue:

> Clearly some things have not been tackled at all. I remember talking to you last time about ... discrimination in relation to sexuality ... I just think ... that's a criminal omission ... I've seen some stuff about race, I haven't seen anything about Child Protection and I've certainly seen nothing about sexuality ... a lot of the culture around kids football is actively and, absolutely, actively and overtly homophobic ... something ought to be done ... and the FA should be taking a lead on that, and I've seen absolutely no developments on that at all ... it would be better if there was a more open confrontation of the issue that a lot of the kids that are playing kids' football are gay or will become gay or will be gay, or will become actively gay, you know ... I just cringe sometimes
>
> (Parent)

This parent's account clearly highlighted concern over the lack of an open forum on such matters, and a sense of fear or confusion about this. As in most sports, 'sexuality' is used as a euphemism for lesbianism in football: there has been comparatively little attention to the male gay 'problem' in the game (Brackenridge *et al.* 2006). This reflects an ostrich-like stance whereby many running the game of football believe that there are no gay men and boys playing football or that, if there are, they are less likely to make themselves visible and so to challenge the status quo. Fortunately, and not before time, since the close of the FA CP project a great deal of work has been done on homophobia and sexuality in the game.[3]

Summary

I hope to have recognized in this chapter the many experiences of girls and women who play, parent, administer and coach football. The voices heard here certainly expose some of the more difficult and testing situations in football that these girls and women have to deal with. It also points out what a powerful force their presence has had on the structure and development of policy and practice alike. Suggest to any girl or woman involved in football that they would be better not doing so and you will find none who agree. It is evident, however, that the FA needs to address the underlying disparities in support and resources for female coaches and to be brave enough to attend to the issues of sexuality in the women's game in an open and calm manner.

Notes

1   Interested readers seeking a more detailed overview are directed to explore such books as Lopez's (1997) *Women on the Ball: A Guide to Women's Football*, Williams and Woodhouse's (1999) *Offside?: The Position of Women in Football*, and Williams' (2003) *A game for Rough Girls?: A History of Women's Football in Britain*.

2   While there is a general belief that girls are at greater risk of abuse than boys, the evidence suggests that boys are equally vulnerable. Figures for 2004–5 indicate that there were more girls on the child protection register in connection with sexual abuse than boys – accounting for eleven per cent of girls on the register at 31 March 2005 and eight per cent of boys. In contrast there were more boys than girls on the register in connection with physical abuse (DfES 2005b).

3   See, for example, Football for All at http://www.theFA.com/theFA/ethicsandsports equity/

Chapter 13

Scouts

Gareth Nutt

The expansion of academic interest and research into football has coincided with a corresponding increase in the social, cultural, economic and political significance attached to an increasingly globalized game. But, although research into football is now well documented, Parker (1996c) reminds us that insightful and substantive revelations about the day-to-day activities of key personnel in football are few and far between. Much of our knowledge of 'life in the game' continues to be informed by the biographies and autobiographies of 'the great and the good'. While many of these publications claim to offer insider accounts of the football world, a large number of them remain heavily mediated, partial and carefully edited versions for commercial consumption. Parker attributes our lack of insight into an occupational culture that sets up barriers and restricts access to forms of research examining 'cultural modes of existence'. Thus, we know very little about the processes that have accompanied the socialization of personnel like managers, coaches and players and the consequences for their social, cultural and professional identities.

Precisely because professional football operates in such an insular world, it seems that the case for 'insider' accounts that critically examine the social structures and processes of working life within English professional football is compelling. Although carrying out a role that remains largely under-researched, professional football scouts are key stakeholders in the recruitment of players and, as such, were chosen for scrutiny as part of the research project. Therefore, this chapter focuses on the scouting process and the centrality of scouting to the organizational structure of football clubs (Monk and Russell 2000). Particular attention is given to the scouting and recruitment of young players with data drawn from interviews conducted with scouts, Academy and Centre of Excellence managers, parents, junior football officials and players. I am also able to draw upon my experiences as a scout for a professional football club. It is a role that I have undertaken on a part-time basis since the 2000/2001 season. My responsibilities lie predominantly in preparing match reports and player assessments for the first team squad although I have occasionally been asked by the Academy Recruitment Manager to report on under-18 FA Academy and FA Youth Cup matches.

Historical emergence of scouting

Although Davies (2000) and O'Donaghue (1999) offer reflections on their careers in the game, football scouts are rarely represented in sports literature beyond the occasional anecdotal references in players' autobiographies. Moreover, many of these appear to have perpetuated a stereotype of a rather avuncular if somewhat solitary individual dedicated to uncovering the 'next best thing' by standing on touchlines in all weathers and venues. Accounts such as these contribute to contradictory views of their role in the recruitment process. On the one hand, scouts are portrayed as key members of 'a rather romantic and somewhat sanitised process of spectacular success' (Conn et al. 2003: 228), while, on the other, they have been instrumental in perpetuating a highly negative view of the way that professional football clubs recruit young players.

Although the extent and organization of early scouting networks is difficult to determine, it is evident that views such as these are rooted in the history of the professional game. According to Kerrigan (2004), the competition for young players increased considerably from the early 1900s in accordance with the financial and cultural importance of the game (Mason 1980, Fishwick 1989). But, while they fulfilled the basic recruitment needs of clubs, Walvin (1975) doubted the degree of professionalism by which this was done. Apparently, scouts adopted a variety of means of recruitment that lacked both forward planning and coherence. Typical was the use made of word of mouth, family connections and personal recommendations. These methods were characteristic of the ways in which football recruited young players.

The contemporary picture of scouting

Contemporary developments, related to the licensing of Academies and Centres of Excellence, might lead one to conclude that scouting today has become more systematic and less reliant on chance, word of mouth and 'tip-offs'. Club scouts certainly pride themselves on being 'in the know' and many have used technology to open up the global market and to build detailed databases for the recruitment of players. Players' agents have also served to add another dimension to their network of contacts. As one Football League scout confirmed, an unwelcome trend has been the number of agents employed by young players seeking professional contracts. He commented:

> The trouble with football now is the dreaded agent and, a lot of the time, if you are going to talk to the boy, you have got to talk to the boy with the agent ... You tend to find now that even the youngest boys, 17, 18 or 19 years of age, have all got agents or advisors of some description. You basically finish up talking to them. We spend most of our time speaking to agents about players and even the ones that we miss we will hear about because somebody

will ring us up and say, 'I represent so and so and he has just been released. Would you be interested in having him down?'

More recently, a number of independent companies have used the internet as a form of recruitment agency. Registered players post their CVs online and clubs are invited to pursue their interests by either using the company as an intermediary or by attending pre-arranged trials. According to one company director we interviewed, internet agencies take their Child Protection (CP) responsibilities very seriously. His view was: 'We believe that we are the only site giving genuine opportunities and chances to young people and protecting them while we do it.' He was adamant that they did not do anything for the younger players without gaining parental permission. For example:

> Well, with a scout, when they come to our trials day, the scout will actually register with us. If that scout is actually interested in a player, they will contact us and we will then check them out, going to the club where appropriate. We then contact the parents.

In a similar way, the Professional Footballers' Association (PFA) has entered into a partnership with an agency to manage the Premier League's Academy 'exit trials' for scholars being released by their clubs. In addition to developing relationships with agents, use of the internet to access commercial agencies, e-mail and mobile telephone technology are now permanent features of a scout's working life. Even so, I am conscious that there remains a strong reliance on some of the more informal networks and traditional methods of information gathering.

Once they have been identified, players will be watched in competition, in training, at pre-arranged trials or invited to attend a trial at the club. During the process, scouts will make judgements about players' technique, their understanding of the game (their ability to read the game) and their physical capacity (speed, agility, strength, stamina, etc.). Steps will also be taken to determine a player's personal and psychological qualities. Quite apart from making judgements about a player's attitude and application during a game, the manner in which the player relates to the management, coaching staff and colleagues is deemed to be an essential prerequisite. Qualities such as being able to 'fit in' with the culture of the dressing room and being a 'team player' are highly valued by professional football clubs.

Scouting structures at professional clubs

As the basic organizational unit within the game, the football club represents an essential determinant of socialization. The actions and behaviour of individuals are subjected to the pressures and expectations generated from within the organizational setting and the general social and cultural pressures relating to how they should act. The organizational culture of the workplace will also have a profound influence upon the criteria used to attach value to the performances of key personnel, including scouts.

The number of scouts employed by clubs varies. Their employment is largely determined by the status of the club and the financial resources made available for the development and maintenance of scouting networks at both the professional and youth team levels. Paradoxically, it is often clubs which have the greatest need to set up scouting networks that are the ones with limited funds to allocate to their scouting and youth development programmes. For many clubs outside the Premier League, a thriving youth development programme might not only be essential for the development of young players for their professional ranks but also key to maintaining a degree of financial stability.

Given their financial constraints, some league and non-league clubs employ a Chief Scout who assumes responsibility for the setting up and management of the club's scouting network, from the youth development programme through to the first team. In cases such as this, the club is likely to employ a small core of volunteers as well as utilizing some of the commercial scouting agencies to view players and to undertake the assessment of forthcoming opposition teams. However, the implications of these systems for CP could be significant, particularly if a Chief Scout knows little about CP policies himself (it is almost invariably a man in this role). As one Chief Scout at a Football League club admitted, his knowledge was 'miniscule' and that he had never been on a CP course. He added: 'Nobody has actually said you must do this, you must do that. It's things I've picked up through just working in football.'

Scouting networks in the Premiership and at the larger Football League Championship clubs are likely to be more extensive and may result in a distinct division of responsibilities between the priorities of supporting the first team squad and managing a comprehensive youth development structure. In these circumstances, the role of Chief Scout is often associated solely with the professional responsibilities of the first team squad. In most cases, the Chief Scout is someone with experience of the professional game, either as a former player or coach, and crucial to the role is their ability to establish and manage a substantial scouting network. Monk and Russell (2000) revealed that one former Premier League club employed over thirty scouts on a nationwide basis, while two other professional clubs had between twelve and twenty scouts, who were part-time. Many Chief Scouts establish a team by developing personal loyalty rather than an affinity with a particular club. This could involve the wholesale transfer of scouting staff should the Chief Scout move from one club to another as Peter Taylor (cited in Murphy 2001: 1) described following his appointment as manager to Leicester City in 1998:

> I've brought 3 scouts with me and Colin (Murphy) has brought in 6 or 7 so their abilities have already been tried and tested. But, of course, we continue

to assess these scouts in terms of their recommendations and by the players that are coming through. Our network covers the whole of the country. We keep the number of scouts relatively small because we want to be in a position to give them plenty of work. We want to make sure that they have always got games to cover and this helps us to retain their loyalty.

A club's scouting network may, at various times, be supplemented by other members of the management and coaching staff and their contacts within the game where favours may be 'called in'. Few staff beyond the Chief Scout will be full-time employees although some might be paid on part-time contracts. Many, like myself, however, are recruited as unpaid volunteers who receive expenses for their contributions. As Taylor (cited in Murphy 2001: 2) confirmed:

> You have to appreciate that most scouts have got full-time jobs outside football. The majority of our scouts get paid so many pence a mile. In addition, some of them get a small retainer. There also tends to be arrangements whereby a scout will get a payment if his recommendation becomes a professional, makes the first team or gets transferred.

In economic terms, Monk and Russell (2000) suggest that these scouts represent a form of producer subsidy, in that the vast majority of their efforts yield little or no payment. Scouts may receive a bonus (typically, a few hundred pounds), but only if someone they recommend is subsequently signed on. In other words, these scouts are only reimbursed for travel and 'out of pocket' expenses. The fact that so many scouts are prepared to spend their time in this way is interesting in itself, particularly as in a typical week they may watch three matches (five hours of football). A similar length of time will be taken up with travel, administration and the completion of individual and match reports (Monk and Russell 2000). The costs to the individual scouts are therefore considerable in terms of time spent and yet revenue gained is small and uncertain.

Academy scouting

The larger the club, the more likely it is that there will be a clearer division of responsibilities between the priorities of the first team professionals and the youth development system. This was exemplified at one Football League club in our research study where the Chief Scout's responsibilities were directed principally at the Professional Game, while overall responsibility for the Academy scouting network lay with an Academy Director. The Chief Scout was even prepared to concede that he did not know enough about youth development scouting and was happy that 'the responsibilities for recruitment were with people with the expertise'. To ensure a degree of coherence between the two, a Director of Football serves as a line manager to whom both are accountable. To enhance the links between to the two roles, the Director of Football's responsibilities extend to the contractual and transfer negotiations of professionals for the first team squad as well as monitoring the club's overseas recruitment of Academy scholars.

In turn, the Academy employs a full-time Academy Recruitment Manager who reports to the Academy Director. His responsibility is to co-ordinate a scouting network that includes six regular part-time scouts and a further six to ten part-time 'contact' scouts appointed to work in specific regions. None of the scouts has been employed to fulfil age-related responsibilities, tending instead to be allocated across the age groups as directed by the priorities set by the Recruitment Manager, Academy Director or Director of Football.

The Academy Director we interviewed confirmed that the employment of Academy scouts still owed much to the informal methods favoured in the traditional game. Since my own recruitment as a scout followed a similar pattern, it is tempting to conclude that the employment of scouts at both professional and Academy levels remains largely informal and illustrative of a 'closed' occupational culture. The Academy Director confirmed:

> Mostly, it comes through contacts. This is probably rife throughout the game. You sort of employ your football mates, who you know and have got a good background; who have recommended good players before.

He also acknowledged that, although it was the club's policy not to advertise, he always followed up letters, telephone calls and recommendations from trusted colleagues and that if he was a 'good guy' they would 'bring him on board'. He was keen to stress that, in his view, Academy scouts require very different skills from those employed to scout the Professional Game. He commented:

> Experienced ex-pros may not be the best people to assess the potential of young players. To actually identify a player and to take into account, say, maturation, is a vastly different skill.

During the recruitment of Academy scouts, considerable attention is given to the quality of a candidate's interpersonal skills. This is in recognition of the pivotal role that they play in attracting players to the club. Unlike scouting for the professional game, which is largely done under a 'cloak of anonymity', Academy scouts are much more likely to be the first point of contact between the club, the player, the player's parents and officials of the junior club or school association. How he presents himself will, in many cases, determine the level of co-operation he is likely to receive from the clubs and the player's parents. Hence, codes of conduct (including a scouting protocol) have been written that both define acceptable standards of behaviour and also promote good practice. Moreover, adherence to these codes also serves to protect scouts from accusations of poor practice or abuse. The following extracts are taken from one professional football club's code of conduct:

> The function of a scout is to identify players with whom the club may wish to enter into negotiations with a view to securing their registrations. Scouts are not themselves entitled to enter into any such negotiations.

In the first instance, when a scout makes an approach to a player at a match or tournament he will make contact with the manager to determine if the player's parent/guardian is in attendance. If the parent/guardian of the player is available, the scout will then speak to them regarding the approach. The scout should formally introduce himself and whom he represents. The scout should not approach the player directly.

Once recruited, best practice determines that scouts undergo a period of induction designed to introduce them to the policies and practices of the club. One Academy manager reported that newly appointed Academy scouts are required to gain CRB clearance and to undergo CP training. Administrative procedures (preparing scouting reports, etc.) are clarified, as are the codes of conduct. Guidance is given on the development of relationships with local associations, schools and clubs as well as strategies for establishing mutual trust between parents and players. Particular attention is also given to the age-specific criteria employed by the club in recruiting young players to the Academy. However, the extent to which an induction process is consistently applied by all professional clubs merits further investigation. One Academy recruitment manager we interviewed confirmed that the monitoring and quality assurance of his scouting network was largely informal.

This resonates strongly with my own experience of 'induction'. While I was required to gain CRB clearance for my role, the club offered nothing in the way of formal training or a programme of induction beyond regular informal contact with the Chief Scout and feedback on my reports. There was no formal process of mentoring and quality assurance other than my value to the club being determined by the quality of my reports. I can only conclude that if, over a period of time, doubts emerged about the detail and accuracy of my written reports, the Chief Scout would have considered the termination of my involvement with the club. I am in no doubt that this remains as relevant now as it was when I started. What remains a concern is that, although ostensibly employed to work at first team level, where 'face-to-face' contact with club officials, parents and under-18 players is not part of my remit, I have, on occasions, been asked to cover under-18 fixtures.

The competitive nature of scouting

In professional football, then, scouts tend to be judged by the accuracy of their team assessments and the quality of players they recommend for recruitment. As with key members of any 'backroom' staff, the expectations of their ability to 'deliver' are high and the demands on their time and commitment considerable. Moreover, the volatile climate of professional football ensures that full-time scouts share many of the job insecurities that are endemic within the game. The pressures and anxieties exerted on managers and coaches are easily transmitted to scouts who might be viewed as core employees and crucial to the club's playing strengths but who, in reality, may have very little security of tenure. For example, scouts whose work is valued by one manager might find themselves out of favour and excluded from the plans of an incoming manager who is keen to surround himself with people 'he can trust'. The scout's sense of vulnerability is heightened further by the pressures clubs are under to recruit the best that is available in the market. They are continually asked to make judgements about players that may, in time, come back to haunt them. This is most evident in the ruthlessly competitive world of the Professional Game but can be just as acutely felt by scouts in youth development who might be accused of letting local talent 'slip through their fingers'. As Daniel points out:

> Academies are not hermetically sealed from the commercial values that determine so much that takes place in the contemporary professional game. Recruitment of young footballers is every bit as much an aggressive and competitive business as the transfer market in senior players.
>
> (Daniel 2004: 210)

While it could be argued that pressures of this sort have always been experienced by scouts at all levels of the game, Daniel (2004) contends that the problems increased when Howard Wilkinson's *Charter for Quality* (FA 1997) advocated that the responsibilities for the development of schoolboy talent were shifted from the ESFA and placed in the hands of the leading professional clubs. Daniel goes on to argue that a commercial imperative had entered the equation with:

> Premiership clubs increasingly viewing youth academies in cost-benefit terms. With the cost of players in the transfer market spiralling out of control, and faced with their own increasingly precarious financial conditions, clubs are looking to their youth development programmes to supply first team players and/or future income.
>
> (Daniel 2004: 207)

Professional football is clearly a highly competitive environment within which to develop talent and for this reason it has been subject to serious criticism. The environment can place excessive demands on the individuals involved, not least scouts, who play a strategic role within youth development programmes. Given this, it is hardly surprising that scouts are often singled out for particular attention.

Criticisms of scouting

While the manner in which schools and junior football are organized may not be entirely immune from criticism, the motives of professional football clubs stand in stark contrast to the values that underpin the work of the ESFA and many junior clubs throughout the country. Youth Academies and Centres of Excellence have the explicit purpose of identifying players of outstanding ability and placing them in a technical and educational programme designed to produce football excellence. The ESFA, however, articulates a more inclusive and participative rationale. Indeed, Daniel (2004: 209) noted that the moment the commercial imperative attached itself to youth football, 'the philosophical gap' became a 'yawning chasm'.

During our research project, 'corrupt', 'exploitative' and 'self-serving', were all terms used by interviewees to describe the culture of the Professional Game. One junior football club coach said: 'the way the professional clubs go about their business is terrible'. It was also suggested that the needs of young players were unlikely to be met until there was a greater degree of openness and public scrutiny of practices.

A central feature of the *Charter for Quality* (FA 1997) was to create opportunities for the recruitment of players from a younger age than the fourteen that it had previously been. In many respects, this was a consequence of a long-held view that the coaching expertise within the Professional Game merited overall responsibility for the development of young players. Having wrested control from 'well-intentioned amateurs', the talent identification and recruitment process in most clubs now starts with players aged seven years and upward. One Academy Recruitment Manager acknowledged that under-7 and under-8 football is a thriving market and, as such, is regularly targeted by his staff even though he accepts that very few of his scouts possessed an in-depth knowledge of the physical, social and emotional characteristics of the developing child across the age ranges. Kees Zwamborn (former Director of Youth Development at Ajax's youth Academy) outlined the challenge facing clubs:

> 'P' is for personality – the 'P' is very important. It's difficult to scout ... a very young player. It's difficult to see. Because when you come here and you must be a grown up player, it's a very hard way, so you have to be a fighter, a winner. Very, very important, but difficult to see when you are a kid of seven years old.
>
> (cited in Stratton *et al.* 2004: 206)

Coaching science literature abounds with talent identification acronyms such as TIPS (technique, intelligence, personality and speed), TABS (technique, attitude, balance and speed) and SUPS (speed, understanding, personality and skill) but, without the ability to apply their knowledge to the scouting process, there is an increasing likelihood that scouts' recommendations will be speculative and prone to error. Children are not, after all, miniature adults.

Also of concern are the limits placed on the participation in other physical and cultural activities by talented children before they even leave primary school. As Warburton (cited in Bent *et al.* 2000: 132) has argued:

> This is a massive area of concern. I would definitely say the balance of the programme we have now, which is games, gymnastics, dance, outdoor pursuits, swimming and athletics, is the ideal for any child. We really need to be giving them a clear balance throughout their time in school, from 4 to 11, with opportunities in all those areas. I'm not a great believer in saying that children can't cope with a lot of physical activity. My concern is that it isn't going to be that balanced. Their whole life is going to be soccer.

Warburton's view is sure to resonate strongly with his colleagues in the education and coaching sectors. As Stevens (cited in Conn *et al.* 2003: 226) confirms:

> A nine year old just concentrating on football intensively to the detriment of any other sport, and to the detriment potentially of other aspects of their personal and social development at that age, I think, is very, very wrong. If you look at some of the academic research that has been done throughout the world now, they would advocate very strongly that probably even up to the age of 11 or 12 a child's involvement in sport should focus on learning fundamentals – the ability to move, the ability to balance, to catch, to run, to jump. They should play lots of different sports and not start to specialise too soon. I think football needs to have a really long hard look at those concepts.

In many respects, these views are not new and, historically, they lie at the heart of the tensions that have existed between professional football and educational organizations such as the ESFA. We revisit just such tensions in the concluding chapter.

The predatory scout

As far back as the Second World War, the actions of scouts from professional football clubs at schoolboy matches were perceived to be intrusive and harmful to the education of young players (Kerrigan 2004). According to the ESFA at the time, it was 'undignified and degrading that scouts should invade the dressing-rooms and ask boys to sign forms that they did not understand' (Kerrigan 2004: 118). While the ESFA's view may have been skewed and motivated by its interest in further consolidating its control over schoolboy football, the professional football clubs' interest in schools football was perceived as a menace. Relationships between the Football League and the ESFA have regularly foundered on the issue of professional clubs' access to young players. Even the 1982 agreement that became the basis of the Associate Schoolboy Scheme did little to alleviate the antipathy between the two organizations or to stem suggestions that some professional clubs had been guilty of financial irregularities by offering inducements during the recruitment of young players. As Kerrigan (2004: 119) concluded:

> The Scheme, which required the co-operation of the boy's parents, his school, the ESFA and the Football League, inevitably gave rise to abuses, misunderstandings and confusions too numerous to be mentioned.

The publication of the FA's *Blueprint for the Future* (FA 1991) emphatically confirmed that the ESFA, the FA and the Football League were unable to reach agreement about the 'the process that develops excellence in elite young footballers' (cited in Kerrigan, 2004: 123). Daniel (2004) contends that the current Academy system continues to be viewed, at best, with suspicion and, at worst, with hostility. It is a position that the Independent Football Commission (IFC 2005) has gone some way to endorsing by recognizing the dangers to junior club football posed by the 'predatory scout'. He is seen as a familiar figure, particularly on the fringes of the some of the larger metropolitan areas of the country. Undoubtedly, finding talented performers is not the problem as the clubs are very well organized and aware of where the talented players can be found. In some cases, however, this has prompted a process of 'trawling' whereby average boys who appear to be talented when playing alongside the very skilful are scouted as well, with apparent disregard for the likelihood that they will be released before reaching the age of sixteen (Daniel 2004). The IFC (2005: 27) presents a graphic image of someone regarded as 'a source of grief, stripping a youth club of its prodigies only to reject them later when the club has broken up with the heart of its talent gone'. One disillusioned Academy player commented:

> They do get too big a batch in, in the hope that one will make it ... The Academies are just a trawl so they don't miss out on a single young player. They are meat markets.
>
> (Daniel 2004: 210)

It is hardly surprising, therefore, that in such a climate of suspicion the recruitment of young players is not always a straightforward process. The suggestion on the part of some is that, all too often, scouting protocols are overlooked in the haste to establish contact with players. As one junior football coach we interviewed reported:

> The professional club should say to the local club, 'You've got a player I want to look at', and then write to us officially, asking to come and see the manager. But they go straight to the parent and, of course, the parent thinks that's brilliant. The pull of the big club means that this happens all the time.

Many junior football club officials are clearly resentful of the ways professional football clubs fail to comply with the guidelines set out for the recruitment of players, particularly as this may have immediate consequences for the playing strengths of their teams. The consequence is that representatives of professional clubs are not always made to feel welcome. One Football League Centre of Excellence scout I interviewed described the lack of co-operation he had received from some junior club team managers who were resistant to the idea that players selected for Centre of Excellence might be denied opportunities of playing for their clubs:

> I've been involved a little bit in the past with managers of teams. Sometimes when you take a scouting role you get bit of a frosty reception because obviously you are taking those lads away from that team; they will no longer be playing for that team.

Daniel (2004) describes the breakdown in relationships between professional clubs and junior league clubs and the impact that the widespread recruitment of young players for Academies and Centres of Excellence can have on the long-term viability of some junior clubs. Stripped of their best players, these clubs are sometimes drawn into a downward spiral in which they cease to retain their competitiveness and find it increasingly difficult to attract enough players for their squads. The realization that many of the boys are unlikely to make their way through the system to become professional footballers seems to have added to the bitterness caused by a player's release from an Academy. Notwithstanding the coaching opportunities that boys may have received during their time at an Academy, the manner in which the release is often managed can heighten the sense, among some managers and parents, that promises have been broken and that their children have been exploited for the benefit of the elite.

In mitigation, one youth development officer from a Football League club whom I interviewed suggested that 'trawling' was more likely to occur among the wealthier clubs as most Football League clubs could ill-afford to take the same risks with recruitment as those with greater financial 'clout'. He actually presented a more conciliatory view:

> We're constantly battling with our local neighbours for the better players obviously. We've got a good rapport with all the clubs, we don't poach each others' players or any of that business, and it's whoever gets in first with the player. We've got a good scouting system and during the last seven or eight years we've had numerous players coming through our centre to play in the first team ... We use every advantage we've got to attract people here.

Moreover, he suggested that the vast majority of clubs at their level might also be victims of the 'poaching' of players from the wealthier clubs that are prepared to pay the compensation set by tribunals. As Conn et al. (2003: 219) contend:

The hunt to find those rare players who might bring success, money or both has bred intense competition among the clubs. They aren't satisfied just to find and develop their own players, they also routinely look to sign players from other academies, with bigger clubs using their power and prestige to lure players from smaller ones.

Yet, scouts are forbidden from spotting young talent at another club. The only time when a representative of one club can 'legally' assess the potential value of young players at another is when the two clubs meet in competition or friendly matches. But, as one coach remarked, there are even methods used to circumvent this ruling. Clubs that hear of emerging talent will ask an unknown scout (from another region) to travel to watch the player in training and report back. Although this is known to go on, the rumours of illegal approaches to players are notoriously difficult to prove, a view endorsed by the Football League's Head of Youth Development, who confirmed:

> Allegations are really quite common but they can only be pursued by the leagues, whether it's the Premier or Football League, on the basis of evidence to corroborate those allegations. Flagrant breaches of the rules are where representatives of the clubs – scouts as they're commonly known – make direct approaches to the parents of players, or indeed even worse, to the players themselves, knowing that those players are at another club and so therefore they know that it is an illegal process. It's totally unacceptable and these sorts of situations put people under pressure and there are massive child protection implications when it's direct approaches to children. I'm afraid that's unacceptable.
>
> (cited in Conn *et al.* 2003: 222)

Bogus scouts

Adults who claim to be representatives of professional clubs also compromise the image of football scouts and the reputation of professional clubs committed to good practice. Without the appropriate training, monitoring and registration with the Premier League and Football League, these fake or 'bogus' scouts are likely to engage in practices that fail to comply with the rules and regulations associated with the recruitment of young players. Their presence at games is often made easier by junior clubs who fail to seek evidence that they are representing who they say they are. As the IFC (2005: 27) noted:

> There are ID systems, and club protocols for scouts. But it does not seem often that a grass roots club enquires of a visiting scout if he has signed up to one, still less whether he would please be careful to observe it.

The prevailing view appears to be that, until such time as managers and officials of junior clubs recognize the importance of checking the credentials of scouts attending youth football matches, children will remain vulnerable. There is also a clear responsibility on the part of the clubs to ensure that the stated codes of conduct and scouting protocols are followed to the letter. For this to happen, a cultural shift is required within the game to put the child first.

Summary

According to Stevens (cited in Conn *et al.* 2003), youth development in English football is too often couched in terms of the clubs' rather than the players' needs. He believes that football has to change its priorities, to take adequate care of the children and young people it now selects from the age of seven upwards. Much more thought needs to be put into managing the recruitment process and supporting a player's development with the player as the single most important person in the process. It will require a radical cultural shift from that described by one FDO we interviewed:

> I think at professional level, we need to change the whole culture of how they look at children, how they treat minors. It has been in the past, to use a football expression, a case of bawl, bark and bollock.

Thus, cultural change, and an increase in awareness of the rights and needs of individual players, are essential prerequisites for creating a more conducive environment for young players. This should be accompanied by a willingness, on the part of professional clubs, to engage with external expertise in a multi-agency approach and to promote a culture in which the sharing of good practice becomes the norm.

Encouragingly, insider accounts are emerging with an altogether more positive interpretation of current practice. Within the Academies, in particular, it appears that the arrival of Education and Welfare Officers has facilitated the development of an explicit focus on CP. Many of these officers are former teaching professionals who are comfortable with child-centred approaches and with sharing good practice: it would seem that they have operated as significant change agents within the professional game. The Academies also promote a range of innovative approaches to the development and implementation of codes of conduct for players, coaches, scouts and parents. In contrast to some of the pejorative views expressed about the practices of professional football clubs, one Academy Welfare Officer suggested:

> I think the Professional Game is leading the way. I think there are a lot of deep thinkers in the Academies, particularly, and I think they're becoming more influential. It's the Professional Game that's taking a holistic approach

to the development of young people, and it's going to take some time for the rest to catch up.

As a result, the role and responsibilities of scouts appear now to be taken more seriously by the clubs. But, while this may reflect a positive cultural shift within the Professional Game, others are more cautious. Daniel (2004), for example, has advocated that part of the 'cure' requires a much stronger commitment on the part of the football authorities to enforcing the existing rules set out in the FA's *Charter for Quality* in which the interests of children are protected.

Rigorous monitoring of the system would seem to be a prerequisite for these changes to become embedded. For example, we need to know more about the effectiveness of club codes and their impact on those they purport to address. The IFC (2005) concluded:

> Some objective measures of the codes' effectiveness would surely be useful, especially in relation to scouts, for example, whose conduct on professional duty will not immediately be observable by the club.
>
> (IFC 2005: 35)

One Welfare/CP Officer concluded:

> I think we're all enthused by the approach they've taken (the FA) while recognizing that Rome wasn't built in a day … Essentially it should be about how to put policies into practice, how to action plan, how to turn rhetoric into reality.

Part III

Reflections

Chapter 14

Managing the research process

Celia Brackenridge

This chapter represents a slight departure from that which precedes it. It is specifically focused on the management of the FA CP project and therefore may appeal more to the research than the practitioner community. Its place here is justified by us because we are not only researchers but also coaches, parents, club officials, referees and scouts. Our roles as researchers are therefore informed by our practical experience and, we hope, enhanced by it.

Managing a complex research project is always challenging for researchers, who usually feel more at home with data and theory than they do with budgets and institutional politics. It was clear from the outset of this research, however, that the strength of the management relationship between the research team and our client – the FA – could make or break the project. Academics tend to ignore or, as best, gloss over such issues in public reports and texts since they are deemed to reside outside their work remit. We took the view, however, that our working relationship with the FA, and with the various stakeholder groups involved in the project, would be crucial factors in shaping the research process and in defining its 'results'. In essence, the management relationship became an integral part of the discourses that we observed and, thus, an important source of data.

I report below on the ethical issues that we anticipated and consider whether and how our ethics protocols helped us to deal with these contingencies. We adopted 'bracketing interviews' as one method by which to anticipate and rehearse such difficulties prior to engaging in fieldwork. Using these and extracts from my own research diary, I attempt to build a chronological reflection of the research process. This reflexive approach is consistent with the 'cultural turn' (Aitchison 2004) in contemporary sociology. We hope that, in laying bare the process of the research, rather than focusing exclusively on its findings, we are not only offering a more honest account of our endeavours but perhaps also, in some small way, helping future researchers and the commissioners of their work to improve their own research management skills and thus to become better collaborators (Ghaye 2006).

Ethical considerations – dilemmas and solutions

Higher Education institutions have recently undergone reform verging on revolution in relation to research ethics: twenty years ago many universities had no ethics committees and no approval procedures for work in the social sciences. All that has changed as consciousness of litigation, negligence and corporate social responsibility has increased.[1] Like many of its post-1992 sector counterparts, the former Cheltenham and Gloucester College of HE succeeded in achieving the designation of 'university' after years of hard work and investment. One of the outcomes of this process was a tightening up of research ethics approvals. The (now) University of Gloucestershire Research Ethics Sub-Committee approved the Ethics Protocol for the FA research project (Appendix 4) and acted as a safety net for ethical issues.[2] It was a surprise to us, however, that the FA did not request an ethics protocol and that it was necessary for us, the contractors, to propose one.

Our major ethical concern was how we should handle the uncovering of abuse or alleged abuse in the course of our fieldwork. The acquisition of what is called 'guilty knowledge' (Fetterman 1984) can plague the holder as it gives information about transgression that cannot be shared without serious consequences. This is the dilemma facing the whistleblower in any organization. It was obvious that we would have to refer any case of abuse or maltreatment of children in our study but we had to find a way of doing this without compromising the confidentiality of our participants, all of whom were promised anonymity as a condition of their consent. The project was most definitely not a prevalence study, setting out to measure the extent of child abuse in football, but this was a potential misconception that we encountered repeatedly. We had to reassure our participants that they were not 'guilty by default' because they had been selected for the project. Although our sampling methods for the clubs and interviews were purposive, selections were based on geographic spread, level and type of football provision (see Chapter 4) and not on some spurious 'hit list' of suspect providers.

We were keen to keep the identities of all participating stakeholders confidential and so avoid any contaminating influence from the FA. Each club and individual approached was asked to complete a written, informed, voluntary consent form in duplicate – one for us and one for them to hold – that committed both parties to confidentiality. Ours were subsequently allocated codes which were then inserted in each transcript. In the course of transcribing interviews or focus groups, researchers removed all identifying features such as names, places or personalized descriptions. The only place where codes and names were held together was in a locked filing cabinet in one of the researcher's offices. In this way, all the transcripts retained anonymity yet, if necessary, the research team could use the various codes to trace back and identify the original source. In the event, it did not prove necessary to do this.

Having made such efforts to assure confidentiality and anonymity, we were taken aback when one researcher arrived at a football club to find a feature in the

Table 14.1 Response rates for bracketing interviews 2002

Sample group	Number contacted	Number responded	Response rate
FA staff	13	4	31%
Researchers	8	8	100%

match programme about being 'selected' for the research project! On another occasion a researcher arrived for an interview and was warmly greeted by a secretary with 'Oh you'll be the one who's here to interview X about child protection'. There was little we could do about such 'leaks' from the research participants but we knew that our own commitment to secrecy had to be absolute if we were to regain access to any problematic research sites in subsequent years.

A second major potential source of worry for us as researchers was the likelihood of media interest or intrusion in the project. I had personal experience of this in the fifteen or so years leading up to this project, during which time I had found contact with journalists to be a dubious privilege (Brackenridge 1999). We were particularly concerned in case there was a disclosure associated with the research project, especially if this involved allegations against a football club staff member, whether paid or volunteer. In order to ensure that the 'wrong' type of information did not leak out to the media, we therefore adopted a media protocol which spelt out a clear chain of command (Appendix 5). This was used only two or three times during the course of the project but it did help to ensure consistency and, perhaps more importantly, gave the FA control over the public face of the research.

Access and accountability – managing expectations

Child protection is clearly a sensitive topic, especially for those volunteers, coaches or administrators for whom soccer, over many years, has become more a vocation than a duty. We were only too well aware that the very fact of the project's existence could be perceived by some in the game as threatening the status quo, challenging their traditional authority and/or practices and appearing to pass judgement. We wished to avoid being seen as the 'thought police', agents of 'political correctness' or spies working for the FA. At the same time, we needed to be able to demonstrate our credentials as FA-approved in order to secure access to our research sites.

In order to prepare for these eventualities, we carried identity badges (ID) and letters of introduction, and also conducted 'bracketing interviews' in advance. Bracketing is a term originally used in hermeneutic phenomenology by Husserl (Moran 2000) to denote the practice of setting aside preconceptions or mentally separating the observer from that which he or she is observing. In our case, we modified this approach and used self-interviews to lay out our own expectations

Table 14.2 Summary of expectations from bracketing interviews against actual findings

Issue: possible impact on the operation of the CP programme and outcomes of
the FA's captive audience of practitioners and members

Expected	Found
FA staff:	
Perception of 'heavy-handedness' leading to negativity	Yes
Variability in the way FA counties operate, therefore likely to be differential uptake of GOAL across the country and differential response to the research ('working with the counties will not be easy')	Yes
Researchers:	
Potential clashes between older/conservative and younger/liberal elements in the game in terms of commitment to and uptake of GOAL	Yes
Potential 'Hawthorn/halo effect' whereby participants in the research behave differently	Some did
Possible information overload and/or top-down edicts producing resistance	Yes
Stakeholders might perceive the GOAL programme as accusing them of abuse	Yes, in clubs
Parents might become complacent if they think or see that CP is now embedded	No
Reluctance to whistle-blow for fear of personal or group reprisals	Yes
Researchers get comprehensive access to people in the game	No

Issue: those within the community of football expected to be most sceptical
about the CP programme

Expected	Found
FA staff:	
Those of long years' standing in the game having entrenched views ('for whom emotional abuse was apparently character-building!')	Yes
Managers who may say one thing and do another	Yes
Grass roots football especially those from minority and disability groups whose voices may not have been heard	Some
Researchers:	
Those in power feeling threatened	Yes
Those insensitive to the needs for CP/in denial about abuse	Yes
Parents, especially where there has been abuse in the family	No
Some children	No
Male coaches especially at club level, who feel threatened by CP	Yes
Some members of the professional game ('there are some not very nice, sceptical, bigoted people in it')	Yes!
Those operating in a climate of 'aggressive masculinity'	Yes
Some county FAs ('who are fiercely protective of their autonomy')	Yes!
Teachers who believe that abuse and poor practice only happens elsewhere	No

Table 14.2 Continued

Issue: 'field constraints' (i.e. practical and/or personal hindrances) that the researchers might expect to confront during the research

Expected	Found
FA staff:	
Unwillingness to talk to researchers or share historic problems	Yes
Lack of awareness/denial/'paedophiles out' issues	Only some
People being prevented/bullied into not talking	Yes
Infrastructure of the FA ('not a well-oiled machine')	Definitely
Infrastructure of the FA counties (many of the administrators ... are not young and many will not have encountered a research project of this nature ... this may lead to uncertainty and trepidation)	Yes
Researchers:	
Uncovering serious abuse	No
Information not forthcoming on time or in enough detail from FA ...	Major issue
or from Lilleshall	Yes, some
Missing peak time for data collection because of off-season	Yes
Apathy by stakeholders/failure to achieve enough replies	Some
Men in the women's game, women in the men's game	Yes
County FA officials resistant to having this project imposed on them by the FA	Yes
Difficulties with access and establishing trusting relationships through gaining credibility ('game credentials')	Yes
'Occupational closure' from those in the professional game	Yes
Wall of silence/lack of answers from respondents	Some
Ethical issues (getting informed consent, honesty of respondents, risk to personal values, confidentiality and right to privacy, the selection and 'labelling' of participants)	Not too bad
Being seen as the 'police'	Yes
Dealing with information uncovered about problems ('guilty knowledge')	No
Personal attacks	Some verbal
Attacks on others in the game/being drawn into personal disputes or asked for advice	Yes
Disclosures of prior or current abuse	No
Not getting the true picture/respondents concealing their real beliefs	Some

of what might confront us and what we might find. In so doing, we hoped to prepare for dealing with any difficult contingency and thus to avoid surprises. (See
Appendices 6 and 7.)[3]

The results of these interviews showed that there was broad agreement
between the FA staff and ourselves about the goals of the research project and
the FA's CP programme. A digest of some of the more contentious expectations
and responses is reported in Tables 14.1 and 14.2. We found the exercise particularly useful as it enabled us to rehearse some of our hopes and fears for the project.
At the end of the first year we could see that most of our predictions had been
accurate. In particular, the anticipation of difficulties with organizational inertia
in the FA itself helped us to cope when problems arose. Moments of friction that
were experienced by many of us were also more readily managed as these had
been thought about in advance. This process of anticipation and control resem-
bles the mental rehearsal of 'what ifs' used by sports psychologists in preparing
performers and coaches.

Thanks to insider knowledge of football traditions and culture in our midst
we were well aware of the importance of FA county secretaries as key gatekeepers for securing access into the field (Foot Whyte 1984). The secretaries of
each of the six selected counties were approached by letter and follow-up telephone calls to request access to clubs on their patch (Professional Game clubs
were approached directly through their Chief Executives). While we tried to
keep the identities of the National Game clubs secret, some county secretaries
wanted to know who was in our sample as a condition of access. Some were
described in the first year's report to the FA as acting like 'robber barons in
their fiefdoms' such was their control over their territories (Brackenridge et al.
2002).

The football community was, in the main, helpful and co-operative about the
research but there were also occasions where our fieldworkers faced rudeness,
including from people in paid positions and/or in positions of significant authority within the FA. One club official threw the back the researcher's ID card
across the table at her; another refused to return numerous telephone calls and
even pretended to be someone else on the telephone in order to avoid being
interviewed. Although these events were stressful for us, they were more easily
managed because of the bracketing exercise.

Research diaries were another coping tool for us and were especially useful
for managing the vagaries of the relationship between the research team, the
FA and our various stakeholder groups. I found it especially frustrating to try to
resolve design and planning issues that created serious financial problems for
the research team while simultaneously maintaining cordial relationships with
the FA and protecting the researchers from management problems. These difficulties are encapsulated in the extracts from my own research diary (Table
14.3).

Table 14.3 Chronology of the research: verbatim extracts from the project director's research diary. This material is from the author's personal research diary and is included to provide the reader with a richer context and background to the research project. Whilst it has been edited for length, the text remains as was written at the time. As such, it remains a personal and subjective account of her experience.

September 2000 ... Initial contact from the FA requesting a research study.

January 2002 ... The notional start date was January 2001. As the months dragged on without a contract the start date was put back several times – to March 1st, then May, then August 2001. I began elated, then got depressed and frustrated then became quite angry and upset about the many and various delays ... There seemed to be no clear reason why things were so slow. In the meantime, the CP work was fast developing and the 'baseline' date for the start of the project was passing.

February 2002 ... The build up to the contract for this project was like Chinese torture but, having finally got this sorted just before Christmas 2001, we have made good progress ... I do worry that [the FA] is almost too confident of us/me sometimes as [they] seem almost prepared to wave through anything I suggest. The lack of a public tendering process for the project reflects this. Perhaps I should simply say 'thanks' but it does make me rather nervous of criticisms from the external research world.

May 2002 ... Watched TV documentary about the financial plight of the game last night and gave serious thought to the possible early curtailment of the project ... not something any of us would welcome but something that we need to think about.

June 2002 ... The county work has perhaps been the most interesting in terms of access issues. Almost everyone has confronted the same blocks from gatekeepers but, once 'inside', there is a thaw and relations seem good ... The bracketing interviews are now analysed and the results are fascinating! Virtually everything that the research team anticipated has happened already ... good and bad. We will repeat the exercise each year as it has helped to frame our thinking ... All in all, I am satisfied about progress but slightly frustrated [by] delays and complications ...

July 2002 ... The FA ... have not delivered ... their [links to allow us] to air the survey site through thousands of websites/e-mails so we have a paltry response and, mainly, unusable data ... The last few weeks have been an intensive data collection time across the board. The club studies have provided plenty of access difficulties and interesting relationship challenges ... the e-mail diary responses have been very poor ... the stakeholder interviews have been moving along well but again with many, many broken appointments. My own first week of interviews was not a success: tape machine problems, audibility problems, missed appointments ... but the second week yielded some really excellent data and one particularly interesting and astounding interview at high level ...

November 2002 ... I was feeling fairly satisfied with the way this year has turned out when – bang! – Adam Crozier resigned from the FA last week. His departure could signal bad news for the project – too soon to say.

March 2003 ... Publicity statement to protect the reputation of the research team – Tony agreed to write something saying the budget cuts were not related in any way to the quality of our work, and put this out on TheFA.com ... I have now read *The Football Business* by David Conn and *Broken Dreams* by Tom Bower. If ever I needed validation of my cynical views of the game then it is in these two books – quite amazing. The hypocrisy and greed of the game is laid bare. Bower's book also raises innumerable questions of logic and sequence that can only be answered by a missing link that keeps making me return to M (from my best interview in year one). I do the follow up interview for that in just a few days and will be interested to test out some of the ideas further.

Table 14.3 Continued

April 2002 ... Research design cut: all Professional Game clubs omitted; stakeholder interviews reduced by half; web checks and e-mail diaries cancelled; internet surveys reduced.

June 2003 ... the FA [has not settled] their invoices. I used an excellent lawyer in the end, courtesy of the Federation of Small Businesses. He gave them a week to pay up and even then they demanded more time. On the day we were due to go to court to sue them the money finally came through to my bank account. The whole business [financial delays, communication problems and so on] has drained me and left me feeling even more cynical about their stated intentions to develop welfare initiatives. England have been warned that they will be kicked out of the European Cup if there is one more pitch invasion or racist incident at a game and that should at least keep the new equity strategy to the forefront but, as for child protection, who knows? Not having confirmation [of the project continuing] for next year makes things even harder and I have told the team to look for other work ... Just when we thought things couldn't get any worse news came through from Tony that he has been given until September 5th to relocate his entire operation to Soho Square. This could be a back-handed compliment as at least it means that the work will be centre stage and thus is likely to continue. The down side is that all the admin staff at Lilleshall will lose their jobs as they are not mobile ... In fact things are worse than they were last year. Tony and his team are now writing a closure plan for Lilleshall and we are fending for ourselves as best we can. The surveys are much, much later than planned going online ... Andy has spent yet more overtime chasing the links for the internet surveys and is at the end of his tether (even he has limits!) so we may well find the quants data are simply not available in time for the analysis week. After all my forward planning last year this is a real sickener. The club studies, on the other hand, are going reasonably well, except for poor Adrian who is suffering the same access difficulties that everyone else had last year ... It would be so good to have news about next year but we'll just have to wait and see.

November 2003 ... Final report submitted. Project closed [because of budget cuts in the FA].

Anyone who thinks that research management is or should be devoid of emotion or value judgement is living in a very different world from that which I inhabited during the project. One criticism of reflexivity is its potential for self-indulgence – indeed one journal editor would not even send a reflexive paper of mine for review and simply returned it with the words 'Too personal' scrawled across the front. But the very experience of friction with the client was a useful stimulus for questions about the FA's attitude to CP overall. It left me asking myself whether some of the senior officers in the game might not be simply using CP as a kind of ethical fig leaf, to cover their embarrassment at the many other problems facing the game – doping, crowd control, 'bungs and fixes' – among others. Perhaps the more the FA could trumpet its work for children, the better it could deflect attention from the uglier side of the game.

Summary

It is one of the strange ironies of research – and especially contract research – that ethical standards, for things like consent and confidentiality, are applied so tightly to our work with participants but so loosely to the management processes. We felt that quality controls on the client side appeared to be seriously lacking in this research project yet the power relations between researcher and client were such that this state of affairs could not be challenged effectively.

The FA is a very large and traditional, hierarchical bureaucracy in which decision-making, at least at the time of the research, was centralized and generally slow. When things were going well, we researchers were able to get on with our jobs and to make rapid strides towards collecting the vast data mountain available to us. But we felt we encountered many challenges ranging from organizational politics to delays with authorizations, to obstructive local attitudes and a plethora of operational difficulties. When these became serious, they undermined both the efficiency and the morale of the researchers and eventually, the viability of the project itself.

What got lost in the midst of the scramble to salvage and restructure CP services in the FA was the demonstrable improvement in the impact of CP on the game that we measured in the second year (reported in Brackenridge et al. 2004). Our results for parents/carers and guardians, and for coaches, managers and teachers, for example, were especially gratifying (Brackenridge et al. 2005), and could have been far more widely publicized, but such was the nervousness about the issue that these findings were not widely disseminated through the game.

Two years on from the end of the research, CP was not only viable but was a growing function within the FA organizational structure. 53,000 people in the game had been Criminal Record Bureau-checked, more than 140,000 had attended the FA's Good Practice and Child Protection workshop and 150,000 had worked through the training programme *SoccerParent* online (Law 2005). This, then, is not an issue that will go away. But, without an evidence base, how will the FA, or indeed any other sport organization, know whether its resources are being well spent and whether children are any safer now than they were before child protection had been heard of in sport?

Notes

1   One of the main drivers for change was the Alder Hey hospital scandal about the use of infant remains for scientific research. Ethics in all sciences became closely scrutinized after these events in the biomedical sciences.
2   Although I was on the staff of the College at the time the contract was offered, I left to set up an independent research company, Celia Brackenridge Ltd, to oversee the work and it was this entity that became the main contractor. All other staff working on the project thus did so in the role of sub-contractors.

3   Comparatively few FA staff returned tapes or written material (Table 14.1) but the results vindicated the decision to conduct these interviews and we fully intended to repeat them in 2003. Sadly, by the time the interview schedules had been distributed in 2003, it had been made clear that the FA would be withdrawing funding from the final three years and the responses to bracketing interview requests dwindled.

Chapter 15

Conclusions

Dream-makers or dream-breakers?

Celia Brackenridge

Events over recent years have been characterised by heated and contradictory debate about both the nature of the problems and what should be done. As a consequence those who are given responsibility for doing something about child abuse, particularly [the FA], have found themselves practising in an area which is increasingly complex, ambiguous, [and] where they have to finely balance actions and interventions which may be constructed as doing too little too late (thus putting children at risk ...), or doing too much too early (and hence being seen as undermining the rights and responsibilities of [coaches] and interfering unwarrantably into the privacy of the [football club].

(Parton in Thorpe 1994: vii, with adaptations in square brackets)

In this concluding chapter, I return to some of the main themes of the book in an attempt to resolve, or at least to synthesize, the arguments and to consider the success or otherwise of football in meeting its child welfare obligations. In so doing, and by way of supplementing the data from the FA Child Protection (CP) project, I consider the findings of the Independent Football Commission (IFC)'s enquiry into CP in Football, conducted over an eighteen-month period after the conclusion of our own research and published in 2005. The IFC's investigation is of particular interest as it arose from within the game and it covered a period of considerable organizational change at the top of the FA.[1]

A framework for understanding approaches to protecting and safeguarding children in sport was proposed in Chapter 2. Because we opened the book with a commitment to honest reflection about the Child Protection in Football Project 2002–2004 it is appropriate, at this point, to look back at the framework to help us make sense of the research findings. In this final chapter, I therefore attempt to assess where and how the child protection work of the FA, as evaluated by our and the IFC's research, is located within the framework. The book closes with some searching questions for those who run youth soccer about the dangers of pursuing talent development over human development among young football players.

The Independent Football Commission report

In July 2005, the Independent Football Commission reported on eighteen months of its own research into the child protection work of the FA.[2] This programme of work, that began some five months after our last report was submitted to the FA, had to be extended because, once started, the IFC investigators realized the immense scope of CP and its reach throughout the football community. This reinforces our view that CP permeates whole organizations and cannot be regarded as simply a bolt-on policy area.

The report was extremely positive about what had happened and gave the FA cause to take pride in its CP record. In many respects, its conclusions echoed ours but they were also written in a much more motivational way, praising and encouraging the major partners in the game. Terms like 'filled with admiration' (p. 8) and 'astonishing progress' (p. 9) must have given pride and encouragement to those CP advocates working within football. Indeed, in the IFC's 2005 Annual Report (IFC 2006) the constituent parties (the FA, the FA Premier League and the Football League) all welcomed the report and, in responding to the IFC's original recommendations, were able to detail a number of further positive actions that they were pursuing, including meetings of a new All-Agency Child Protection Forum.

But the purpose of social scientific investigation is to use its own independent stance to raise questions beyond the level of provision. Inevitably, the IFC was able to gain smoother access than us into many parts of the professional game, notably county FA Secretaries. It is difficult to assess precisely how the IFC research methods were designed or the data analysed. Large amounts of information were collected, through individual interviews and focus groups, and the IFC also drew extensively from the data presented in our own FA CP projects reports (Brackenridge et al., 2003, 2004b). Not surprisingly, then, many of the IFC's comments on good practice and future challenges echoed our own.

Common areas of good practice included:

- county FA CP Officer structures which, by 2005, had become consolidated
- the FA's own CP Unit (now Equality and Child Protection Department)
- the education and training programme, especially the awareness-raising workshop, and
- the Charter Standard club system through which codes of conduct and CP policy and procedures are promulgated.

Challenges identified by both sources included:

- the importance of recruiting and rewarding appropriately qualified CP Officers within the county FAs
- the sheer difficulty of reaching to the outer limits of the affiliated game
- following up training workshops in a timely and efficient manner

- Introducing a functional and foolproof national ID system
- Attrition rates among the ageing volunteer force and the difficulty of attracting new volunteers to replace them
- Fully embedding referees within the CP system
- Involving professional footballers as role models for CP work
- Checking and updating Charter Standard requirements in an efficient and effective manner
- Managing scouts, who often operate at the margins of the affiliated game, and
- Partnership working across the constituent bodies in the game.

Children in football – workers or players?

The emergence of the 'preventative state' (Parton 2005: 6) has had interesting consequences for sport, the introduction of formal CP procedures being just one. In order for us to consider sport as falling under the regulation of wider child pro-tection systems we must first define it as part of the state apparatus. The history of amateur British sport from about the late 1930s, with the foundation of the Central Council for Recreative Physical Training (CCRPT), to the formation of the Sports Council in 1972, and since, has been characterized by serious and con-tinued wrangling over autonomy between the two organizations, but we have now reached a point where sport is, de facto, an extension of government policy (Sport England 2004c).

The appropriation of sport for state purposes is certainly not new but has arguably been given added impetus by the drive of New Labour to control its construction and use. Even governing bodies as powerful as the FA have not escaped requirements to contribute to a host of political agendas, from ending childhood obesity to reducing diabetes, racism and homophobia to promoting out-of-school learning (FA Learning http://www.thefa.com/TheFA/FALearning/ retrieved 27 June 2006).

How do the findings of our and the IFC's work reflect upon child welfare and the question of children in football as consumers, citizens, workers or players? Donnelly (1997) used the child labour laws in Canada to critique youth sports and a similar exercise in the Britain might readily throw up similar issues of over-training and exploitation (David 2005). But exceptions are readily made in sport, where children may 'play' much harder, and for much longer, than many of us who 'work' in offices:

> Child maltreatment is culturally relative. Some behaviours are viewed as normal in one culture that may not be regarded so in another. Cultural rela-tivism does not mean that 'anything goes', however.
>
> (May-Chahal and Coleman 2003: 15)

Although written with reference to national cultures, we might also apply this quote to the different stakeholder 'cultures' apparent within football. In Chapter 2, I suggested that, under a utilitarian ideology, child maltreatment might be rationalized as normal or acceptable in order to achieve competitive success. There is certainly ample evidence from our research that some young footballers are being treated more as workers than players. But how far can or should we press this neo-Marxist-flavoured claim? Not one person involved in our research would have willingly signed up to the view that children in football are units of economic production. Yet many argued that others in the game treat them this way. Examples included club officials who urged us to study 'X club down the road because they treat kids terribly' and league officials who readily pointed the finger at other colleagues for flouting codes of practice or CP policies. A senior FA official also described CP as being used at the highest level as a kind of front or 'frippery' to deflect attention away from some of the game's other problems like fraud, corruption and financial greed. There is a game of buck-passing going on here that can detract seriously from the quality of the young person's footballing experience.

The contrasts between the utilitarian (competitive) and humanistic (child-centred and reforming) ideologies in sport (Table 2.2) are evident among the different stakeholder groups whom we have studied in football and they have led to different views about the worth of CP for the game. But it would be wrong to suggest that each stakeholder group or subculture was necessarily homogenous. We found caring coaches and punitive parents just as we found caring parents and punitive coaches, for example. In other words, all groups contained both dream-makers and dream-breakers. But, as has been evidenced repeatedly in Part II, there was a tendency for the competitive ideology to hold sway among rather too many involved in junior football. Despite the many intrinsic benefits of football for children, the professional exemplar inevitably leads to interest in, and for some obsession with, potential extrinsic gains. These material rewards undoubtedly set the tone for much that happens in the junior game. As talented young players progress towards the higher echelons of the game they become more and more subject to the scrutiny and control of the business of football, cast more and more as investments and less and less as human beings.

The quote at the head of this chapter indicates that CP presents sport with a delicate balancing act. Doing too little, adopting a permissive approach (Brackenridge 2004b), leaves children open to abuse; yet doing too much, adopting a prescriptive approach, can give rise to accusations of interference and bureaucracy. Further tensions arise between 'command and control' and 'support and development' styles of managing CP in sport (Brackenridge et al. 2002). Overall, advocates of CP in football appear to achieve different balances in their attempts at implementation (see Figure 15.1):

it's the dilemma that governing bodies have that, on the one hand we're a policing organization, we're a control body, we fine, we police, we adhere to regulations, we develop regulations. On the other side we try to be a touchy feely service and support organization and that often is difficult.

(Administrator)

'Command and control' aspects of CP include:

- mandatory CP training
- mandatory CRB checks
- compulsory policy and CP posts
- surveillance and disciplinary procedures
- minimum or no consultation
- minimum or no ownership from grass roots stakeholders.

'Support and development' aspects include:

- emphasis on education and training
- staged implementation
- flexible targets
- negotiated timescales
- personal development advice, e.g. learning logs
- widespread consultation with key stakeholders
- widespread ownership of the CP initiative.

Those in football more comfortable with the first approach perceive CP as a regulatory mechanism to rid the game of abuse and/or to protect it from infiltration by undesirable individuals. Those more comfortable with the second perceive CP as an agenda for personal education and development, the promulgation of good practice and cultural change in football. There is clearly a delicate balance to be

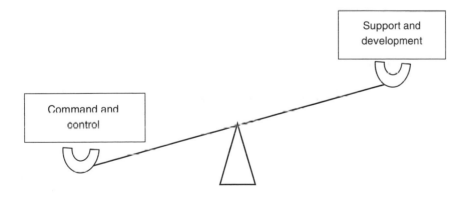

Figure 15.1 The child protection balancing act

Table 15.1 Advantages and disadvantages of different approaches to CP

Approach	Advantages	Disadvantages
Command and control	Procedures embedded quickly	Consultation curtailed or partial
	Lines of referral clear	Ownership reduced
	Feelings of security increased	Some people feel threatened
	Bad practice curtailed	Can establish punitive culture
		Can overlook internal risks
Support and development	Consultation comprehensive	Consultation slows down implementation
	Stakeholders listened to	Can overlook external risks
	People feel included	Can appear 'soft'
	Good practice celebrated	

achieved, since both approaches have merits and limitations for different situations (Table 15.1).

We found both strong and weak stakeholder groups in respect of engagement with CP in football. There was consensus, however, that the FA's CP Strategy would increase safety for children in the game.

In the putative voluntary sector, with its traditions of political and financial autonomy, and a commitment to virtue ethics over contractarianism (McNamee 1996), laborious requirements for CRB checking, paper-driven procedures and fears of false allegations have been known to result in a backlash against CP (Finkelhor 1994) where the balance has tipped too far towards command and control. Some sports, for example, have found their volunteers unwilling to help with junior sections or coaches steering clear of working with children, all because of CP. In short, there is a real question for the football authorities about the counterproductive potential of CP. [3]

Talent development or human development

Long Term Athlete Development (Balyi and Hamilton 2003) has been adopted by Sport England as *the* major underpinning framework for sport performance development. At face value, it is a panacea for the ills of burn-out, pressure, over-training and over-exposure and offers an integrated approach to physical, physiological, psychological and technical development for the individual athlete. However, it can also be conceived as a dehumanizing practice that has as its end point *performance outcomes*, essentially focused on human *doing* rather than human *being* (Ingham *et al.* 1999). A more reflexive approach might actually allow more constructive engagement with the subjects of youth sport, children themselves.

Power, authority and control in football, as in many other sports, still rest with rival institutions and individuals whose sectarian in-fighting leaves little time or energy for those young players who hold the key to the future.[4] Consultation, when it does happen, is easily used as a mask for continuing paternalism by those for whom radical change would threaten their power base. For example, the FA's annual Child Protection conference in October 2003 was entitled 'Putting Children First' but three years on it was still unclear to us precisely how children had had a direct influence on policy changes. Perhaps this is an example of our adult obsession with controlling childhood that arises from our uncertainty about the fate of adulthood as we come to terms with social fracturing in late modernity (Parton 2005).

Despite the oft-cited statistic that only one per cent of the game is at the elite level, that one per cent exerts a huge influence over the other ninety-nine per cent, whether it be through sales and sponsorship pressure, competitive aspirations or mimicry of skills and tactics. The marketization of children's football has led us away from the notion of the child as consumer, or even as citizen, as advocated in Chapter 2, and towards a view of the child as worker (the scholarization of childhood).

The performance emphasis of sport, as evidenced in talent identification and development schemes, takes us back to our earlier arguments about a discursive shift from child protection to safeguarding. For example, a Charter Standard club that refused membership to children who were not deemed to be of a high enough playing standard was privileging, in a very direct way, football performance over child welfare.

Forster (1998: 165) argues that prolonged paternalism in the name of CP can communicate to children that they are incapable of taking responsibility for their own actions. One author, Frank Furedi, has even gone so far as to equate contemporary CP measures with the government's anti-terror laws (Buie 2005: 1). In sport, it seems that paternalism is actually the modus operandi which would help to explain why participation continues to be depoliticized, adult athletes so often seem child-like and sport persists as a never-never land. But, in football, paternalism is mediated by an even more serious issue, that of performance success. Children in football are protected as individual rights bearers but safeguarded as talented commodities.[5] Since talent is such an overriding concern for football, it appears that the child's worker status or asset value must be safeguarded at all costs.

In Table 2.3 I contrasted the care and control perspectives on childhood that underpin the analysis of CP and safeguarding set out in Chapter 2. In that chapter, I suggested that:

> uncritical acceptance of the safeguarding label plays directly into the government's youth control agenda in ways that might actually reduce rather

Table 15.2 Common themes in the recent history of children and sport

	Children in society	Children in sport
C17 onwards	Tension between individual liberty and need for social discipline	
C18	Emergence of schooling separates the child from adult society	Emergence of organized sport separates the child from community leisure
Mid C18	Child constructed as both victim (in need of guidance) and villain (in need of control)	Physical training constructed for both social development and social control
C18–C19	Family reconfigured as an instrument rather than a model of government	Physical training reconfigured as an instrument of government rather than separate from it Physical training segues into physical education
Mid C20	Professionalization of social work (the 'fifth social service' Townsend 1970)	Professionalization of sport
Late C20	Socialization of civil society through quantitative techniques and risk management (social government)	Tension between sport for personal fulfilment and sport for the greater social economic good Social government of sport through cost–benefit analysis Scientific rationality and biopolitics underpin the 'more medals mantra' and Long Term Athlete Development
Early C21	Child protection segues into safeguarding Safeguarding a political panacea/social insurance	Physical education segues into youth sport Safeguarding in sport serves personal and political agendas Sport the sixth social service?

After Parton (2005)

than enhance the possibility of sport organizations achieving any aspirations for individual development and autonomy among their athletes.

It seems clear that, not just in football but in youth sport more generally, both personal and political agendas are now served by safeguarding (Table 15.2). Safeguarding simultaneously serves the interests of the child footballer (providing personal safety), the game of football (optimizing commodity value) and society (reducing worklessness and social disruption). Within this mix, there is precious little space for child-centred or child-directed football play. In short, youth sport, never better exemplified than in football, may now have assumed the status of the 'sixth social service' (Townsend 1970).[6]

This is a serious point on which to close but one that we feel requires further examination by both the football authorities and their less prominent partners in British sport if we are to be honest about the value and purposes of the children's game. The cultural changes that we tracked within football, over a relatively short period of two years, gave cause for optimism and showed that good CP policies and sound implementation can have a dramatic and positive impact on the youth game. Children's football is the stuff of dreams: long may this continue.

Notes

1   The Independent Football Commission was established in 2001 by the governing bodies of football in England – the Football Association (FA), the FA Premier League (PL) and the Football League (FL) – a development that was agreed by the government. Its purpose is to scrutinize the performance of the three constituent governing bodies, especially in relation to their role in providing for the needs of the football community. The role of the IFC is to evaluate the effectiveness of the self-regulatory framework of football and to propose improvements. See www.theifc.co.uk

2   The path to ethical sport is paved with good intentions. The FA, and its former Equity and Ethics Department, in particular, invested huge amounts of human and financial resources into designing and implementing the world's largest governing body CP programme. Its decision to include monitoring research from the start of the programme roll out was visionary and should have equipped it with longitudinal evidence of beneficial outcomes. While this began to happen in the second year of our research, the project was cut short by the financial crisis associated with the departure of FA Chief Executive Adam Crozier. The England men's team manager, Sven Goran Eriksson, was awarded a £1m pay rise and other claims on the organization's finances suffered: the research project was just one of them. The CP monitoring void was filled by the IFC.

3   The only way to allay such fears is to collect systematic, longitudinal, impartial evidence of the incidence and prevalence of different types of abuses in football and of the impact of CP on different stakeholder groups. This is precisely what the FA intended when it first commissioned the project that provided much of the data for this book.

4   For example, despite the largely positive comments about the IFC CP work, the FA Premier League could not resist a dig at its partners, the FA and the FL:

... the Premier League will not, of course, be prepared to dilute in any way its commitment to, and pursuit of, best practices in the safeguarding of children, and still wishes to maintain a direct relationship with the IFC on this issue.

(IFC Annual Report 2006: 51)

... to which the IFC replied: 'The IFC does not feel that this concern is justified.'

(IFC 2006: 24).

5   The awarding of the 2012 Olympic and Paralympic Games to London has presented British sport with a set of unique opportunities and but also many challenges. The political gains from hosting such an event are seen by bidding governments to far outweigh the financial burdens that inevitably accrue. Civic pride is a strong political motivator. No doubt the Games themselves will act as a genuine catalyst for increased engagement in sport and physical activity in the population. They will certainly be used to add momentum to the many sport-related policy initiatives such as crime reduction and community safety, economic impact and regeneration, and social capacity and cohesion (Value of Sport Monitor, www.sportengland.org/vsm/vsm_intro.asp retrieved 31 August 2005). There is also a danger that the utilitarian ideology will become dominant in the preceding years, that any vestiges of play in youth sport will be eradicated and that extrinsic values will replace intrinsic ones.

6   In 1970 Peter Townsend reviewed the Seebohm proposals for changes in social work and argued that social work, alongside health, housing, education and social security, had become 'the fifth social service'.

Appendices

Sample survey

Parents and carers 2002

Please complete all the questions for a chance to win a World Cup 2002 shirt!

Q1 What is your main role/preferred activity within football? (Click only 1)
- ❏ *Mainly helping on the playing side (training, collecting balls, running the line)*
- ❏ *Mainly helping with off-field duties (washing kit, catering, driving children to matches)*
- ❏ *Mainly just attending matches and supporting team*
- ❏ *None*
- ❏ *Other*

Q2 Please identify your main/preferred level of activity in football (click only 1)
- ❏ *With adults in the professional game (Barclaycard Premiership, Nationwide Football League)*
- ❏ *With under-18s in the professional game (Barclaycard Premiership, Nationwide Football League)*
- ❏ *In schools football – primary*
- ❏ *With adult women in the National Division, Northern or Southern Divisions*
- ❏ *With women under 18 in the National Division, Northern or Southern Divisions*
- ❏ *Other football schemes (soccer schools, camps, tournaments)*
- ❏ *With adults in the semi-professional game (Conference league/Unibond/Ryman/Dr Martens)*
- ❏ *With under-18s in regional, county or district leagues (including junior youth teams)*
- ❏ *Other*
- ❏ *With adults in regional, county or district leagues (including women in Combination leagues)*
- ❏ *With under-18s in semi-professional game (Conference league/Unibond/Ryman/Dr Martens)*
- ❏ *Don't know*
- ❏ *University football*
- ❏ *In schools football – secondary*

Q3 Have you heard about the FA's GOAL initiative?
No ❑
Not sure ❑
Yes ❑

Q4 In general, how satisfied are you with the treatment of children/young people in football?
Very satisfied ❑
Not satisfied ❑
Fairly satisfied ❑
Don't know ❑

Q5 Are you able to recognize the signs of...?

	Yes	No	Not sure
Physical abuse	❑	❑	❑
Emotional abuse	❑	❑	❑
Sexual abuse	❑	❑	❑
Neglect	❑	❑	❑
Bullying	❑	❑	❑

Q6 Do you know that there is an FA/NSPCC telephone helpline?
Yes ❑
No ❑
Not sure ❑

Q7 Do you have a Child Protection/Welfare Officer at your child's club/school/scheme?
Yes ❑
Not sure ❑
No ❑
Don't belong to a club/school/scheme ❑

Q8 How confident are you that you could respond appropriately if you came across child abuse in football?
Very confident ❑
Not at all confident ❑
Somewhat confident ❑
Don't know ❑

Q9 How well do you think the FA is managing the treatment of children/young people at the moment?
Very well ❑
Not well ❑
Quite well ❑
Don't know ❑

Q10 What do you think might be the main outcomes of the FA Child
Protection Strategy? (Click up to 3)
- ❏   *Extra paperwork for us*
- ❏   *Improved practice/behaviours*
- ❏   *False allegations*
- ❏   *Coaches leaving the sport*
- ❏   *Increased safety for children*
- ❏   *Over-protection of children*
- ❏   *Wasted time*
- ❏   *Bad coaches removed from the game*
- ❏   *Wasted money*
- ❏   *More involvement from parents/carers/guardians*
- ❏   *Don't know*
- ❏   *Other*

Please specify

Q11 Has your child's club/school/scheme incorporated the FA Policy,
Procedures and Practices for child protection?

Yes	❏
No	❏
Not sure	❏
Don't belong to a club/school/scheme	❏

Q12 Have you ever used The FA/NSPCC helpline?

No	❏
Don't know	❏
Yes	❏

Q13 In your view, which of the following are most likely to improve the treat-
ment of children/young people in football in the next year? (Click up to 3)
- ❏   *A strategic plan for child protection*
- ❏   *Child Protection/Welfare Officers in every club/school/scheme*
- ❏   *Police checks/screening of coaches and others working in football*
- ❏   *A telephone helpline for young people*
- ❏   *Videos/posters and booklets about child protection*
- ❏   *Carefully selected and trained workshop tutors*
- ❏   *Disciplinary and support systems for those involved in child abuse*
- ❏   *Talking with young people about child protection*
- ❏   *Don't know*
- ❏   *Other*

Please specify

Q14 Have you received a job description/role clarification or information about your child protection responsibilities in football?

No ❑
Yes ❑
Not sure ❑

Q15 How happy are you with the way that your child is treated by her or his football coaches or teachers?

Very happy ❑
Not happy ❑
Fairly happy ❑
Not sure ❑

Q16 How happy are you with the way that your child is treated by her or his agent?

Very happy ❑
Not sure ❑
Fairly happy ❑
Doesn't have an agent ❑
Not happy ❑

Q17 Who do you feel has the main responsibility for ensuring your child's welfare in football? (Click up to 3)

❑ Me as a parent/carer/guardian
❑ Football coach or teacher
❑ Child Protection/Welfare Officer at club
❑ Referees
❑ FA as an organization
❑ Team-mates
❑ Everyone involved in football
❑ Not sure
❑ Other

Please specify

Q18 How happy are you with the way that your child is treated by scouts?

Very happy ❑
Not sure ❑
Fairly happy ❑
Hasn't been seen by a scout ❑
Not happy ❑

Q19 How well do the following groups treat children/young people in football?

	Very well	OK	Not very well	Don't know	Not applicable
Parents/carers/ guardians	❑	❑	❑	❑	❑
Scouts	❑	❑	❑	❑	❑
Agents	❑	❑	❑	❑	❑
Teachers	❑	❑	❑	❑	❑
Coaches/Managers	❑	❑	❑	❑	❑
Football Development Officers	❑	❑	❑	❑	❑
Child Protection/ Education Welfare Officers	❑	❑	❑	❑	❑
Volunteers/Other adult helpers	❑	❑	❑	❑	❑
Medics/physiotherapists	❑	❑	❑	❑	❑
Administrators	❑	❑	❑	❑	❑
Players over 18	❑	❑	❑	❑	❑
Young people	❑	❑	❑	❑	❑
Referees	❑	❑	❑	❑	❑

Q20 What is your age?
18–24   ❑
25–40   ❑
41+   ❑

Q21 What is your gender?
Female   ❑
Male   ❑

Q22 What is your ethnic group? (Source: Census 2001)
❑   White (British, Irish, other white background)
❑   Mixed (White and Black Caribbean, White and Black African, White and Asian, other mixed background)
❑   Asian or Asian British (Indian, Pakistani, Bangladesh, any other Asian background)
❑   Black or Black British (Caribbean, African, any other Black background)
❑   Chinese or other ethnic group (Chinese, any other background)

Q23 The Disability Discrimination Act (1995) defines a disabled person as anyone with a physical or mental impairment which has a substantial and long-term adverse effect upon their ability to carry out normal day-to-day activities. Do you consider yourself to be...?

Visually impaired   ❑
Learning disabled   ❑
Hearing impaired   ❑
Disabled (other)   ❑
Physically disabled   ❑
Not impaired or disabled at all ❑

Q24 Which of these educational qualification is the highest one that you have?
   ❑   *None, I'm still at school/college/university*
   ❑   *School Ed: CSEs/'O' levels/GCSEs or equivalent*
   ❑   *Further Ed: 'A'/AS levels/Higher School Cert/NVQ/ GNVQ/HNC/ HND/RSA/OCR/BTEC/City and Guilds/Edexecel*
   ❑   *Higher Ed: first degree (BA/BSc/BEd) or higher degree (Postgrad Cert/Diploma/MA/MSc/MBA/PGCE/PhD)*
   ❑   *No formal qualifications*

Q25 In which of these football regions are you most involved? (Click only 1)
   ❑   *North (including Yorkshire, North East and North West)*
   ❑   *South (including London, South East and South West)*
   ❑   *Midlands (including East Midlands and West Midlands)*
   ❑   *Not sure*

Thank you for completing this survey. By clicking on the SUBMIT button your survey will automatically go to the Prize Draw page. If you click on the SUBMIT button and nothing happens this is because you have not answered all of the questions. Please go back and complete the questions you have missed.

Sample survey
Football Development Officers 2002

Please complete all the questions for a chance to win a World Cup 2002 shirt!

Q1   What is your main role/preferred activity within football? (Click only 1)
- ❑ *Local authority Football Development Officer*
- ❑ *County-based Football Development Officer*
- ❑ *Club-based Football Development Officer*
- ❑ *General Sport Development Officer working in football sometimes*
- ❑ *Football in Community Officer*
- ❑ *Other*

Q2   Please identify your main/preferred type of activity in football (click only 1). We acknowledge that you may work in both areas but we need to identify your main activity. If you are working within the women's or girls' game please go to Q3, if you are working within the men's or boys' game please go to Q4.
- ❑ *Women's or girls' game*
- ❑ *Men's or boys' game*

Q3   Within the women's or girls' game, which is your main/preferred type of activity (click only 1). If you work across all levels of the game, select 'other'.
- ❑ *With adult women in the National Division, Northern or Southern Divisions*
- ❑ *With women under 18 in the National Division, Northern or Southern Divisions*
- ❑ *In schools football – primary*
- ❑ *With adults in regional, county or district leagues (including women in Combination leagues)*
- ❑ *University football*
- ❑ *Other football schemes (soccer schools, camps, tournaments)*
- ❑ *With under-18s in regional, county or district leagues (including junior youth teams)*
- ❑ *In schools football – secondary*
- ❑ *Other*
- ❑ *With disabled young people (under the age of 18)*

Q4   Within the men's or boys game, which is your main/preferred type of activity (click only 1). If your work is across all levels of the game, select 'other'.
❑   *With adults in the professional game (Barclaycard Premiership, Nationwide Football League)*
❑   *With under-18s in the professional game (Barclaycard Premiership, Nationwide Football League)*
❑   *In schools football – primary*
❑   *With adults in the semi-professional game (Conference league/Unibond/Ryman/Dr Martens)*
❑   *With under-18s in regional, county or district leagues (including junior youth teams)*
❑   *Other football schemes (soccer schools, camps, tournaments)*
❑   *With adults in regional, county or district leagues*
❑   *With under-18s in semi-professional game (Conference league/Unibond/Ryman/Dr Martens)*
❑   *Other*
❑   *University football*
❑   *In schools football – secondary*
❑   *With disabled young people (under the age of 18)*

Q5   Have you heard about the FA's GOAL initiative?
No   ❑
Not sure   ❑
Yes   ❑

Q6   If yes please identify how this information was given to you (click as many as appropriate). If no, please go to Q7
❑   *E-mail from county FA officer*
❑   *E-mail from other FA official*
❑   *Attendance at FA conference*
❑   *Attendance at other conferences*
❑   *Formal letter from club/association*
❑   *League/county Child Protection Officer*
❑   *Formal letter from club/association*
❑   *League/county Football Development/In the Community Officer*
❑   *Through your club/association/league administrator*
❑   *Word of mouth*
❑   *Informal chat with club/association/county Child Protection Officer*
❑   *Informal chat with club/association/county Football Development/In the Community Officer*
❑   *The FA website*
❑   *FA qualifications (coaching, refereeing, physio, etc.)*
❑   *Other, please specify*

Q7   Are you able to recognize the signs of...?

	Yes	No	Not sure
Physical abuse	❏	❏	❏
Emotional abuse	❏	❏	❏
Sexual abuse	❏	❏	❏
Neglect	❏	❏	❏
Bullying	❏	❏	❏

Q8   Do you know that there is an FA/NSPCC telephone helpline?
Yes   ❏
No   ❏
Not sure   ❏

Q9   Do you have a designated person for Child Protection/Welfare Officer at your club/school/scheme?
Yes   ❏
Not sure   ❏
No   ❏
Don't belong to a club/school/scheme ❏

Q10 How confident are you that you could respond appropriately if you came across child abuse in football?
Very confident   ❏
Not at all confident ❏
Somewhat confident   ❏
Don't know   ❏

Q11 Who would be your first contact point if you did come across child abuse on football? PLEASE SPECIFY THE PERSON'S ROLE AND NOT THEIR NAME

Q12 Do you think the FA is being proactive about managing the treatment of children/young people at the moment?
Yes   ❏
Somewhat   ❏
Not at all   ❏
Don't know   ❏

Q13 What do you think might be the main outcomes of the FA Child
Protection Strategy? (Click up to 3)
- ❏ *Extra paperwork for us*
- ❏ *Improved practice/behaviour from parents*
- ❏ *Improved practice/behaviour from coaches*
- ❏ *More false allegations*
- ❏ *More coaches leaving the sport*
- ❏ *Increased safety for children*
- ❏ *Over-protection of children*
- ❏ *Wasted time*
- ❏ *Bad coaches removed from the game*
- ❏ *Wasted money*
- ❏ *More involvement from parents/carers/guardians*
- ❏ *I have not noticed any changes*
- ❏ *Don't know*
- ❏ *Other*
Please specify

Q14 Has your club/school/scheme incorporated The FA Policy, Procedures and
Practices for child protection?
Yes ❏
No ❏
Not sure ❏
Don't belong to a club/school/scheme ❏

Q15 Have you ever used the FA/NSPCC helpline?
No ❏
Don't know ❏
Yes ❏

Q16 If yes, how satisfied were you with the service? If no, please go to Q17
Not satisfied ❏
Satisfied ❏
Not sure ❏

Q17 In your view, which of the following has improved the treatment of children/young people in football in the past year? (Click up to 3)
- ❑ *The FA taking the lead in child protection*
- ❑ *Child Protection/Welfare Officers in every club/school/scheme*
- ❑ *Screening of coaches and others working in football*
- ❑ *A telephone helpline for young people*
- ❑ *Videos/posters and booklets about child protection*
- ❑ *Good quality education and training workshops, and materials*
- ❑ *Disciplinary and support systems for those involved in child abuse*
- ❑ *Talking with young people about child protection*
- ❑ *I have not noticed any improvement in the treatment of children/young people in football*
- ❑ *Don't know*
- ❑ *Other*
Please specify

Q18 Have you received a job description/role clarification or information about your child protection responsibilities in football?

No ❑

Yes ❑

Not sure ❑

Q19 If yes, how did you receive this information? If no, please go to Q20

Q20 How happy are you with the way that children and young people are treated by the football club(s)/organizations(s) that you work with?
- ❑ *Very happy*
- ❑ *Not happy*
- ❑ *Somewhat happy*
- ❑ *Don't know*
- ❑ *There are no young people in my club/school/scheme*

Q21 Do you think that in general parents/carers/guardians in football are...
- ❑ *Over-involved (pushy/excitable/fanatical)?*
- ❑ *Moderately involved (supportive in a good way)?*
- ❑ *Under-involved (uninterested or not very supportive)?*
- ❑ *There are no young people in my club/school/scheme*

Q22   How well do the following groups treat children/young people in football?

	Very well	OK	Not very well	Don't know	Not applicable
Parents/carers/guardians	❏	❏	❏	❏	❏
Scouts	❏	❏	❏	❏	❏
Agents	❏	❏	❏	❏	❏
Teachers	❏	❏	❏	❏	❏
Coaches/managers	❏	❏	❏	❏	❏
Football Development Officers	❏	❏	❏	❏	❏
Child Protection/ Education Welfare Officers	❏	❏	❏	❏	❏
Volunteers/other adult helpers	❏	❏	❏	❏	❏
Medics/physiotherapists	❏	❏	❏	❏	❏
Administrators	❏	❏	❏	❏	❏
Players over 18	❏	❏	❏	❏	❏
Young people	❏	❏	❏	❏	❏
Referees	❏	❏	❏	❏	❏

Q23   When working with children or young people in football which of the following, if any, are a worry or cause for concern to you? (Click on up to 3)
- ❏ One to one meetings with players
- ❏ Going into changing rooms
- ❏ Appropriate touching
- ❏ Reporting bad practice of other colleagues
- ❏ Working with vulnerable children
- ❏ Developing close intimate relationships with players
- ❏ Taking children away in cars
- ❏ Dealing with child abuse disclosures
- ❏ False allegations
- ❏ I don't work with young people
- ❏ I don't have any worries or concerns
- ❏ Other

Q24   Have you undertaken any Child Protection/Welfare training courses?
Yes   ❏
No   ❏

Q25 If yes, please indicate the training organization. If no, please go to Q26
- ❑ *The FA*
- ❑ *Sportscoach UK (Formerly NCF)*
- ❑ *Social services*
- ❑ *NSPCC*
- ❑ *Local Education Authority*
- ❑ *Other, please specify*

Q26 Which of the following is your greatest cause for concern in relation to the FA's work in Child Protection? (click only 1)
- ❑ *Being seen as an FA informer on other professionals/colleagues*
- ❑ *Increased bureaucracy/too many initiatives*
- ❑ *Restriction of role – my judgment is being questioned*
- ❑ *Maintaining high personal standards of child protection/welfare*
- ❑ *Having to improve standards with current resources*
- ❑ *I don't agree with the need for the work in child protection/welfare*
- ❑ *Lack of consultation on the development of the work in child protection/welfare*
- ❑ *Lack of communication regarding the work in child protection/welfare*
- ❑ *I have no concerns*
- ❑ *Other, please specify*

Q27 What has changed the most over the last year since the introduction of the FA Child Protection work? (Click up to 3)
- ❑ *Increase in personal standards of child protection/welfare*
- ❑ *Increase in paperwork*
- ❑ *Greater awareness of other CPO/EWO's behaviours*
- ❑ *Greater consultation with my peers*
- ❑ *Greater awareness of child protection/welfare issues*
- ❑ *Greater strain on financial resources*
- ❑ *Greater confidence to report child protection/welfare concerns*
- ❑ *Greater concern over personal behaviour*
- ❑ *Greater concern among peers*
- ❑ *Restriction of role – my judgment is being questioned*
- ❑ *More false allegations*
- ❑ *More child protection/welfare referrals*
- ❑ *I don't think there have been any changes over the past year*
- ❑ *Don't know*
- ❑ *Other, please specify*

Q28 What is your age?
18–24	❑
25–40	❑
41+	❑

Q29 What is your gender?
Female ❑
Male ❑

Q30 What is your ethnic group? (Source: Census 2001)
❑ *White (British, Irish, other white background)*
❑ *Mixed (White and Black Caribbean, White and Black African, White and Asian, other mixed background)*
❑ *Asian or Asian British (Indian, Pakistani, Bangladesh, any other Asian background)*
❑ *Black or Black British (Caribbean, African, any other Black background)*
❑ *Chinese or other ethnic group (Chinese, any other background)*

Q31 The Disability Discrimination Act (1995) defines a disabled person as anyone with a physical or mental impairment which has a substantial and long-term adverse effect upon their ability to carry out normal day-to-day activities. Do you consider yourself to be...?
❑ *Visually impaired*
❑ *Learning disabled*
❑ *Hearing impaired*
❑ *Disabled (other)*
❑ *Physically disabled*
❑ *Not impaired or disabled at all*

Q32 Which of these educational qualification is the highest one that you have?
❑ *None, I'm still at school/college/university*
❑ *School Ed: CSEs/'O' levels/GCSEs or equivalent*
❑ *Further Ed: 'A'/AS levels/Higher School Cert/NVQ/GNVQ/ HNC/HND/RSA/OCR/BTEC/City and Guilds/Edexecel*
❑ *Higher Ed: first degree (BA/BSc/BEd) or higher degree (Postgrad Cert/Diploma/MA/MSc/MBA/PGCE/PhD)*
❑ *No formal qualifications*

Q33 In which of these football regions are you most involved? (Click only 1)
❑ *North (including Yorkshire, North East and North West)*
❑ *South (including London, South East and South West)*
❑ *Midlands (including East Midlands and West Midlands)*
❑ *Not sure*

Thank you for completing this survey. By clicking on the SUBMIT button your survey will automatically go to the Prize Draw page. If you click on the SUBMIT button and nothing happens this is because you have not answered all of the questions. Please go back and complete the questions you have missed.

Appendix 2

Sample interview or focus group schedule

Introduction

Hello. My name is .... and I would like to hear your opinions about how young people are treated in football. Thanks very much for agreeing to take part in this discussion. It should take about 20 minutes. Before we start can I please remind you that:

- there are no right or wrong answers
- all views are welcome
- all individuals' names, places or other identifying features will be removed from the information that I collect.

I will be around for a while at the end so please ask if you have any questions.

Question areas and prompts

1. Background information
   Role, background in football, career background
2. What do you consider to be the key issues in the treatment of young people in football?
3. How does your club/organization/league approach these issues?
   Are young people involved in the running of the club/organization?
   Are there people that young people can go to if they need help or support?
   Are parents involved in the ways things run?
4. What do you understand child protection to involve/concern?
   Give definition if they can't – 4 types of abuse + bullying
   How does your club/organization deal with these kinds of things?
   Are there specified CP roles?
   Is there a specific CP policy?
   Do they know anything about the helpline?
   Do you get regular information and materials from the FA about CP?
   Do they know about the FA CP Strategy and the GOAL campaign?
5. Can you identify particular examples of good practice from your club/organization/league?

What happens when there are social events – is there alcohol?
Is there swearing or bad behaviour and are young players exposed to this?
How do young players get home after training/matches/events?
6.   How well are child protection policies being implemented?
In your club/organization?
Nationally?
How seriously are CP roles taken?
How well supported by the FA do you feel relation to child protection?
What more do you think the FA could do to make juniors safer in football?
7.   Any other comments...

Close and thanks + confirm response to information requests (e.g. 'So can you tell me about the GOAL campaign then?')

Consultation methods for children

Although the focus of much of our consultation work with children and young people was the semi-structured interview, researchers on the project had some success with a range of other techniques designed to engage and empower our participants.

For example, one consultation session incorporated the following three exercises:

1. The use of an 'ideas box', labelled 'Keeping Football Safe'. This was in reality a shoe box with a slit where children were asked to post their ideas on pieces of paper.

2. A Code of Conduct exercise. Children were presented with a large chart, on which they were encouraged to record their thoughts on the following:

    *   Rights of coach
    *   Responsibilities of coach
    *   Rights of players
    *   Responsibilities of players.

3. Football resource game. Children were given an image of a football (below), and asked to record their ideas on the following issues on the panels of the ball.

    *   Five ways my coach can keep football safe
    *   Five ways my parents/carers can help keep football safe
    *   Five ways football can be made safer
    *   Five ways football can be made more enjoyable.

Appendix 4

Ethics and data protection protocol

1. The principles of the University of Gloucestershire's (U Glos) Research Ethics Sub Committee (RESC) will be adhered to strictly. No covert empirical research will be undertaken. This protocol will be reviewed periodically. Any changes will be taken to RESC for approval. The Chair of U Glos RESC will act as an advisor to the project.

2. All members of the project team, including any student researchers and their supervisors, will be required to sign a confidentiality agreement before joining the project. The team are forbidden from discussing, outside the confines of the project team and or Advisory Group, any details of the data collected in the course of the project. Public research seminars and presentations by members of the project team may refer to the general research design and methods.

3. All members of the project team will undergo training on the Data Protection Act and the secure handling of data in both hard copy and electronic formats.

4. Where research partners are engaged to assist with remote data collection, whether by electronic or other means, they will be expected to abide by the same ethical procedures as the contractor.

5. Any student dissertations or similar coursework projects conducted as part of this project may, at the discretion of the FA, be subject to an embargo of up to two years before being placed in the relevant University Learning Centre for public access. The research team will normally discuss dissertation titles in advance with the project Steering Group. Embargo decisions will be made by the Steering Group at the appropriate meetings in each academic year.

6. All participants in the project will be asked to sign voluntary informed consent forms prior to their involvement.

7. No disclosures of child abuse or illegal practices uncovered in the course of data collection, whether by formal or informal means, will be reported to the client. Where the project team has evidence or suspicions of abuse or 'significant harm' to any child arising from the research these suspicions will be referred immediately to the FA Child Protection helpline on an anonymous basis. In addition, the Child Protection or Welfare Officer at the closest organizational point to the incident will be notified.

[Note: definitions of 'abuse' 'poor practice' and 'significant harm' will be those adopted in FA Child Protection awareness training courses.]

Researchers reporting suspicions or allegations in this way will complete an incident report form that will be held securely by Celia Brackenridge Ltd. In the event of any member of the research team being called to appear as a witness by a case conference, police enquiry or court of law, a copy of this incident report form will be supplied to the authority concerned.

8. All members of the research team will undergo Subject Access Checks through the FA and/or the Criminal Records Bureau once it becomes operational.

9. Raw data derived from the project may be used by researchers after the termination of the project, at the FA's discretion.

10. Any breach of this protocol by a researcher will be regarded as a disciplinary offence and may lead to immediate dismissal from the project team.

Appendix 5

Media protocol

The FA and research team anticipate press interest in the event of a disclosure associated with the research project, especially if this involves allegations against a staff member, whether paid or volunteer. A clear chain of command and procedures will be adopted whereby:

1. No one in the research organization or the FA responds to such media enquiries other than the nominated person (Tony Pickerin) or the FA's Press Officer or other FA post-holder designated by the CEO. The only response to Press enquiries by other people will be 'No comment';
2. Any research staff member being targeted by the media about abuse disclosures will notify the FA (Tony Pickerin or his personal assistant) as soon as possible, if possible within two hours;
3. The FA will keep a record of frequently asked media questions about welfare, child protection and safety issues and develop agreed answers to these that can be used in staff training events and public meetings;
4. Any FA staff who speak to the media on behalf of the Association will be:
    *   familiar with any past and ongoing cases and disclosures and up-to-date with current investigations;
    *   thoroughly familiar with the FA Strategy, Policy and Procedures for Child Protection and with the national context of these issues in sport;
    *   informed about the rights of the individuals involved in the each case;
    *   in touch with relevant others (county FA CP Officers, clubs, parents/carers) and aware of their views and actions and of any statements they have made to the media about specific cases;
    *   skilled at preparing and issuing media releases/information;
    *   experienced at speaking with journalists and giving interviews, and at resisting pressure to disclose personal information from cases.
5. No FA or research staff will divulge any identifiable features of the research data (names, places, clubs, etc.) to the media (see Ethics Protocol (Appendix 4)).

Bracketing interview schedule 2002

Child protection in football – impact research

Pre-project questions for FA personnel

Kindly give as much time to this exercise as you can, thinking carefully about your answers in advance without conferring with your FA colleagues. It is important for us to uncover disagreements or ambiguities at this early stage so we can attempt to iron them out. Please complete the consent form then tape your answers onto the blank cassette and return it with the questionnaire to the project team at Cheltenham within the next month. If you would prefer to write answers, or to send any additional notes then that is fine. All thoughts are welcome at this point to help us clarify the precise nature and scope of the research. Your answers will be anonymous and all tapes will be destroyed on completion of the audit stage of the work. No personal or other information will be used by which you might be identified to others. Researchers working on the project will all be expected to sign a confidentiality agreement.

Informed consent

I hereby consent to be provide answers for this study of child protection in football. I understand that my comments will not be traceable and that no identifying features will be divulged in reports or written material. I also understand that the raw tapes and notes from this interview will be destroyed at the conclusion of the audit stage of the project.

NAME.. DATE................

SIGNED ....

Key:

'Programme' = the FA's child protection work
'Project' = the research commissioned to monitor the impact of the programme

1. What do you think is the overall goal for this CP programme?
2. By what yardstick will you consider that it has succeeded?
3. What do you think is the overall goal for this research project?
4. By what yardstick will you consider that the research has succeeded?
5. The FA has a captive audience of practitioners and members:
    a) what difference might this make to the way the CP programme operates and to its outcomes?
    b) how might this affect the data collected in the research?
6. What do you perceive are the intended outcomes for the CP programme:
    a) long term?
    b) short term?
7. What unintended outcomes of the CP programme do you think the researchers might observe?
8. What would you say are the key research questions for the FA?
9. Who within the community of football do you expect to be most sceptical about :
    a) the CP programme?
    b) the research project?
10. What 'field constraints' (i.e. practical and/or personal hindrances) might the researchers expect to confront during the research?
11. What reasons might there be for the research team to report to another agent inside the FA instead of Tony Pickerin?
12. How will you feel if the research uncovers extensive poor practice and abuse?
13. How confident are you that Soho Square will take on board the findings of this research?
14. What possible disputes might there be during the research project?
15. What dispute resolution mechanism should be agreed (ideally before the research commences)?

Thank you very much for your time

Kindly return with tape and any supporting papers or notes to:
Celia Brackenridge, Leisure and Sport Research Unit, Cheltenham and Gloucester College of HE, Francis Close Hall, Swindon Road, Cheltenham, GL50 4AZ

Bibliography

Aicinena, S. (2002) *Through the Eyes of Parents, Children and a Coach: A Fourteen Year Participant–Observer Investigation of Youth Soccer*, Lanham: University Press of America.

Aitchison, C.A. (2004) *Gender and Leisure: A Social-Cultural Nexus*, London: Routledge.

Albermarle, Lady (1960) *The Youth Service in England and Wales (The Albermarle Report)*, London: HMSO.

Alderson, P. (2004) 'The adult's tin ear', *The Guardian*, 19 April, p. 15.

Allen Collinson, J., Fleming, S., Hockey, J. and Pitchford, A. (2005) 'Evaluating Sports-based Inclusion Projects: Methodological Imperatives to Empower Young People', in K. Hylton, J. Long and A. Flintoff (eds) *Evaluating Sport and Active Leisure for Young People*, Eastbourne: Leisure Studies Association.

Allison, J. and James, A. (2004) *Constructing Childhood: Theory, Policy and Social Practice*, London: Palgrave.

Allison, M. (1999) *The Contribution of Sport to Health*, sportscotland research digest no. 39, Edinburgh: SportScotland, www.sportscotland.org.uk

Armstrong, G. (1998) *Football Hooligans: Knowing the Score*, Oxford: Berg.

Bailey, P. (1978) *Leisure and Class in Victorian England: Rational Recreation and the Contest for Control 1830–1885*, London: Routledge.

Bale, J. (1993) *Sport, Space and the City*, London: Routledge.

Balyi, I., and Hamilton, A. (2003) 'Long Term Athlete Development Update: Trainability in childhood and adolescence', *Faster, Higher, Stronger*, Issue 20, July, pp. 6–8.

Becker, H. (1963) *Outsiders*, New York: Free Press.

Bent, I., McIlroy, R., Mousley, K. and Walsh, P. (2000) *Football Confidential*, London: BBC Books.

Bernandes, J. (1997) *Family Studies: An Introduction*, London: Routledge.

Bishop, J. and Hoggett, P. (1986) *Organising Around Enthusiasms*, London: Comedia.

Boocock, S. (2002) 'The Child Protection in Sport Unit', *Journal of Sexual Aggression*, 8(2): 99–106.

Bourdieu, P. (1986) *Distinction: A Social Critique of the Judgement of Taste*, London: Routledge.

—— (1990) *The Logic of Practice*, Cambridge: Polity Press.

Bower, T. (2003) *Broken Dreams: Vanity, Greed and the Souring of British Football*, London: Simon and Schuster.

Brackenridge, C.H. (1999) 'Managing myself: Investigator survival in sensitive research', *International Review for the Sociology of Sport*, 34(4): 399–410.

—— (2000) 'Exposing the "Olympic family": a review of progress towards understanding risk factors for sexual victimisation in sport', presented to The Victimisation of Children and Youth: An International Research Conference, Family Research Laboratory and Crimes Against Children Research Centre, University of New Hampshire, 25–28 June.

—— (2001a) *Spoilsports: Understanding and Preventing Sexual Exploitation in Sport*, London: Routledge.

—— (2001b) 'Child Protection and Welfare', unpublished report to the Youth Sport Trust.

—— (2002) '"So what?" Attitudes of the voluntary sector towards child protection in sports clubs', *Managing Leisure – An International Journal*, 7(2): 103–124.

—— (2004a) 'Silent voices', presented to the annual conference of the Leisure Studies Association, Leeds Metropolitan University, 13–15 July.

—— (2004b) *Burden or Benefit? The Impact of sportscotland's Child Protection Programme with Governing Bodies of Sport*, Research Report 94, Edinburgh: sportscotland.

—— (2006) 'The Parents' Optimum Zone: Measuring and optimising parental engagement in youth sport', presented to the Commonwealth Games Conference, Melbourne, Australia, 13–15 March.

Brackenridge, C.H., Bringer, J.D. and Bishopp, D. (2005) 'Managing cases of abuse in sport', *Child Abuse Review*, 14(4): 259–274.

Brackenridge, C. H., Bringer, J. D., Cockburn, C., Nutt, G., Pawlaczek, Z., Pitchford, A. and Russell, K. (2002) 'Child Protection in Football Research Project 2002', unpublished report to the Football Association.

—— (2004) 'The Football Association's Child Protection in Football Research Project 2002–2006: Rationale, design and first year results', *Managing Leisure – An International Journal*, 9(1): 30–46.

Brackenridge, C.H., Cockburn, C., Collinson, J.A., Ibbetson, A., Nutt, G., Pawlaczek, Z., Pitchford, A. and Russell, K. (2003) 'Child Protection in Football Research Project 2003', unpublished report to the Football Association.

Brackenridge, C.H. and Fasting, K. (2002) 'Sexual harassment and abuse in sport – the research context', in C. Brackenridge and K. Fasting (eds) 'Sexual Harassment and Abuse in Sport – International Research and Policy Perspectives', Special Issue, *Journal of Sexual Aggression*, 8(2): 3–15.

Brackenridge, C.H., Rivers, I., Gough, B. and Llewellyn, K. (2006) 'Driving down participation: Homophobic bullying as a deterrent to doing sport', in C. Aitchison (ed.) *Sport and Gender Identities: Masculinities, Femininities and Sexualities*, London: Routledge.

Brailsford, D. (1992) *British Sport: A Social History*, Cambridge: Lutterworth Press.

Bridle, B. and Burgoyne, D. (2004) 100 Years: A History of Schools Football in St Albans, St Albans: St Albans Primary Schools Sports Association.

Buie, E. (2005) 'Children are "Living in a Security State"', *Times Educational Supplement*, 23 September, p. 1.

Burstyn, V. (1999) *The Rites of Men: Manhood, Politics and the Culture of Sport*, Toronto: University of Toronto Press.

Caillois, R. (1961) *Man, Play and Games*, New York: The Free Press.

Campbell, N. (2006) 'No case to answer? The only way is out for sour Sweetenham', *The Guardian*, Sport, 12 January, p. 7.

Carter, J. (1974) 'Problems of Professional Belief', in J. Carter (ed.) *The Maltreated Child*, Huntingdon: Priory Press.

Central Council for Physical Recreation (1960) *Sport in the Community, the Report of the Wolfenden Committee on Sport*, London: CCPR.

Cheal, D. (1991) *Family and the State of Theory*, London: Harvester Wheatsheaf.

Chief Secretary to the Treasury (2003) *Every Child Matters*, (Cmnd 5862), London: HMSO.

Children and Young People's Unit, Department for Education and Skills (2001) *Learning to Listen: Core Principles for the Involvement of Children and Young People*, London: DfES.

Children's Legal Centre (January 2002) *Working with Young People: Legal Responsibility and Liability*, 5th edn., Colchester: CLC.

Child Protection in Sport Unit (2002) *Sportscheck: A Step by Step Guide for Sports Organisations to Safeguard Children*, London: Sport England/NSPCC.

Child Protection in Sport Unit (2003) *Standards for Safeguarding and Protecting Children in Sport*, London: Sport England/NSPCC.

Coalter, F. (ed.) (1989) *Freedom and Constraint: The Paradoxes of Leisure. Ten Years of the Leisure Studies Association*, London: Comedia/Routledge.

—— (1998) 'Leisure Studies, leisure policy and social citizenship: the failure or the limits of welfare', *Leisure Studies*, 17(11): 21–36.

Cockburn, C. (2002) Fieldwork diary, 'Child Protection in Football Research Project', unpublished.

Cohen, S. (1972) *Folk Devils and Moral Panics: The Creation of the Mods and Rockers*, London: MacGibbon and Kee.

Collier, R. (1999) 'Men, heterosexuality and the changing family', in G. Jagger and C. Wright (eds) *Changing Family Values*, London: Routledge.

Collina, P. (2003) *The Rules of the Game*, London: Pan MacMillan.

Collins, M. (1995) *Sports Development Locally and Regionally*, Reading, ILAM.

Collins, M. (2003) *Modern Love: An Intimate History of Men and Women in Twentieth Century Britain*, London: Atlantic Books.

Colwell, S. (1999) 'Stalking Referees: Resolving Refereeing Problems', in *Singer and Friedlander Football Review 1998–99 Season*, University of Leicester: http://www.le.a/c.uk/crss/sf-review/98-99/98article3.html retrieved 18 April 2006.

Commission for Equality and Human Rights (2006) *Equality Act 2006*, London: HMSO, www.cehr.org.uk retrieved 1 May 2006.

Commission for Racial Equality (2000a) *Racial Equality Charter for Sport*, London: CRE/Sport England.

—— (2000b) *Achieving Racial Equality: A Standard for Sport*, London: CRE/ Sport England.

Conn, D. (1997) *The Football Business*, Edinburgh: Mainstream Publishing.

Conn, D., Green, C., McIlroy, R. and Mousley, K. (2003) *Football Confidential 2: Scams, Scandals and Screw-ups*, London: BBC Books.

Cooke, D. (2001) 'Exchange value as pedagogy in children's leisure: Moral panics in children's culture at century's end', *Leisure Sciences*, 23: 81–98.

Cooper, D. (1971) *The Death of the Family*, London: Allen Lane.

Coote, D. and Folwell, J. (2005) 'Loneliest Job in the World', http://www.bbc.co.uk/ nottingham/content/articles/2005/09/28/referees_wanted_feature.shtml retrieved 18 April 2006.

CPSU (2006) *Strategy for Safeguarding Children and Young People in Sport*, Child Protection in Sport Unit, Leicester: NSPCC/Sport England.

Critcher, C. (2003) *Moral Panics and the Media*, Buckingham: Open University Press.

Cross, G. (1993) *Time and Money: The Making of Consumer Culture*, London: Routledge.

Cushion, C. (2001) 'The Coaching Process in Professional Youth Football', unpublished doctoral thesis, Brunel University, London.

Daly, C. and Hamilton, C. (February 2003) *The Child Protection System: A Guide to the Law*, Colchester: Children's Legal Centre.

Daniel, P. (2004) 'Football for children or children for football? A contemporary boys' league and the politics of childhood', in S. Wagg (ed.), *British Football and Social Exclusion*, London: Routledge.

David, P. (2001) 'The promotion and protection of the human rights of child athletes', presented to the Council of Europe seminar 'The Protection of Children, Young People and Women in Sport: How to Guarantee Human Dignity and Equal Rights for These Groups', Hanaholmen, Finland, 14–16 September.

—— (2005) *Human Rights in Youth Sport: A Critical Review of Children's Rights in Competitive Sport*, London: Taylor & Francis.

Davies, L. (2000) *My Name is Len Davies, I'm a Football Scout*, Blackpool: Skelton/Davies.

Davis, J. (2006) Personal communication, 10 April 2006.

De Koren, B. (2005) *Junkyard Sports*, Champaign, IL: Human Kinetics.

Deloitte & Touche (2003a) *National Governing Bodies of Sport – Success Criteria/Model Framework 1.2*, 22 July, London: UK Sport.

—— (2003b) *Investing in Change – High Level Review of the Modernization Programmes for Governing Bodies of Sport*, London: UK Sport.

DfES (2005a) *Youth Matters*, (Cmnd 6629), London: HMSO.

—— (2005b) *Statistics of Education. Referrals, assessments and children and young people on child protection registers: Year ending 31 March 2005*, Norwich: HMSO.

—— (2003) *Every Child Matters: Green Paper*, London: HMSO: www.dfes.gov.uk/everychildmatters retrieved 16 June 2004.

—— (2004a) *Every Child Matters: The Next Steps*, London: HMSO.

—— (2004b) *Every Child Matters: What You Said*, London: HMSO.

Department of Health (2000) *Quality protects: Disabled Children, Numbers and Categories*, London: Department of Health.

Donnelly, P. (1997) 'Child labour, sport labour: Applying child labour laws to sport', *International Review for the Sociology of Sport*, 32(4): 389–406.

Duffy, J. (2001) 'The Child Safety Catch', BBC News, 7 February, http://news.bbc.co.uk/1/hi/uk/1156063.stm accessed 2 May 2006.

Duncan, N. (1999) *Sexual Bullying: Gender Conflict and Pupil Culture in Secondary Schools*, London: Routledge.

Dunning, E., Murphy, P. and Williams, J. (1988) *The Roots of Football Hooliganism*, London: Routledge.

Dunning, E. and Sheard, K. (1979) *Barbarians, Gentlemen and Players*, London: Martin Robertson.

Dyck, N. (2000) 'Home Field Advantage? Exploring the social construction of children's sports', in V. Amit (ed.) *Constructing the Field: Ethnographic Fieldwork in the Contemporary World*, London: Routledge.

Elleray, D. (2004) *The Man in the Middle*, London: Time Warner Books.

Embrey, C. (1986) 'The nature of dissent: a study of school and junior soccer', in Evans, J. (ed.) *Physical Education, Sport and Schooling: Studies in the Sociology of Physical Education*, Lewes: Falmer Press.

Entwhistle, R. (1999) *I'm Not God, I'm Just a Referee: A Lifetime in the Middle*, Manchester: Empire Publications.

Evans, J. (1993) *Equality, Education and Physical Education*, London: Falmer Press.

Evans, R. and Bellion, E. (2005) *The Art of Refereeing: Techniques and Advice for Every Soccer Referee*, London: A and C Black.

Fajerman, L. and Treseder, P. (2002) *Children are Service Users Too: A Guide to Consulting Children and Young People*, London: Save the Children.

Fetterman, D.M. (ed.) (1984) *Ethnography in Educational Evaluation*, Beverley Hills, CA: Sage.

Finkelhor, D. (1994) 'The "backlash" and the future of child protection advocacy', in J.E.B. Myers (ed.) *The Backlash: Child Protection Under Fire*, London: Sage.

Fishwick, N. (1989) *English Football and Society, 1910–1950*, Manchester: Manchester University Press.

Fleming, S. (1997) 'Qualitative Research of Young People and Sport: the Ethics of Role-Conflict', in A. Tomlinson and S. Fleming (eds) *Ethics, Sport and Leisure: Crises and Critiques*, Aachen: Meyer & Meyer.

Fletcher, R. (1973) *The Family and Marriage in Britain: An Analysis and Moral Assessment*, Harmondsworth: Penguin.

Foot Whyte, W. (1984) *Learning from the Field: A Guide from Experience*, London: Sage.

Forster, K. (1998) 'Protecting children: Some ethical challenges for schools arising from child protection policies', *Professional Ethics*, 6(3&4): 155–171.

Foucault, M. (1979) *Discipline and Punish: the Birth of the Prison*, (translated by Alan Sheridan), London: Penguin.

Franklin, B. (1995) *The Handbook of Children's Rights: Comparative Policy and Practice*, London: Routledge.

Fraser, S., Lewis, V., Ding, S., Kellett, M. and Robinson, C. (2004) *Doing Research with Children and Young People*, London: Sage/Open University.

Frosh, S., Phoenix, A. and Pattman, J. (2002) *Young Masculinities*, London: Palgrave.

Furedi, F. (1999) 'Watch out, adults about', *Independent on Sunday*, 22 August.

—— (2001) *Paranoid Parenting*, London: Allen Lane.

—— (2005) 'Making Sense of Safety', keynote address to a conference Cotton Wool Kids, hosted by Generation Youth, Hampden Park Stadium, Glasgow, 20 September.

Gardner, P. (1998) 'Classroom teachers and educational change 1876–1996', *Journal of Education and Teaching: International Research and Pedagogy*, 24(1): 33–49.

Gathorne-Hardy, J. (1998) *Sex the Measure of all Things: A Life of Alfred C. Kinsey*, London: Chatto & Windus.

Ghaye, A. (2006) 'From private to public – writing a reflective account?', *Reflective Practice*, 7(1): 1–7.

Gibson, G. (2002) 'Determining the role of the parents in preparing the young elite player for a professional AFL career', in W. Spinks, T. Reilly and A. Murphy (eds) *Science and Football IV*, London: Routledge.

Gil, G. J. (2002) 'Soccer and kinship in Argentina: The mother's brother and the heritage of identity', *Soccer and Society*, Autumn (3): 11–25

Giulianotti, R. (1999) *Football: A Sociology of the Global Game*, London: Polity.

Giulianotti, R., Hepworth, M. and Bonney, N. (1994) (eds) *Football, Violence and Identity*, London: Routledge.

Gold, J. (2004) 'Pupils have their say' *The Guardian*, 22 April, p. 25.

Green, S. and Hogan, D. (eds) (2005) *Researching Children's Experience*, London: Sage.

Griffin, P. (1992) 'Changing the game: Homophobia, sexism, and lesbians in sport', *Quest*, 44: 251–265.

Gruneau, R. (1983) *Class, Sports and Social Development*, Amherst, Mass: University of Massachussetts Press.

Guttman, A. (1996) *The Erotic in Sport*, New York: Columbia Free Press.

Hamil, S., Michie, J., Oughton, C. and Warby, S. (2000) *Football in the Digital Age: Whose Game is it Anyway?* London: Mainstream Publishing.

Hamilton, C. (May 2001) *Offering Children Confidentiality: Law and Guidance*, Colchester: Children's Legal Centre.

Hamilton, C. and Fiddy, A. (November 2002) *Children at Work: A Guide to the Law*, Colchester: Children's Legal Centre.

—— (October 2002) *At What Age Can I? A Guide to Age-based Legislation*, Colchester: Children's Legal Centre.

Hamilton, C., Hopegood, L. and Rimmington, H. (2000) *Bullying: A Guide to the Law*, Colchester: Children's Legal Centre.

Hargreaves, J. (1986) *Sport, Power and Culture*, Cambridge: Polity.

Harold, M. (2004) *Raising Children in an Affluent Society*, Dublin: Blackhall Publishing.

Harris, N. (1971) *The Charlton Brothers*, London: Stanley Paul.

Hart, R. A. (1992) *Children's Participation from Tokenism to Citizenship*, UNICEF.

Hart, S. (2005) 'China's children still paying for gold', www.telegraph.co.uk retrieved 5 December 2005.

Hawtin, A. and Wyse, D. (1997a) 'Children's Rights: A National and International Perspective: Overview of Children's Rights in the UK', The British Council, Governance and Law, www.britcoun.org/governance/chlrghts/cr02.htm

—— (1997b) 'Children's Rights: A National and International Perspective: Identification and Analysis of Issues', The British Council, Governance and Law, www.britcoun.org/governance/chlrghts/cr02.htm

Haywood, L., Kew, F., Bramham, P., Spink, J., Capenerhurst, J., and Henry, I. (1995) *Understanding Leisure*, Cheltenham: Stanley Thornes.

Hellestedt, J. (1987) 'The coach/parent/athlete relationship', *The Sport Psychologist*, 1: 151–160.

—— (1990) 'Early adolescent perceptions of parental pressure in the sport environment', *Journal of Sport Behaviour*, 13(3): 135–144.

Hendrick, H. (1997) *Children, Childhood and English Society 1880–1990*, Cambridge: Cambridge University Press.

Home Office (2004) *Child Abduction: Understanding Police Recorded Statistics*, London: HMSO.

Hopcraft, A. (1968/2006) *The Football Man*, London: Simon and Schuster (2nd edn. Aurum Press).

Howell, S., and McNamee, M. (2003) 'Local justice and public sector leisure policy', *Leisure Studies*, 22(1): 17–35.

Hughes, E. (1980) *Crazy Horse*, London: Arthur Baker.

Huizinga, J. (1938 [1955]) *Homo Ludens: A Study of the Play Element in Culture*, Boston: Beacon Press.

Independent Football Commission (2005) *Report on Child Protection in Football*, Stockton-on-Tees: IFC.

—— (2006) Annual Report 2006, Stockton-on-Tees: IFC.

Ingham, A. G., Blissmer, B. J. and Wells Davidson, K. (1999) 'The expendable prolympic self: Going beyond the boundaries of the sociology and psychology of sport', *Sociology of Sport Journal*, 16: 236–268.

International Olympic Committee Medical Commission (2005) *Consensus Statement on Training the Elite Child Athlete*, Lausanne: IOC.

Ives, J. (2004) 'Focus on children's services', Editorial, *Leisure News*, March, 11–17: 1.

Jagger, C. and Wright, C. (eds) (1999) *Changing Family Values*, London: Routledge.

Jambor. E. (1999) 'Parents as children's socialising agents in youth soccer', *Journal of Sport Behaviour*, XXII(2): 350–359.

James, A. and Prout, A (eds) (1990) *Constructing and Reconstructing Childhood: Contemporary Issues in the Sociological Study of Childhood*. London: Falmer.

Jefferson Lenskyj, H. (1994) 'Sexuality and femininity in sport contexts: Issues and alternatives', *Journal of Sport and Social Issues*, 18: 356–376.

Jeffreys, S. (1990) *Anticlimax: A Feminist Perspective on the Sexual Revolution*, London: The Women's Press.

Jenks, C. (1996) *Childhood*, London: Routledge.

Jennings. A. (1996) *The New Lords of the Rings*, London: Simon and Schuster.

Kay, T. (2004) 'The family factor in sport: A review of family factors affecting sports participation', in N. Rowe (ed.) (2004) *Driving Up Participation: The Challenge for Sport*, London: Sport England.

Kennedy, M. (1989) 'The abuse of deaf children', *Child Abuse Review*, 3: 3–7.

Kerr, A. (1999) *Protecting Disabled Children and Adults in Sport and Recreation: The Guide*, Leeds: National Coaching Foundation.

Kerr, A. (2000) *Coaching Disabled Footballers*, Leeds: National Coaching Foundation.

Kerrigan, C. (2000) 'Thoroughly good football': teachers and the origins of elementary school football', *History of Education*, 29(6): 517–541.

—— (2004) *Teachers and Football: A History of the English Schools Football Association*, London: ESFA.

King, A. (1998) *The End of the Terraces: The Transformation of English Football in the 1990s*, Leicester: Leicester University Press.

Kirby, P., Lanyon, C., Cronin, K. and Sinclair, R. (2003) *Building a Culture of Participation: Involving Children and Young People in Policy, Service Planning, Delivery and Evaluation. Research Report*, London: National Children's Bureau.

Kirk, D. (1999) *Schooling Bodies*, Leicester: Leicester University Press.

Knight, T. (2005) 'Olympics: Pinsent upset at Chinese "abuse"', www.telegraph.co.uk, retrieved 5 December 2005.

Laming, Lord (2003) *The Victoria Climbié Inquiry: Report of an Inquiry by Lord Laming*, (Cmd 5730), London: Stationery Office.

Larson, O. (2001) 'Charles Reep: A major influence on British and Norwegian football', *Soccer and Society*, 2(3): 58–78.

Law, S. (2005) 'The State of Junior Football', BBC Radio 5 Live, 19 December.

Lewis, V., Kellett, M., Robinson, C., Fraser, S. and Ding, S. (2004) *The Reality of Research with Children and Young People*, London: Sage/Open University.

Lopez, S. (1997) *Women on the Ball: A Guide to Women's Football*, London: Scarlet.

McIntosh, M. (1978) 'The state and the oppression of women', in A. Kuhn and A. Wolpe (eds) *Feminism and Materialism*, London: Routledge and Kegan Paul.

McKechnie, J. 'Children's voices and researching childhood', in B. Goldson, M. Lavalette and J. McKechnie (eds) (2002) *Children, Welfare and the State*, London: Sage.

McKendrick, J., Bradford, M. and Fielder, A. (2000) 'Kid customer? Commercialisation of playspace and the commodification of childhood', *Childhood*, 7(3): 295–314.

McKinstry, L. (2002) *Jack and Bobby – A Study of Brothers in Conflict*, London: Harper Collins.

McNamee, M. (1995) 'Theoretical limitations in codes of ethical conduct', in G. McFee *et al.*, *Leisure Cultures: Values, Gender, Lifestyles*, Brighton: Leisure Studies Association, Vol. 54.

Mason, M. (2000) 'Teachers and the myth of modernisation', *British Journal of Educational Studies*, 48(2): 155–170.

Mason, T. (1980) *Association Football and English Society, 1863–1915*, Brighton: Harvester.

May-Chahal, C. and Coleman, S. (2003) *Safeguarding Children and Young People*, London: Routledge.

Mayall, B. (2000) *Towards a Sociology for Childhood*, Buckingham: Open University Press.

Messner, M. (1992) *Power at Play: Sports and the Problem of Masculinity*, Boston: Beacon Press.

Michel, E. and Hart, D. (2002) *Involving Young People in the Recruitment of Staff, Volunteers and Mentors*, London: NCB.

Miller, D. (1989) *Stanley Matthews: The Authorized Biography*, London: Pavilion.

Monk, D. and Russell, D. (2000) 'Training apprentices: Tradition versus modernity in the football industry', *Soccer and Society*, 1(2): 62–79.

Moran, D. (2000) *Introduction to Phenomenology*, London: Routledge.

Morgan, G. (undated) *The Easy Guide to Your Kids' Rights at Work*, London: Abbey National.

Mount, F. (1982) *The Subversive Family: An Alternative History of Love and Marriage*, London: Jonathon Cape.

Murdoch, G. P. (1965) *Social Structure*, New York: Free Press.

Murphy, P. (2001) Developing Football Talent: Patrick Murphy interviews Peter Taylor, Former England Under 21 Coach, the Manager of Leicester City and Coach to the Full England Team, Singer and Friedlander Football Review, Season 2000–01, www.le.ac.uk/crss/sf-review/00-01/01article5.html retrieved 18 April 2006.

Murray, B. (1994) *Football: A History of the World Game*, Aldershot: Scolar Press.

Myers, J. and Barrett, B. (2002) *In at the Deep End: A New Insight for all Sports from Analysis of Child Abuse Within Swimming*, NSPCC: London.

Myers, J. and Edwards, H. (2003) *Safeguarding: Another buzz word or a concrete way of ensuring the protection of children?* NSPCCInform, www.nspcc.org.uk/Inform/OnlineResources/InformationBriefings/Safeguarding retrieved 20 February 2006.

National Children's Bureau (2001) *The Emperor's New Clothes: A Report on Three Conferences Exploring Children's Rights*, London: NCB.

—— (1998) *Young Opinions, Great Ideas*, London: NCB.

National Children's Bureau and PK Research Consultancy Ltd. (2003) *Listening to Change: A Study of Ways of Involving and Consulting Children and Young People in Central Government Initiatives*, London: DfES.

National Working Group on Child Protection and Disability (2003) *It Doesn't Happen to Disabled Children: Report of the National Working Group on Child Protection and Disability*, London: NSPCC. Available at www.nspcc.org.uk/Inform/Publications/Downloads/ItDoesntHappenToDisabledChildren_pdf_gf25304.pdf

Nichols, G. (2004) 'Crime and punishment and sports development', *Leisure Studies*, 23(2): 177–194.

Nottinghamshire FA (2006) www.nottinghamshirefa.com/football retrieved 10 May 2006.

Oakley, A. (1974) *The Sociology of Housework*, London: Martin Robertson.

—— (1976) *Subject Housewife*, Harmondsworth: Penguin.

Odendahl, T. and Shaw, A. M. (2002) 'Interviewing elites', in J. F. Gubrium and J. A. Holstein (eds) *Handbook of Interview Research: Context and Method*, London: Sage Publications.

O'Donaghue, F. (1999) (2nd ed) *Scouting for Glory*, Poole: Firebird Books.

Office of National Statistics (2001) www.statistics.gov.uk/census2001/demographic_uk.asp retrieved 10 June 2004.

Ollé, H. (2002) *Young Europe: What Young People Between the Ages of 9 and 14 Think about Participation, Politics and Europe*, London: NCB.

Oram, K. (2001) *The Effects of the Organisational and Cultural Shift from the Youth Trainee to Academy System on Young Professional Footballers*, unpublished masters thesis, University of Gloucestershire.

Orr, J. (2005) 'China's abuse of its athletes is no different to British public schools, says Olympic chief', www.telegraph.co.uk retrieved 5 December 2005.

Pahl, R. (1995) *After Success: Fin de Siècle Anxiety and Identity*, Cambridge: Polity Press.

Parker, A. (1996a) Professional football club culture: Goffman, asylums and occupational socialization, *Scottish Centre Research Papers in Sport, Leisure and Society*, 1: 123–130.

—— (1996b) 'Sporting masculinities, gender and the body', in C. Hickey, L. Fitzclarence and R. Matthews (eds) *Where the Boys Are: Masculinity, Sport and Education*, Geelong: Deakin Centre for Education and Change.

—— (1996c) *Great Expectations: Grimness or Glamour? The Football Apprentice in the 1990s*, www.umist.ac.uk/sport/Parker.html retrieved 13 June 2006.

—— (2000) 'Training for glory, schooling for failure? English professional football, traineeship and educational provision', *Journal of Education and Work*, 13(1): 61–76.

—— (2001) 'Soccer, servitude and sub-cultural identity: Football traineeship and masculine construction', *Soccer and Society*, 2(1): 59–81.

—— (2002) 'Pressures, problems and the PhD process: Tales from the training ground', in G. Walford (ed.) *Doing a Doctorate in Educational Ethnography*, London: Elsevier.

Parsons, T. (1971) *The Social System*, London: Routledge and Kegan Paul.

Parton, N. (1985) *The Politics of Child Abuse*, London: Macmillan.

—— (1996) *Social Theory, Social Change and Social Work*, London: Routledge.

—— (2005) *Safeguarding Childhood: Early Intervention and Surveillance in a Late Modern Society*, London: Routledge.

Physical Activity Task Force (2003) *Let's Make Scotland More Active: A Strategy for Physical Activity*, Edinburgh: Scottish Executive, www.show.scot.nhs.uk/sehd/PATF/Index.htm

Piper, C. (2005a) 'Investing in children: rationing and risk', seminar to the Interdisciplinary Centre for Child and Youth Focussed Research, Brunel University, Uxbridge, 30 November.

—— (2005b) 'Assumptions about children's best interests', in H. Hendrick (ed.) *Child Welfare and Social Policy*, Bristol: The Policy Press.

Pitchford, A. (2005) 'Referee Training and Development in England', unpublished document, University of Gloucestershire.

Pitchford, A., Brackenridge, C., Bringer, J. D., Cockburn, C., Nutt, G., Pawlaczek, Z. and Russell, K. (2004) 'Children in Football: Seen but not heard', *Soccer and Society*, 5(1): 43–60.

Pollard, R. (2002) 'Charles Reep (1904–2002): pioneer of notational and performance analysis in football', *Journal of Sports Science*, 20(1): 853–855.

Pollert, A. (1981) *Girls, Wives, Factory Lives*, London: Macmillan.

Prescott, P. and Hartill. M. (2004) '"It gets sorted in-house": Sport, Child Protection Policy and the Case for Evaluation', unpublished report.

Pronger, B. (1990) *The Arena of Masculinity: Sports, Homosexuality and Meaning of Sex*, London: GMN Publishers Ltd.

Prout, A. (2005) *The Future of Childhood*, London: RoutledgeFalmer.

Qvortrup, J. (1991) *Childhood as a Social Phenomenon – An Introduction to a Series of National Reports*, Eurosocial Report 36/1991, Vienna: European Centre.

Renold, E. (1997) '"All they've got on their brains is football": Sport, masculinity and the gendered practices of playground relations', *Sport, Education and Society*, 2(1): 5–23.

Richardson, D. and Reilly, T. (2001) 'Talent identification, detection and development of youth players – sociological considerations', *Human Movement, Polish Scientific Physical Education Association*, 1(3): 86–93.

Ritzer. G. (1998) *The McDonaldisation Thesis*, London: Sage Books.

Robson, B. with Harris, B. (1991) *Against the Odds*, London: Stanley Paul.

Robson, G. (2000) *'No One Likes Us, We Don't Care': The Myth and Reality of Millwall Fandom*, Oxford: Berg.

Rose, L. (1991) *The Erosion of Childhood: Child Oppression in Britain 1860–1918*, London: Routledge.

Rowe, N. (ed.) (2004) *Driving Up Participation: The Challenge for Sport*, London: Sport England.

Ryle, G. (1949) *The Concept of Mind*, Chicago: University of Chicago Press.

Savage, M., Barlow, J., Dickens, P. and Fielding, T. (1992) *Property, Bureaucracy and Culture: Middle Class Formation in Contemporary Britain*, London: Routledge.

Save the Children (2002) *Children are Service Users Too: A Guide to Consulting Children and Young People*, London: Save the Children.

Schindler, C. (2001) *Fathers, Sons and Football*, London: Headline.

Scottish Executive (2004a) *Protecting Children and Young People: The Charter – Explanatory Booklet*, Edinburgh: Scottish Executive.

—— (2004b) *Protecting Children and Young People: The Charter*, www.scotland.gov.uk/childrenscharter

Scraton, P. (ed.) (1997) *'Childhood' in 'Crisis'?*, London: UCL Press.

Scraton, P. and Haydon, D. (2002) 'Challenging the criminalization of children and young people: Securing a rights-based agenda', in J. Muncie, G. Hughes. and E. McLaughlin (eds) *Youth Justice: Critical Readings*, London: Sage.

Seddon, P. (1995) *A Football Compendium*, London: British Library.

Shaoul, M. and Williamson, T. (2000) *Forever England: A History of the National Side*, Stroud: Tempus Publishing.

Shier, H. (2001) 'Pathways to participation: openings, opportunities and obligations. A new model for enhancing children's participation in decision-making, in line with

Article 12.1 of the United Nations Convention on the Rights of the Child', *Children and Society*, 15(2): 107–117.

Simson, V. and Jennings, A. (1992) *The Lords of the Rings*, London: Simon and Schuster.

Sinclair, R. and Franklin, A. (2000) *Young People's Participation: Quality Protects Research Briefing*, London: Department of Health.

Sir Norman Chester Centre for Football Research (2002) *Fact Sheet 15: Refereeing*, University of Leicester, www.le.a/c.uk/so/css/resources/factsheets/fs15.html retrieved 18 April 2006.

Skelton, C. (2000) 'A passion for football: dominant masculinities and primary schooling', *Sport, Education and Society*, 5(1): 5–18.

SkillsActive (2004) *Community and Sport Development Research Project*, London: SkillsActive.

Smith, M. K. (2001) 'Club work', the *Encyclopedia of Informal Education*, www.infed.org/association/clubwork.htm.

Sparkes, A. C. (2002) *Telling Tales in Sport and Physical Activity: A Qualitative Journey*, Champaign, IL: Human Kinetics Press.

Sport England (2003a) *Young People and Sport National Survey 2002: Headline Findings*, London: Sport England.

—— (2003b) *Sports Volunteering in England in 2002*, London: Sport England.

—— (2004a) *The Equality Standard: A Framework for Sport (The Standard)*, London: Sport England.

—— (2004b) *Excellence Framework for Sport and Recreation Services: The Case for Sport and Recreation*, London: Sport England, www.sportengland.org.taes_framework_document

—— (2004c) *Driving up Participation: The Challenge for Sport. Academic Review Papers Commissioned by Sport England as Contextual Analysis to Inform the Preparation of the Framework for Sport in England*, London: Sport England.

Sport England (2006) *What Sport England Actually Does*, www.sportengland.org retrieved 1 May 2006.

Sports Council (2003) *Women and Sport: Policy and Frameworks for Action*. London: Sports Council.

Stratton, G., Reilly, T., Williams, A. M. and Richardson, D. (2004) *Youth Soccer: From Science to Performance*, London: Routledge.

Stroot, S. (2002) 'Socialisation and participation in sport', in A. Laker (ed.) *The Sociology of Sport and Physical Education*, London: RoutledgeFalmer.

Sugden, J. (1997) 'Field workers rush in (where theorists fear to tread): The perils of ethnography', in A. Tomlinson and S. Fleming (eds) *Ethics, Sport and Leisure: Crises and Critiques*, Aachen: Meyer & Meyer.

Sugden, J. and Tomlinson, A. (2003) *Badfellas: FIFA Family at War*, Edinburgh: Mainstream Publishing.

Sullivan, P. M. and Knutson, J. F. (2000) 'Maltreatment and disabilities: a population based epidemiological study', *Child Abuse and Neglect*, 24: 1257–1273.

Sussex County FA (2004) *Child Protection Checks and Training*, http://www.sussexfa.com/referees/links retrieved 17 February 2006.

The Children Act 1989, London: HMSO.

The Children Act 2004, London: HMSO.

The Football Association (1991) *Blueprint for the Future*, London: the Football Association.

—— (1997) *Football Education for Young Players – A Charter for Quality: Recommendations*, London: the Football Association.

—— (2000a) 'Strategic Plan', unpublished document, London: the Football Association.

—— (2000b) *The FA Child Protection Policy*, London: the Football Association.

—— (2000c) *Child Protection Procedures and Practices Handbook*, London: the Football Association.

—— (2000d) 'Strategic Plan for the Protection of Children/Young People and Disabled People in Football', unpublished document, London: the Football Association.

—— (2001) *The FA Football Development Strategy 2001–2006*, London: the Football Association.

—— (2002) *Child Protection Action Plan*, unpublished document, London: the Football Association.

—— (2003) *Junior Football Trends*, London: the Football Association.

—— (2005a) *Disability Football Strategy 2004–2006*, London: the Football Association.

—— (2005b) *Football for Disabled People: Strategy update*, The London: the Football Association.

—— (2005c) *The FA Annual Review 2004–2005*, London: the Football Association.

The FA.com (2005) www.thefa.com/Euro2005/NewandFeatures/Postings/2005/06/Euro2005_EnglandPlayersReception.htm retrieved 8 August 2005.

The FA.com (2006a) www.thefa.com/Womens/Reference-FAQ/Postings/2003/11/Participation+Figures.htm retrieved 13 June 2006.

—— (2006b) www.thefa.com/TheFA/FALearning/ retrieved 27 June 2006.

The Referees' Association (2001) *FAQs – Child Protection and CRB*, www.football.referees.org retrieved 18 April 2006.

Thompson, E. P. (1991) *The Making of the English Working Class*, Harmondsworth: Penguin.

Thompson, K. (1998) *Moral Panics*, London: Routledge.

Thomson, G. (1998) *The Man in Black: A History of the Football Referee*, London: Prion Books.

Thorpe, D. (1994) *Evaluating Child Protection*, Buckingham: Open University Press.

Thorpe, S. (2004) 'Pick the best, forget the rest? Training field dilemmas and children's football at the turn of the century', in S. Wagg (ed.) *British Football and Social Exclusion*, London: Routledge.

Tolley, E., Girma, M., Stanton-Wharmby, A., Spate, A. and Milburn, J. (1998) *Young Opinions, Great Ideas*, London: National Children's Bureau.

Townsend, P. (1970) *The Fifth Social Service: A Critical Analysis of the Seebohm Proposals*, London: The Fabian Society.

UK Sports Council/International Working Group on Women and Sport (1998) *Women and Sport. From Brighton to Windhoek: Facing the Challenge*, London: UK Sports Council.

UK Youth Parliament (2004) www.ukyouthparliament.org.uk/4655/46854.html retrieved 8 June 2004.

United Nations (1989) *Convention on the Rights of the Child*, www.unicef.org.crc/bg008.htm

Vertinsky, P. (1988) '"Of no use without health": Late nineteenth century medical prescriptions for female exercise through the life span', *Women and Health*, 14(1): 89–115.

Walvin, J. (1975) *The People's Game*, London: Allen Lane.

Index

Watson, N., Weir, S. and Friend, S. (2005) 'The development of Muscular Christianity in Victorian Britain and beyond', *Journal of Religion and Society*, 7. moses.creighton.edu/JRS/toc/2005.htm, retrieved 29 March 2006.

Westcott, H. (1993) *Abuse of Children and Adults with Disabilities*, London: NSPCC.

Whitaker, R. (2002) *Mad in America: Bad Science, Bad Medicine, and the Enduring Mistreatment of the Mentally Ill*, Cambridge, MASS: Perseus Publishing.

White, A. (2003) 'Women and sport in the UK', in I. Hartman-Tews and G. Pfister (eds) *Sport and women: Social issues in International Perspective*, London: Routledge.

Wigglesworth, N. (1996) *The Evolution of English Sport*, London: Frank Cass.

Wilkinson, H. (1996) 'But will they vote? The political attitudes of young people', *Children and Society*, 10(3): 242–244.

Williams, J. (2003) *A Game for Rough Girls? A History of Women's Football in Britain*, London: Routledge.

Williams, J., Hopkins, S. and Long, C. (eds) (2001) *Liverpool FC and the Transformation of Football*, Oxford: Berg.

Williams, J. and Woodhouse, J. (1999) *Offside? The Position of Women in Football*, London: Routledge.

Winter, J. (2006) *Who's the B*****d in the Black?* London: Ebury Press.

Wynne, D. (1998) *Leisure, Lifestyle and the New Middle Class*, London: Routledge.

Learning Resources
Centre